Transforming Malaysia

The **Institute of Southeast Asian Studies (ISEAS)** was established as an autonomous organization in 1968. It is a regional centre dedicated to the study of socio-political, security and economic trends and developments in Southeast Asia and its wider geostrategic and economic environment. The Institute's research programmes are the Regional Economic Studies (RES, including ASEAN and APEC), Regional Strategic and Political Studies (RSPS), and Regional Social and Cultural Studies (RSCS).

ISEAS Publishing, an established academic press, has issued more than 2,000 books and journals. It is the largest scholarly publisher of research about Southeast Asia from within the region. ISEAS Publishing works with many other academic and trade publishers and distributors to disseminate important research and analyses from and about Southeast Asia to the rest of the world.

Transforming Malaysia

Dominant and Competing Paradigms

EDITED BY

ANTHONY MILNER
ABDUL RAHMAN EMBONG
THAM SIEW YEAN

INSTITUTE OF MALAYSIAN & INTERNATIONAL STUDIES (IKMAS)
Malaysia

INSTITUTE OF SOUTHEAST ASIAN STUDIES
Singapore

First published in Singapore in 2014 by
ISEAS Publishing
Institute of Southeast Asian Studies
30 Heng Mui Keng Terrace, Pasir Panjang
Singapore 119614

E-mail: publish@iseas.edu.sg • Website: bookshop.iseas.edu.sg

Jointly with Institute of Malaysian & International Studies (IKMAS)
Universiti Kebangsaan Malaysia
43600 UKM Bangi, Selangor Darul Ehsan, Malaysia

ISEAS Library Cataloguing-in-Publication Data

Transforming Malaysia : dominant and competing paradigms / edited by Anthony Milner, Abdul Rahman Embong and Tham Siew Yean.
1. Malaysia—Race relations.
2. Malaysia—Politics and government.
3. Malaysia—Economic policy.
4. Malaysia—Foreign relations.
I. Milner, A. C. (Anthony Crothers), 1945-
II. Abdul Rahman Embong.
III. Tham, Siew Yean.
DS595 T77 2014

ISBN 978-981-4517-91-1 (soft cover)
ISBN 978-981-4517-92-8 (E-book PDF)

Cover images: Artist's impression and photo taken by Lin Chew Man. Reproduced with permission.

Typeset by International Typesetters Pte Ltd
Printed in Singapore by Mainland Press Pte Ltd

CONTENTS

LIST OF TABLES AND FIGURES

Tables

Figures

PREFACE

Seeking to become a high income, developed and united country by 2020, Malaysia seems trapped. It is still viewed as a state searching for a nation — a country deeply divided into ethnic or racial blocs which do not share a national vision. Malaysia's challenge is enormous, as this volume explains. But it is also a challenge of ideas rather than straightforward social fact. The racial structure of Malaysia is in a critical way ideologically created — a paradigm — and the task of building a united nation state and national economy is one that cannot be left entirely to specialists in economics and political institutions.

As can be seen in the run up to, and the aftermath of the 13th general election held on 5 May 2013, the race paradigm has been raised sharply to the fore again as a weapon of mobilization, including by the right wing elements in the ruling UMNO and their supporters. The relevance of the debate on the race paradigm — which is the central theme in this volume — is immediately apparent in these developments. This volume examines the manner in which Malaysia's race paradigm was formulated and promulgated, and achieved dominance. It notes as well the presence and competition — and failure — of other societal paradigms, and then goes on to test whether or not the dominant paradigm is losing influence in specific practical areas of Malaysian life.

The volume focuses on ideas, but recognizes too that paradigms are formulated and contested in a political and economic context. The history of ideas has been neglected in Malaysian studies — and yet, in certain ways, it can help open up new possibilities. The mere reminder that the current Malaysian configuration is a construct — and has been challenged in the past — can be liberating. Examining the race paradigm in process, and in practice — also helps to identify ways in which it might be qualified or modified in the future, when economic and political imperatives seem to demand structural challenge.

This volume is the latest in the series of books emerging from IKMAS's collaborative projects under the auspices of the Pok Rafeah chair, and is in line with IKMAS overall framework of globalization and social transformation. It may be recalled that the first chairholder, Professor J.H. Mittelman, who was at IKMAS in 1997 and 1999 collaborated with IKMAS Fellows to produce the book *Capturing Globalization,* edited by J.H. Mittelman and Norani Othman (2001). The second collaboration — with Professor Joan Nelson who occupied the Pok Rafeah chair from 2006 to 2007 — resulted in the publication of another book entitled, *Globalization and National Autonomy: The Experience of Malaysia*, edited by Joan M. Nelson, Jacob Meerman, and Abdul Rahman Embong. This book was jointly published in 2008 by the Institute of Southeast Asian Studies (ISEAS), Singapore and IKMAS, Bangi, and won the "Best Co-published Work" award from the ASEAN Book Publishers Association in 2009. It is our hope that the present volume, will provoke serious rethinking and reflections about the kind of paradigm Malaysia needs to guide policy-making and socio-political action to engage with globalization and promote social cohesion. Our objective for Malaysia must be to partake successfully in the process of globalization and transform the country into a competitive high-income nation.

Anthony Milner, Abdul Rahman Embong and Tham Siew Yean
9 September 2013

ACKNOWLEDGEMENTS

This book would not have been possible without the excellent ideas contributed by Professor Milner, the lead editor of this book. As in the case of research collaborations, vital ideas are frequently exchanged during the series of workshops held to deliberate on the draft chapters for this book, as well as during coffee and lunch breaks or even along the corridors. IKMAS is indeed fortunate to have Professor Milner as he provided the necessary synergy to bring together a collegial project such as this. We are also grateful to the Pok Rafeah Foundation as it is their funding that enabled the establishment and operations of the Pok Rafeah chair, for which Professor Milner was its fourth holder.

As in all previous IKMAS book projects, this book owes its completion to many able helpers. We would like to put on record our thanks in particular to all the administrative and support staff of IKMAS who arranged the numerous workshops and gave assistance in various other ways. We also would like to thank Universiti Kebangsaan Malaysia for partially funding the publication of this book through its annual budget for the Insitute. This book has benefitted tremendously from the comments and criticisms by Professor Terence Gomez from the University of Malaya, and Profesor Abdul Halim Ali, adjunct professor from Universiti Malaysia Sarawak who attended the special workshop held to discuss and comment on the final draft of the book. To both of them, a special thank you. We also would like to thank the two blind reviewers appointed by the publishers for their valuable comments and criticisms. Whilst efforts have been made to improve the various chapters in accordance with the comments and criticisms, mistakes and other ommissions remain, for which we as editors and individual book chapter writers are solely responsible. Finally, we would also like to thank Lin Chew Man for his creative ideas for our book cover.

LIST OF CONTRIBUTORS

Abdul Rahman Embong, Ph.D. (Sociology of Development at Universiti Malaya), is Emeritus Professor and Principal Research Fellow at the Institute of Malaysian and International Studies (IKMAS), Universiti Kebangsaan Malaysia (National University of Malaysia). His research focuses on development, middle class, democratization, ethnicity, nation-state and globalization. His books include *Southeast Asian Middle Classes: Prospects to Social Change and Democratisation* (editor, 2001); *State-led Modernization and the New Middle Class in Malaysia* (2002); *Globalisation, Culture and Inequalities: In Honour of the Late Ishak Shari* (editor, 2004), and *Malaysia at a Crossroads: Can We Make the Transition?* (co-editor, 2011).

Anthony Milner (Ph.D. in History at Cornell University) is Basham Professor of Asian History at the Australian National University and Professorial Fellow at the University of Melbourne. One focus of his research has been the history of ideas and political culture in the "Malay World". His publications include *The Invention of Politics in Colonial Malaya* (2002); *Kerajaan: Malay Political Culture on the Eve of Colonial Rule* (1982, 2008); *The Malays* (2011); and *Bangsa and Umma: Development of People-grouping Concepts in Islamized Southeast Asia* (co-editor, 2011). He was recently co-editor of the report: *Our Place in the Asian Century: Southeast Asia as The Third Way* (2012).

Azizah Kassim (Ph.D. in social anthropology at the School of Oriental and African Studies, University of London) is a Visiting Professor at IKMAS, Universiti Kebangsaan Malaysia (National University of Malaysia). Her current research interests focuses on international migration. Her publications include "Public Universities in Malaysia: Their Development and Internationalization", in *Internationalization of Higher Education in Malaysia: Understanding, Practices and Challenges*, edited by Tham Siew Yean (2013); and "Trans-National Migration and the Contestation for Urban Space: Emerging Problems and Possible Solutions", in *Malaysia at the Crossroads: Can We Make the Transition*, edited by Abdul Rahman Embong and Tham Siew Yean (2011).

K.S. Nathan (Ph.D. in International Relations, Claremont Graduate University, USA; LL.B Hons. and LL.M, London) is a Professor and Principal Research Fellow at the Institute of Ethnic Studies (KITA), Universiti Kebangsaan Malaysia (National University of Malaysia). His research interests include Malaysian politics and foreign policy, U.S. relations with Asia, and ASEAN regional security. His publications include: *The European Union, United States and ASEAN: Challenges and Prospects for Cooperative Engagement in the 21st Century* (2002); *Religious Pluralism in Democratic Societies: Challenges and Prospects for Southeast Asia, Europe, and the United States in the New Millennium* (editor, 2010).

Helen Ting (Ph.D. in Political Science, Sciences-Po, Paris) is a Research Fellow at the Institute of Malaysian and International Studies (IKMAS), Universiti Kebangsaan Malaysia (National University of Malaysia). She was a Visiting Fellow at the Institute of Asian and African Studies, Humboldt University in Berlin from September 2012 to January 2013. Her research interests include identity politics, nationalism, gender and inter-ethnic relations. Among her publications are: "Institutional Reforms and Bi-party Political System: Beyond 'Expedient Multiculturalism'", in *Malaysia at a Crossroads: Can We Make the Transition?* (2011). Her latest book *Women in Southeast Asian Nationalist Movement: A Biographical Approach*, co-edited with Susan Blackburn, was published in 2013.

Ragayah Haji Mat Zin (Ph.D. in Economics, Vanderbilt University, USA) is a recently retired professor from the Institute of Malaysian and International Studies (IKMAS), Universiti Kebangsaan Malaysia (National University of Malaysia). Her research interests include income distribution, poverty, trade and industrial development. Some recent publications include *Malaysia's Development Challenges: Graduating from the Middle* (co-editor, 2012); "Recent Trends in the Demand of International Students for Higher Education in Malaysia", in *Proceedings of the 2nd International Conference on Global Trends and Challenges in Higher Education and Quality Assurance*, edited by Nasir Ahmad Khan (co-author, 2012).

Tham Siew Yean (Ph.D. in Economics, University of Rochester) is a Professor and Principal Research Fellow at the Institute of Malaysian and International Studies (IKMAS), Universiti Kebangsaan Malaysia (National University of Malaysia). Her research interests include free trade agreements, foreign direct investment, services trade and liberalization, especially in private higher education. Some recent publications include *Malaysia's Development Challenges: Graduating from the Middle* (co-edited with Hal Hill and Ragayah Haji Mat Zin, 2012); *Internationalizing Higher Education in Malaysia: Understanding, Practices and Challenges* (editor, 2013), and "Internationalizing Higher Education in Malaysia: Government Policies and University's Response", *Journal of Studies in International Education*, published online, 27 February 2013.

1

INTRODUCTION

Anthony Milner, Abdul Rahman Embong, and Tham Siew Yean

An issue persistently focused on in public discussion in Malaysia today is the challenge of becoming a high-income country and a developed nation — and to do this by the year 2020. Time is running out, and yet influential Malaysians feel they have "become stuck" or "trapped" at a middle stage in the developmental trajectory. What is it that holds Malaysia back and prevents the country from achieving its promise? Attention is repeatedly drawn to the ethnic or racial structure of its population, and the policy demand on the government that arises because of the inequalities in this structure. Blame for Malaysia having become trapped is often attributed to the consequences of a demographic fact — to the country having a 'plural society' driven by racial or communal difference and contest, and a damaging structure of race-stirring politics generated by that society. But are we dealing here with givens? What of human agency — and, in particular, of the role of ideas and ideological skillfulness?

This book argues that the ideological aspect of the "Malaysia question" has been neglected, and that there is a need to examine closely the construction of what became established as the dominant societal paradigm of social and political life in the country. The authors consider first, the way the race paradigm — the rigid structure of "Malay", "Chinese" and "Indian" — has been both constructed and contested; and secondly, the particular manner in which the paradigm continues to be employed in a range of practical, policy areas. Although the range of issues examined in the second half of the book is by no means comprehensive or exhaustive, nevertheless, they include significant areas in the policy discourse — namely poverty eradication and income distribution; foreign workers; trade policy formulation; and foreign policy. Each of the issues throws light on whether there are signs that the race paradigm is becoming less influential; and, also, what other ideological constructions are available — constructions which might be of greater strategic value to a country determined to achieve a new level of economic and political development? Seen in this way, each chapter provides some insight into the workings or impact of the race paradigm in official discourse and policy formulation as well as public and academic deliberations.

This book is based on a research project that was initiated and sponsored by the Institute of Malaysian and International Studies (IKMAS) at Universiti Kebangsaan Malaysia (National University of Malaysia), and it has to be positioned in the context of the Institute's previous work. Research undertaken by IKMAS in the late 1990s, under the auspices of the Distinguished Pok Rafeah Chair in International Studies, addressed the question of how developing countries including Malaysia should engage with globalization in order to be active participants, rather than its captives (Mittelman and Norani Othman 2001). Still working within the framework of globalization and social transformation, a second IKMAS project concentrated on constraints on national autonomy, namely the issue of how to insure a degree of national autonomy in a period of intense globalization — and concluded that despite Malaysia's "rapid and extensive integration into the world economy after 1970, thus far pressures of economic globalization have not severely constrained the government's freedom to establish and pursue preferred objectives" (Nelson 2008, p. 302). In particular, so this second study observed, the government "steered economic policies" in ways that helped the "restructuring of society" and also "political patronage" (p. 304). In education and industry it adopted policies "designed to promote Malay and other Bumiputra progress" (p. 305) — and yet foreign direct investment did not slow, and a great increase in exports took place (with a growing share of manufacturing as well) (p. 305).

While these two earlier projects focused on constraints on autonomy, today in Malaysia it seems to be the domestic constraints on Malaysia's global competiveness — including on Malaysia's success or otherwise in the "global competition for talent" (World Bank 2011, p. 13) that are of greatest importance. A World Bank report on Malaysia in April 2011 identified the government's policies favouring a certain section of society as holding back the economy: in particular the report held these policies responsible for a massive brain drain, namely of Chinese and Indians, which has limited foreign investment. World Bank senior economist Philip Schellekens said that foreign investment could be five times the current levels if the country had a more competitive talent base. He also argued that Malaysia lacked a real meritocracy and this was a "fundamental constraint" on Malaysia's expansion because "competition is what drives innovation" (Malaysian Insider 28 April on World Bank 2011). There is a sense here again of Malaysia becoming "trapped" or "stuck" on its progress to realize Vision 2020. The political and economic dimensions of this entrapment — namely, the challenges faced by the country in graduating from a middle-income to a high-income economy — was a topic explored in a third IKMAS project in 2009/10, involving Hal Hill from the Australian National University (Hill, Tham and Ragayah 2012).

In 2009, a fourth IKMAS project also addressed this sense of entrapment, and suggested Malaysia had come to a "crossroads" — a point where the country might or might not move forward to become a "developed, democratic, socially-just, ethnically-united, accountable and globally competitive nation" (Abdul Rahman Embong and Tham 2011, p. 17). Malaysia, the project volume argued, faced a "critical transition" — a transition that would mean "significant and even fundamental changes and transformation in the social structure and relations, politics, economy, culture and mindset of the society" (p. 17). With this in mind, the volume focused sharply on the issue of Malaysia's economic competitiveness — particularly in the context of the rise of China and India (as well as intra-ASEAN rivalry for foreign investment) — and confirmed the "need to promote merit and excellence irrespective of ethnicity" (p. 16). The book noted the Najib government's "1Malaysia" aspiration, as well as the New Economic Model and Government Transformation Plan — which together have been described (by the government) as being designed to bring fundamental change, and a stronger economic competitiveness. But the book also observed that while these reform moves highlight "the people" (the *rakyat*) — rather than one or more "races" — in October 2010, Prime Minister Datuk Seri Najib Razak assured the General Assembly of the ruling United Malays National Organization (UMNO) that the rights of the Malays would not be questioned (p. 16). Reconciling

"1Malaysia" aspirations with this assurance, it might be observed, may not be impossible — but it is not easy. In considering the prospect of being able to achieve a successful "critical transition", the fourth IKMAS project stressed the need for a "firmly committed" leadership with "the support of the people"; or, alternatively, the option of looking to an agency "from outside the ruling elite" (p. 18).

Whichever of these directions is taken, the task of gaining public consensus for change will be difficult — and this has a lot to do with the continuing power of Malaysia's race paradigm, the central concern of this present volume. A paradigm, of course, is something that helps a community to make sense of the world, to find patterns there — it helps to define what is important, what problems deserve attention, and how they might be solved (Kuhn 1996, chapters 2 and 3). There is likely to be more than one paradigm competing for influence in a community; but a dominant paradigm can have the effect of making others seem unrealistic or confused. The dominant paradigm tends to screen out data and perspectives that do not fit its patterns. Thinking about why it is important to focus on Malaysia's race paradigm, it is helpful to note the distinguished historian of ideas, John Pocock's observation that a paradigm "distributes authority so as to favour certain modes of action and those said to be engaged in them" (2009, p. 72). We should also recall that the process of breaking down a paradigm is in part a contest of ideas, in which skillful argument (with audience-sensitive rhetoric) plays a central role.

It is often overlooked that Malaysian history includes numerous instances of virtuosity in ideological work — instances where deep structural change has been implemented. Examples are the reconstitution of the Peninsular sultanates during the British period, the creation of a trans-sultanate racial unity, and the particular construction of the plural society itself (Milner 2011, chapters 5 and 6; Milner 2002, chapter 8; Milner 2003*a*).

In Malaysia, there are certainly numerous personal advantages to be gained from sustaining racial or communal thinking: at least in the short and medium term the defence of specifically racial interests can also attract votes. This bears, of course, on the larger challenge of changing a deeply-entrenched public mindset. Today we see the race paradigm employed explicitly or implicitly at almost every turn. Its presence is implied in many of the criticisms advanced outside and inside the national Government, often complaining of the damage done to non-Malays and even Malays themselves on account of the "special treatment" given to the favoured section of the Malaysian community. But it should be noted that the paradigm is present too, of course, in the statements of Government leaders. For instance, in his 2010 UMNO speech — at a time when he was vigorously promoting the idea of 1Malaysia — the Prime Minister told his party members to "come together to strengthen the (Malay) race" and reminded them that they were a "race chosen to lead a plural society". He spoke as well of the Federal Constitution: Malaysia, he said, is "a country based on the principles enshrined in the Constitution", and he explained that the "position of the Malays and the Bumiputra and other races in terms of politics has been clearly enshrined (there)". "Sealed in the Constitution", he said, was a "national social contract" between Malays and non-Malays — between "our founding fathers who represented the various races at the start of Independence" (The Sun Daily, 22 October 2010).

The Najib's governmental call for a "1Malaysia" in itself gave prominence to the race paradigm. In communicating the idea of one rather than more than one Malaysia — in suggesting the vision of a united rather than divided Malaysia — it immediately recalled the current divisions in the society, and in Malaysia it is race or ethnicity rather than regional or class divisions that are encountered in public and most private discussion. In Malaysia when division is referred to, what is generally meant is the manner in which the society and politics of the country are structured around race — most commonly the "Malay", "Chinese" and "Indian" races. Thus, when the Malaysian government speaks of "1Malaysia", or of delivering good policy programmes on behalf of "the people" of the country, the implication is clear: the divisions that are to be transcended are those separating these three racial groups.

The seemingly inclusive "1Malaysia" rhetoric gives way to the more abrasive and overt race paradigm in particular when certain interests are threatened. For example, most recently, when referring to the results of the 13th general election held on 5 May 2013, many commentators noted with regret how the race paradigm was used by Prime Minister Najib Razak himself, who blamed his government's losses on what he called "the Chinese tsunami" (Anand 2013). On its part, the UMNO-owned Malay paper, *Utusan Malaysia*, on 7 May 2013 published a provocative front-page headline with the words in red, "Apa Lagi Cina Mahu?" (What More Do the Chinese Want?). Several commentators debated this racialized interpretation of the election results, arguing that it was an "urban Malaysian tsunami" rather than "a Chinese tsunami" that caused the defeat of many BN candidates in the election.

Moving from such national leadership formulations to the everyday working of the race paradigm, John Gullick's classic overview of Malaysia described its power long ago: in Malaysia, he said, conflicts of economic and social interest "are shut into a communal and monolithic opposition of one group against another". Even reform "when it comes is the fruit of communal bargaining" (Gullick 1981, p. 129). In the primary school system "there has been an active process promoting the reproduction of ethnic differences and the polarization of ethnic groups" (Shamsul and Anis 2011, p. 25). In politics, parties continue to "organize their campaigns along ethnic lines and deliver messages to specific ethnic communities, often playing on the security of one community against the other for political gain" (Welsh 2004, p. 145). In academic analyses, an ethnic or race perspective has been dominant, for instance, in studies of politics and history — there is "hardly the language to speak of transethnic solidarities let alone political community in Malaysia" (Mandal 2004, p. 53; Khoo 1995, p. xvii). It is so much the case that "ethnicity" is the "*modus operandi* in Malaysian society" that when new elements are being incorporated — for instance, the Orang Asli "Semai" group — what takes place is an "intensification of their sense of identity" rather than "cultural homogenization" (Gomes 2009, p. 318). Certainly, professional opinion polling suggests a large majority of Malaysians conceptualize their society in starkly racial terms — each "race" expressing a substantial degree of distrust toward the others, and most people quite comfortable employing racial stereotyping (Merdeka Centre 2006).

With respect to public discussion in Malaysia, the 2010/11 furor over a Malay-language novel, *Interlok* — written in 1971 by the celebrated author, Abdullah Hussain — underlined the continued salience of the race paradigm. The book was used in government schools and, it must be said, does portray Malaysian society in terms of the classic three-race structure. The author conveys the purpose of wishing to reconcile the different peoples of Malaysia — the Malays, Chinese and Indians — but the book employs language and character description which non-Malays, especially Indians, find repugnant. It happens to be an "Indian" protagonist in the text who sees the need to "become involved in the struggle to form a single Malayan society, where everybody could live in peace and harmony" (p. 388), and the novel also attempts to portray the forging of warm personal relationships between members of the different "races". But the use of the word "pariah" in the dialogue of the story is frequently cited as unacceptable to the Indian community, and the way the text is taught in schools is said to make *Interlok* in general a lethal instrument for the denigration of one race by another. Whatever the intentions of the author may have been, his book has gathered its own grim momentum.

Potent as the race-based paradigm is in these various ways; it is nevertheless a paradigm — and not a mere statement of demographic and sociological reality. Paradigms, it is true, are often simply taken-for-granted — treated as mere fact. This helps account for their power. Pocock makes the point that although a paradigm is "historically conditioned" it tends to "suppress awareness of the conditions governing its existence" (2009, p. 72). In the case of Indonesia it has been argued that the inability "to recognize the constructedness of social identities" helps to explain the violence of communal divisions (Heryanto 2006, p. 32; Mandal 2004, p. 56). With respect to Malaysia, Sumit Mandal has observed with justification that the lack of "critical examination of race has meant that it assumes a murky space in society with potentially harsh social and political consequences" (2004, p. 57). One step toward challenging or at least moderating the race paradigm — a step we take in this book — might therefore be to historicize it, to show how it was constructed over time.

There have been many accounts of the formation of Malaysia's plural society — usually stressing the pattern of "Chinese" and "Indian" immigration into the country, particularly during the colonial period, and some pointing to the exacerbation of race relations as a result of a British "divide and rule" approach. In fact, there was already much immigration from China and the Indian subcontinent before the establishing of British control in the Peninsular states in the 1870s (Khoo 2009). The British did make a contribution, but it could be argued that it was their ideological one which remains the most fundamental and potent. They played a critical role in helping to forge, and to give political significance and prominence to the terms "Malay", "Chinese" and "Indian" — rendering increased rigidity and inflexibility to these (and other) "racial" categories. The creation of Malaysia's plural society, it should be stressed, cannot be understood only in terms of patterns of immigration, settlement and occupation. Certainly, most of the Peninsular states and the Straits Settlements were remarkable for the rich mixture of peoples they attracted — and for the range of cultural and religious influences that worked against social homogeneity. But the so-called "Malay", "Chinese" and "Indian" communities were themselves far from homogeneous — and were still only in the process of being consolidated in the period of British dominance.

If we go back to the pre-colonial period — to the early nineteenth century and before — the most influential societal paradigm on the Peninsula and in some other regions of the Archipelago was the sultanate or *kerajaan*, and it was not race-based (Gullick 1965; Milner 1982; Milner 2011*a*, chapters 3 and 4). Nor was it focused primarily on a territorially-defined state. The *kerajaan* was conceptualized in terms of the personal relationship between ruler and subject (*rakyat*) — and not a relationship with a specific race. There were numerous *kerajaan* on the Peninsula and elsewhere in the Archipelago — royal capitals (or centres) might move from one location to another, and royal subjects often abandoned one ruler and joined the subjects of another. Racial definition — like territorial delineation — was not the key. As discussed in Chapter 2 in this book, a person of Orang Asli, Batak, Arab, Indian or Chinese background — and many others as well — could become incorporated in a *kerajaan,* obeying its rules and even taking an elevated title in the royal hierarchy.

The British ideological input to the development of the race paradigm began from the earliest years of their administrative engagement on the Peninsula. Particularly from the late eighteenth century, Europeans increasingly categorized mankind in terms of races, and the process was given serious "scientific" status. Even some political leaders — Napoleon is one example — now tended to map out the world in racial rather than dynastic units. Thomas Stamford Raffles and other European officials in Southeast Asia were influenced by these trends, and thus sought to describe the region's peoples in this manner, defining "Malay", "Javanese" and other "races" in both cultural and physical terms. As the British established political control over the Peninsula, they introduced numerous types of administrative measures that reinforced the racial paradigm: the categories in the official census and the special legislation protecting Malay land ownership — just like the establishing of a "Chinese Protectorate" — are examples of measures that had this impact (Shamsul 1996; Shamsul 1998; Milner 2011*a*, chapter 5). The census categories moved slowly but steadily toward the exclusive highlighting of "race" — the term "race" first appeared in an appendix containing instructions to enumerators in the 1891 census, and by the 1911 census the people were classified essentially into just "Malays", "Chinese" and "Indians" (Hirschman 1987, p. 561).

The imposition of the British race ideology took place with respect to a wide range of peoples across the Empire (Bayly 2004, p. 110; Hannaford 1996) — including in Sarawak and North Borneo (Sabah), the future East Malaysia. As Tim Babcock has explained, in colonial Sarawak people who were once identified with a particular place or regional name were now subject to a European attempt to impose "bounded, permanent and stable ethnic identities" (1974, p. 197). Fines were used to discipline racial classification (Pringle 1970, pp. 296–98); in 1950 the anthropologist Edmund Leach boasted that the ethnic structure he advocated for Sarawak "almost entirely dispense[d] with all the 200 odd minor "tribal" names which clutter up the earlier literature" (1950, pp. 52–53). The racial engineering in Sabah — under the North Borneo Company — differed from that of the Brooke regime in Sarawak. While the category "Malay" was implemented in Sarawak, Muslims in Sabah continued to be called "Brunei", "Bajau" and so forth (Pringle 1970, p. xix). The British administrators of the British North Borneo Company also employed the Malay word "Dusun" with reference to the majority rural population — though the people themselves had employed no common name. It was in the 1950s — in the years leading to Independence — that the term "Kadazan" began to be used by political leaders to promote a broad social identity among non-Muslim peoples in Sabah (Reid 1997). In Sarawak, the Brookes — in seeking an ethnic classification to replace local (often river-based) identities — used "Iban", and in recent decades, the term "Iban" has gradually gained acceptance over "Dayak" (Pringle 1970, pp. xviii, 19, 20).

The Malay/Chinese/Indian race paradigm — which quickly became dominant on the Peninsula, and then emblematic of modern Malaysia, was enunciated with particular clarity by Frank Swettenham at the opening of the twentieth century. Identifying the three main groups, he attributed to each a cluster of dominant characteristics. In fact, essentialist motifs such as the Malay "disinclination to work" and the Chinese "energy and industry" (Swettenham 1907, pp. 136, 232) — and many more — appear again and again in the colonial period, in local as well as British writings. Westerners initiated the racializing process — and it was resisted in various ways, including (at least initially) by the royal courts. The evolution of the race paradigm involved collaboration — an "epistemological partnership" between foreign and local knowledge — to use Tony Day's phrase (Day 2002, p. 101). Local ideologues helped, for instance, to define the "Malay race" and give it emotive content; to embed it in the public mind (Milner 2011*a*, chapter 5; Milner 2002). The post-Independence history of the paradigm was influenced by the 1969 race riots and the launching of the New Economic Policy — aimed at restructuring Malaysian society by lifting the economic condition of the Malays. In 1986 the use of the term "social contract" — by a senior member of the governing UMNO party — to describe the so-called ethnic bargaining between Malays and non-Malays in the lead up to Independence also helped to harden race categories. Further reinforcement came from the increased use of the phrase "*ketuanan Melayu*" (Malay sovereignty) over the last couple of decades — and also the deploying of the term "*pendatang*" (immigrant) to refer to Chinese and Indians, no matter how long their families have lived in Malaysia.

When Malaysia's racial dynamic is understood as a paradigm rather than a demographic fact, the task of traversing the "crossroads" becomes at least in part an ideological one. When race is employed constantly in public and policy discussion as well as academic analysis we need to recall that it is a construct — a product largely of the British colonial presence in the nineteenth and twentieth centuries. Social and economic complexity can be seen to be essentialized in terms of "Malay", "Chinese" and "Indian" interests and perspectives — and the interaction between these three communities. When Malaysia is conceptualized as a "plural society" — and it is done so time and again, including in royal and prime ministerial speeches (*New Straits Times*, 6 December 2010; "Special Statement", Yang di-Pertuan Agong, 3 July 2011) — we can approach this as an ideological creation and challenge, not a mere statement of fact.

In the manner of dominant paradigms, the potency of this race paradigm has been such that rival interpretations — or structures of interpretation — have tended to be rejected immediately as inadequate. But the fact that there has been so much talk in Malaysia recently of fundamental, structural change does raise the question of whether this paradigm is at last beginning to wane in influence. With this in mind a principal objective of this book is to examine how far the social and economic dynamics of Malaysia have finally begun to change in ways that challenge the race paradigm. Does it remain analytically adequate — adequate for academic and policy purposes, and also as a foundational motif in public discussion? Or is a case building up for conceptualizing Malaysia in terms of a single "national" community with "national" interests, perhaps as a single "*rakyat*", to appropriate the old "feudal" term for a polity's "subjects" (see chapters 2 and 3)? Is there better reason now to speak of Malaysia as a "cosmopolitan" society of equal citizens, or a people differentiated by class rather than race? These and other formulations — urged in recent years, but failing for a long period to gather sufficient ground against the race paradigm — may conceivably be gaining a greater explanatory capacity today.

The first three chapters in this book are concerned primarily with ideas. Chapter 2 relates the history of the construction of the race paradigm and the contest it faced with other possible paradigms, elaborating on some of the observations in this Introduction. The chapter spells out the view that a history of ideas has the potential to broaden the context in which rethinking can be carried out, and that there is a genuine need today to enrich public discussion about the challenges and options which Malaysia faces. To take some specific examples, this history of ideas suggests that such concepts as "*bangsa*", "*Melayu*" and even "Ruler" have assumed an unwarranted rigidity in present-day political discourse. (For an interesting current discussion of the concept of "*bangsa*" as used in Malaysia, see Kessler 2012; see also Milner 2011*b*).

Chapter 3 examines the particular post-Merdeka evolution of the *rakyat* paradigm — the feudal concept of 'the people'. In Rahman Embong's view, this paradigm — in its reconstructed form — might just have the capacity to be a "local idea" with the capacity to realize the Malaysian dream of achieving social cohesion and unity. An inclusive paradigm embedded in the *kerajaan* (or ruler-centred) paradigm of the pre-colonial feudal era, it has the potential — according to this chapter — to be tapped creatively for the purpose of building and maintaining social cohesion in the diverse multi-ethnic Malaysia. To understand the progressive content of the rakyat paradigm, Rahman takes a historical sociology approach, examining in particular the history of ideas and their social forces in different periods of Malaysian society. He shows the usefulness of the *rakyat* paradigm as an analytical construct — and as a contribution of local ideas and concepts towards social science knowledge.

In Chapter 4 Helen Ting focuses on the role of the state and politics in shaping the race paradigm, examining the way institutional mechanisms have reinforced not a greater sense of national unity but rather the socially-divisive, tension-promoting race paradigm. In agreement with Catherine Verdery's contention that state efforts to forge a national identity institutionalize a particular social frame in the generation of ethnic identities, this chapter examines the institutional mechanism which has applied and reinforced the race paradigm in a divisive manner. It argues that the nation-building policies in Malaysia, rather than doing away with the race paradigm and forging a greater sense of national unity, have reinforced and deepened the race paradigm and created more tension and division within the nation.

The following chapters examine where and how far the race paradigm continues to be employed in current public and academic deliberation. Chapter 5 by Ragayah considers approaches to poverty and income distribution, noting the different paradigms that are employed in one context or another internationally. In Malaysia, it was the New Economic Policy's dual objectives of both eradicating poverty and restructuring society that saw culmination in the use of the race paradigm. Estimating its continuing role in government policy is difficult because the government's Economic Planning Unit as custodians of economic data, especially by ethnic groups, was reluctant to share data until recently. However, it is important to note that the race paradigm appears to continue to operate alongside other frameworks such as the overall poverty incidence and income distribution, or analysis by class, state, or region.

In Chapter 6 by Azizah the analysis moves to the issue of foreign workers in Malaysia. In 1992 a policy on foreign workers was introduced to regulate recruitment and employment. The increasing use of foreign workers has frequently been attributed to the shortage of domestic workers in the country and their reluctance to work in certain types of jobs. Azizah contends the government (and academic) concern about security and economic criteria appears to take precedence over the race paradigm — but the chapter also argues that in fact the race paradigm is embedded in the security perspective, which is the ultimate foundation of foreign worker policy in Malaysia.

Chapter 7 by Tham Siew Yean turns to trade policy formulation, noting that both economic and race imperatives were accommodated in Malaysia's trade policy before the establishment of the World Trade Organization. Today, international agreements of various types are impinging on Malaysian governmental mechanisms that are intended to protect domestic industries. Some of these industries — such as the Proton car — have been designed in part to further the objectives of the race-focused New Economic Policy. Looking ahead, export competitiveness will matter most if such industries are to survive, and prosper — and, after all, trade is fundamental to the economic growth that has long been recognized as necessary in the ethnic restructuring of the economy.

The final chapter by K.S. Nathan turns to foreign policy, and insists that while the race paradigm is helpful in understanding the internal dimension of "national security" thinking, the conduct of foreign policy — though largely in Malay hands — is governed above all by a shrewd, rational and pragmatic calculation of how best to advance the national interest. In particular, the quest for recognition of Malaysia's shift from the status of "object" to "subject" in international relations supersedes the preoccupation with ethnicity that so dominates domestic politics. Some might argue that the 'national interest' is at least partly shaped by the race paradigm — nevertheless, the argument in this chapter chimes with the everyday observation that it is when Malaysians deal with foreigners (living or traveling in other countries) that they feel most "Malaysian".

While internally the race paradigm is being contested, it is in Malaysia's international engagement — in foreign policy and trade — that we see the race paradigm facing the strongest competition. Some would argue that it is practical challenges that matter most in episodes of paradigmatic transition, and that real change is most likely to take place as a consequence of economic or security crises in the international sphere (for example, the fall of the Shah in Iran in 1979; the 11 September 2001 attacks). From such a perspective, ideological deliberation could well be seen as making no serious independent contribution. The historical record does demonstrate the importance of such challenges — the economic downturns of the 1980s and late 1990s, for instance, had an acute destabilizing impact on Malaysia — but it also warns against factoring out developments in the realm of ideas. Ideological work tends to play a special role in the "process by which a paradigm disintegrates and comes to be replaced". To be effective, that work has to be able to "import elements of reality which (the paradigm) fails to order" or "expose previously unsuspected flaws in (the paradigm's) ordering of reality" (Pocock 2009, p. 72).

This book follows both tracks — seeking, on the one hand, to test how far the societal race paradigm is still able to "order reality" in the face of the social and economic change that has been taking place in Malaysia; and, on the other, in the chapters that focus on ideas, to recover some of the complexity of the Malaysian ideological story. Highlighting the way in which the race paradigm was constructed, including the strategic suppressing of alternative conceptualizations, underlines its contingent character — and holds out the possibility of future revision and reconstruction. Uncovering the complexity has the further possible advantage of identifying earlier, discarded conceptualizations or understandings that might prove fruitful in future planning.

In its ideological concerns this volume contributes to a larger project — a quest for a greater degree of elbow room within the ideological architecture of Malaysia; a quest that entails what might be termed an exercise in "hermeneutic retrieval". For instance, a recent book, *Sharing the Nation* (Norani Othman et al. 2008) argues that Malaysians have thought too rigidly about the so-called Malay-non-Malay "social contract" which was critical in forging the constitutional compromise on which the nation is based. It might be conceptualized rather as a "covenantal idea of mutuality — the notion that the lives of all citizens are interdependent" and thus the basis of a "shared nationhood" (p. 88). Another area where there has been a call for greater flexibility is the understanding of the term "bumiputra" (or "sons of the soil"). Assuming that the term continues to be used for those who are seen to have the right to special treatment from the government, the suggestion has been made that it could be reconstructed and made more inclusive "so that the constitution can now protect all rather than the few". It is certainly not just Malays, insists Azly Rahman, who today "toil for the soil" (2009, p. 439). In the religious sphere, Ahmad Fauzy Abdul Hamid has criticized the "legalist Islam practiced by the present Malaysian state" (2011, p. 80) and suggests that the Sufi-influenced Islam dating back to the Melaka sultanate has much to offer today when there is a need for "enhancing tolerance and accommodation among Malaysians" (p. 87).

The race paradigm, we would predict, is not about to be overthrown: some of the essays here offer a reminder of its continued potency. Nevertheless, in stressing the constructed nature of the race paradigm, and narrating how it has become entrenched — sometimes in contest with other types of national blueprint — we seek to reinforce the view that the ideological landscape in which policy can be developed in Malaysia is a lot richer than many assume. Furthermore, in analysing practical ways in which the race paradigm is influential (or less influential) today the book issues a warning that new economic and political developments — new realities — may well call for adjustments in the way Malaysians conceptualize their society and nation. The race paradigm — strong as it has been — could well be undermined both from within and without.

References

Abdul Rahman Embong and Tham Siew Yean, eds. *Malaysia at a Crossroads: Can We Make the Transition?* Bangi: Penerbit Universiti Kebangsaan Malaysia, 2011.

Abdullah Hussain. *Interlok*. Kuala Lumpur: Dewan Bahasa dan Pustaka, 1971.

Ahmad Fauzi Abdul Hamid. "Malay Racialism and the Sufi Alternative". In *Melayu: The Politics, Poetics and Paradoxes of Malayness*, edited by Maznah Mohamad and Syed Muhd Khairudin Aljuneid. Singapore: National University Press, 2011.

Anand, Ram. "When Najib Failed as a Statesman". *Malaysiakini*, 7 May 2013.

Azly Rahman. "The 'New Bumiputraism' as Pedagogy of Hope and Liberation: Teaching the Alternative Malaysian Ethnic Studies". In *Multiethnic Malaysia: Past, Present and Future*, edited by Lim Teck Ghee, Albert Gomes and Azly Rahman. Petaling Jaya: Strategic Information and Research Development Centre, 2009.

Babcock, Tim G. "Indigenous Ethnicity in Sarawak". *Sarawak Museums Journal* 22, no. 43 (1974): 191–202.

Bayly, C.A. *The Birth of the Modern World 1780–1914*. Oxford: Blackwell, 2004.

Day, Tony. *Fluid Iron: State Formation in Southeast Asia*. Honolulu: University of Hawai'i Press, 2002.

Gomes, Alberto. "Ethnicisation of the Orang Asli: A Case Study of the Semai". In *Multiethnic Malaysia: Past, Present and Future*, edited by Lim Teck Ghee, Albert Gomes and Azly Rahman. Petaling Jaya: Strategic Information and Research Development Centre, 2009.

Gullick, J.M. *Indigenous Political Systems of Western Malaya*. London: Athlone Press, 1965.

———. *Malaysia: Economic Expansion and National Unity*. London: Ernest Benn, 1981.

Hannaford, Ivan. *Race: The History of an Idea in the West*. Washington: Woodrow Wilson Center Press, 1996.

Heryanto, Ariel. *State Terrorism and Political Identity in Indonesia: Fatally Belonging*. Abingdon: Routledge, 2006.

Hill, H., Tham S.Y. and H.M.Z. Ragayah, eds. *Malaysia's Development Challenges: Graduating from the Middle*. Abingdon: Routledge, 2012.

Hirschman, Charles. "The Meaning and Measurement of Ethnicity in Malaysia: An Analysis of Census Classifications". *Journal of Asian Studies* 42, no. 3 (1987): 555–82.

Kessler, C.S. *What Every Malaysian Needs to Know about "Race"*. Bangi: Institute of Ethnic Studies (KITA), Universiti Kebangsaan Malaysia, 2012.

Khoo Boo Teik. *Paradoxes of Mahathirism*. Kuala Lumpur: Oxford University Press, 1995.

Khoo, Kay Kim. "The Emergence of Plural Communities in the Malay Peninsula before 1874". In *Multiethnic Malaysia: Past, Present and Future*, edited by Lim Teck Ghee, Albert Gomes and Azly Rahman. Petaling Jaya: Strategic Information and Research Development Centre, 2009.

Kuhn, T.S. *The Structure of Scientific Revolutions*. Chicago: University of Chicago Press, 1996.

Leach, E.R. *Social Science Research in Sarawak*. London: His Majesty's Stationery Office, 1950.

Mandal, Sumit K. "Transethnic Solidarities, Racialization and Social Equality". In *The State of Malaysia: Ethnicity, Equity and Reform*, edited by Edmund Terence Gomez. London and New York: RoutledgeCurzon, 2004.

Merdeka Center. *Public Opinion Poll on Ethnic Relations*. Bangi, Selangor, 2006.

Milner, Anthony. *Kerajaan: Malay Political Culture on the Eve of Colonial Rule*. Tucson: University of Arizona Press for the Association for Asian Studies, 1982.

———. "Inventing Politics: The Case of Malaysia". *Past and Present*, vol. 132, no. 1 (1991): 104–29.

———. "'Malayness': Confrontation, Innovation and Discourse". In *Looking in Odd Mirrors: The Java Sea*, edited by V.J.H. Houben, H.M.J. Maier and W. Van der Molen. Leiden: Rijksuniversiteit, 1993.

———. *The Invention of Politics: Expanding the Public Sphere in Colonial Malaya*. Cambridge, New York and Melbourne: Cambridge University Press, 2002.

———. "How 'Traditional' is the Malaysian Monarchy?" In *Malaysia: Islam, Society and Politics*, edited by Virginia Hooker and Norani Othman. Singapore: Institute of Southeast Asian Studies, 2003*a*.

———. "Who Created Malaysia's Plural Society?" *Journal of the Malaysian Branch of the Royal Asiatic Society* 76, no. 2 (2003*b*): 1–24.

———. *The Malays*. Oxford: Wiley-Blackwell, 2011*a*.

———. *Malaysia's Dominant Societal Paradigm: Invented, Embedded, Contested*. Bangi: Penerbit Universiti Kebangsaan Malaysia, 2011*b*.

Mittelman, J.H. and Norani Othman, eds. *Capturing Globalization*. London and New York: Routledge, 2001.

Nelson, Joan M. "Conclusions". In *Globalization and National Autonomy: The Experience of Malaysia*, edited by Joan M. Nelson, Jacob Meerman and Abdul Rahman Embong. Singapore: Institute of Southeast Asian Studies and Bangi: Institute of Malaysian and International Studies, 2008.

Norani Othman, Mavis C. Puthucheary and Clive S. Kessler. *Sharing the Nation: Faith, Difference, Power and the State 50 Years after Merdeka*. Petaling Jaya: SIRD, 2008.

Pocock, J.G.A. *Political Thought and History: Essays on Theory and Method*. Cambridge: Cambridge University Press, 2009.

Pringle, Robert. *Rajahs and Rebels: The Ibans of Sarawak under Brooke Rule*. Ithaca: Cornell University Press, 1970.

Reid, Anthony. "Endangered Identity: Kadazan or Dusun in Sabah (East Malaysia)". *Journal of Southeast Asian Studies* 28, no. 1 (1997): 120–36.

Shamsul A.B. "Debating about Identity in Malaysia: A Discourse Analysis". *Southeast Asian Studies* 34, no. 3 (1996): 8476–499.

———. "Ethnicity, Class, Culture or Identity? Competing Paradigms in Malaysian Studies". *Akademika* 53 (1998): 33–59.

Shamsul A.B. and Anis Y. Yusoff. *Managing Peace in Malaysia: A Case Study*. Bangi: Institute of Ethnic Studies, 2011.

Swettenham, Sir Frank. *Malaya: An Account of the Origin and Progress of British Influence in Malaya*. London: John Lane and Bodley Head, 1907.

Welsh, Bridget. "Real Change? Elections in the *Reformasi* Era". In *The State of Malaysia: Ethnicity, Equity and Reform*, edited by Edmund Terence Gomez. London and New York: RoutledgeCurzon, 2004.

World Bank. *Malaysia Economic Monitor: Brain Drain*. Washington, D.C.: The World Bank, 2011.

Newspapers

Lee Wei Lian. "Malaysia's brain drain getting worse, says World Bank". *Malaysian Insider*, 28 April 2011.

"Najib's speech at 61st UMNO General Assembly". *The Sun Daily*, 22 October 2010. <http://www.thesundaily.my/node/137039>.

New Straits Times, 6 December 2010; "Special Statement", Yang di-Pertuan Agong, 3 July 2011.

Zulkiflee Bakar. "Apa Lagi Cina Mahu?" *Utusan Malaysia*, 7 May 2013.

2

RACE AND ITS COMPETING PARADIGMS
A Historical Review

Anthony Milner and Helen Ting[1]

Can Malaysian society and politics ever move beyond a race-based paradigm? The need to do so has been stressed by many of those who are working to move Malaysia to a new developmental stage — but, as the Introduction to this book points out, the potency of this paradigm should not be underestimated. How then has the race paradigm become embedded, and in what ways has it been contested and defended? Is it possible to conceptualize Malaysians in terms other than "Malay", "Chinese" and "Indian" (with allusions to a list of further indigenous groupings)? This last question is often asked. Some analysts have begun to envisage a national "transethnic solidarity" (Loh 2010, p. 11; Mandal 2004, p. 49), a "growing feeling of multi-racialism" (Gomez 2004, p. 21), a move from a "plural to a multiethnic society or nation" (Ong 2009, p. 478), a "nation of equal citizens" (Ong 2009, p. 478), a more "inclusive citizenship" (Hefner 2001, pp. 45, 48), an emerging "language of inclusion and civility" (Abdul Rahman 2001, pp. 72, 81), and a greater stress on "cosmopolitanism" (Yao 2003). In the past, there have been attempts to imagine a "Malayan" citizenship, a "Malayan Union", a multiethnic identity under a "Melayu" label, a "Malaysian Malaysia", a "Bangsa Malaysia" (a Malaysian "race" or "nation") — and in recent years the federal government constantly invoked the idea of a "1Malaysia".

The formulation or countering of these concepts has of course been shaped by specific economic or political circumstances — the aftermath of the Japanese Occupation, the Communist Insurgency, the 1969 race riots, dramatic downturns in the economy, and so forth. Insisting that ideas and the way they are debated are significant and deserving of analysis in their own right is not to deny their context. The issue is one of focus, and our concern is to examine the manner in which the race paradigm came into being, and then a number of the various attempts that have been made to replace it. To recover both the history of the race paradigm and the range of other conceptualizations operating or advocated in the past makes sense right now — not only for historical purposes, but because of the contribution it could make to the practical deliberations at present taking place in Malaysia. The ideological formulations of the Najib government's signature policy, "1Malaysia", conveyed the impression that a new race-transcending template for this country is under serious consideration. A contest of ideas is likely to be central to achieving any fundamental change, and a "history of ideas" approach to the race issue offers the potential to enrich that contest — at least by suggesting added possibilities, perhaps assisted by long-ignored flexibilities.

THE RACE PARADIGM

The Introduction to this book recalled the pre-colonial context in which the race paradigm began to be established in the nineteenth century — and noted that far-reaching "racial engineering" was initiated by the British in Borneo as well as the Peninsula, with the promotion of "Dayak" and "Dusun" as well as "Malay" and other ethnic identities. Our principal concern, however, is the Malay/Chinese/Indian paradigm which is so often seen to structure social, economic and political life in Malaysia.

Looking at the region in terms of its precolonial history, the area covered by the present-day Malaysia, Indonesia and Brunei consisted of kingdoms and chieftainships of one form or another, not races or even territorially-defined states. On the Peninsula, Sumatra and Borneo rulers of sultanates or *kerajaan* came from a range of backgrounds, including Arab and Indian. The kerajaan polity was based on the concept of personal relations with the ruler. A ruler referred to himself as a ruler, not the ruler of a state (or a specific race or ethnic group). To use the language of royal letters of the time, in the *kerajaan* polity a ruler would describe himself as "Yang Di Pertuan Sultan X, who sits in state on the throne of the kerajaan that is in the settlement/country (negeri) Y" (Ahmat Adam

2009, pp. 86, 104, 192, 265; Gullick 1965; Milner 1982). The ruler did not describe himself as the "Sultan of Johor" or the "Sultan of Perak", or the "Sultan of the Malays". In this *kerajaan* paradigm, for all its lack of stress on geographic or ethnic definition, the community was bonded together through various hierarchical relations between ruler and subject — relations that were carefully enunciated in ceremonies, texts, clothes styles and so forth. The people would announce themselves as "subjects of a ruler" (*rakyat*). Status was determined in relation to the ruler, and some court texts suggest that status in this world influenced one's position in the next. In the words attributed to the loyal official of the Sultan of Melaka, Hang Tuah: "we who live under *rajas* do whatever work we have to do as diligently as possible, for as the old people say: it is good to die with a reputation (*nama*) which is good" (Kassim Ahmad 1968, p. 319). The Sultan who accumulated subjects would also seem to have enhanced his own status.

Subjects of a Sultan (*rakyat*), in many cases living close to a river, were of course often identified with that river — as "*orang Terengganu*" and so forth — and the name "*orang Melayu*" may well have had such a river origin. There is no strong evidence, however, that so-called "*orang Melayu*" viewed themselves in the pre-colonial *kerajaan* period as members of a trans-Sultanate race or ethnicity (Milner 2011, chapter 4). They used the phrase in a Melaka-Johor context, and people who lived in Patani or Kedah do not appear to have referred to themselves as "*orang Melayu*", at least until the nineteenth century. When "*Melayu*" did begin to be employed by some commoner "Malay" leaders as a trans-*kerajaan* category — influenced by European racial thinking — it was also initially opposed by the *kerajaan* elites on the Peninsula (as well as on Sumatra and Borneo) (Milner 2011, chapters 4 and 5).

In the nineteenth century because of European influence (as discussed in the Introduction), the term "Malay" — which tended to have been used with reference to the people of Melaka, and polities linked to Melaka — began increasingly to refer to the idea of a trans-sultanate Malay racial identity. Abdullah Abdul Kadir, "Munshi Abdullah" — who was much influenced by the European elite in Singapore and Melaka — was a pioneer in this building of the "Malay race" (*bangsa Melayu*). Writing in the 1830s and 1840s, Abdullah — unlike traditional authors at the courts on the Peninsula and elsewhere in the Archipelago — described the world in terms of race: he was concerned in particular with the fortunes of the Malays, and not of one kingdom (*kerajaan*) or another. He and many later Malay leaders feared the competition of "other races" and he felt Malays had much to learn from the British race. Especially from the first decades of the twentieth century, a series of ideologues (starting with the Singaporean, Mohd. Eunos Abdullah) engaged in a long and challenging process of propagating the idea of the "Malay race" — defining it, and injecting in it a high emotive value. People were urged to be loyal to their race — sometimes urged to do so in the old language once used specifically to describe loyalty to a monarch. Aspirations and anxieties were also enunciated in racial terms — with immigrant peoples, especially the "Chinese race", often portrayed as a threat to the Malays, particularly in economic areas (Khoo 1981; Roff 1994; Milner 2002).

The category "Malay race" is now treated as a given in Malaysian social discourse. For some it has assumed a formidable rigidity — and yet knowing the ideological history of the concept may be a step toward greater flexibility. The fact that "Malay" came to mean something different in East Sumatra, the Riau Archipelago, Singapore and Sri Lanka — and that its meaning continues to be debated in Malaysia (Kahn and Loh 1992, pp. 5–6; Shamsul 1997; Milner 2011) — also underlines the observation that it is a man-made concept rather than a mere biological reality. We will return to this issue of flexibility.

As "the Malays" were gradually constituted as a racial entity, so a similar dynamic was present among other peoples. The building of a "Chinese" cultural and political identity in Malaya was a process which took place largely in the twentieth century — and it too was influenced by European thinking about race, transmitted in this case largely through Japan (Yen 2000, p. 12; Tan 1988, pp. 21–23). Foreigners had long called "Chinese" people "Tang People" (which referred to the Tang dynasty of the seventh to tenth centuries) — and "Chinese" sometimes began to refer to themselves in this way (Tan 2000, p. 66). In China itself neither race nor ethnicity were "well-defined" categories, and the "boundaries separating the Han and the non-Han were merely cultural constructions shifting along specific historical situations" (Shen and Chien 2006, p. 57). It is only in modern times, in the context of rising anti-colonial nationalism, that the idea of the "Han" — shaped by the Western concept of "race" — became a "biological category" (p. 57). At the turn of the twentieth century, there was no word in the Chinese vocabulary to denote the concept of race — or a people sharing common ties of descent, language and culture — and the word *minzu* was coined (Tan 1988, p. 23). In his discussion of nationalist ideology, the widely-respected Chinese nationalist, Dr Sun Yat Sen — who was committed to uniting the "Chinese people" — insisted that the Chinese belonged to "the blood-stock of the yellow race", sharing a common language, religion and customs. Sun argued that China was the only country where "race" and "nation" coincided (Purcell 1980, p. 295).

In colonial Malaya, marriages between Hokkien, Cantonese, Hainanese and Teochew groups had tended to be rare — as were those between Tamil, Malayali, Telugu and Sikh groups (Khoo 2009, p. 25). Solidarity within dialect groups was enhanced by the "inability to communicate with people of other dialect groups", and by the tensions that often existed between these groups (Lee 1978, p. 46). Besides these dialect-based differences, there was a further distinction within the so-called "Chinese" community (certainly during the 1930s) between the Straits-born and the "newer immigrants" — some of the former sharing "Malay blood" and "far more intimately linked to the Colony" than the latter (Emerson 1964, p. 282).

The socially constructed nature of "race" in Malaysia is evident again when the historical development of the "Indian race" is examined. The so-called "Indian" community in Malaya included Tamils, Malayalees, Telegus, Punjabi Sikhs, Gujeratis, Sindhis, Marathis and Bengalis, as well as the division between castes — and those people came from what is now Pakistan, Bangladesh, and Sri Lanka as well as India. A number of the Muslims among these groups began to identify with the "Malay" rather than "Indian" community. Attempts made to unify the "Indian" community sometimes exacerbated tensions. For instance, those seeking to bring Hindu practices into conformity with elite Brahmanic norms have met resistance — especially from powerful Tamil groups, promoting a Tamil religion free from reliance on Brahmannic ritual or Sanskrit language (Arasaratnam 1993; Brown 1993).

The Indian Association of the Federated Malay States founded in 1906 was an early initiative to bring Indians together. From the 1920s, Hindu Tamil leaders succeeded in getting "Indian" representation on the legislative bodies of the Federated Malay States and the Straits Settlements (Tate 2008, pp. 45–46) — which probably in itself helped to promote the imagining of the term "Indian race" as a classifier, though it did not manage to unite "the Indians" as a community, even at elite level. The first organization which could claim to represent all the disparate "Indian" groups on the Malay Peninsula, the Central Indian Association of Malaya (CIAM), was founded in late 1936. Within a few months, however, a Pan-Malayan Dravidian association was formed — which reflected the dynamics of Dravidian versus Indian nationalist tension on the Indian subcontinent (Tate 2008, p. 25). Political rivalry plagued even the "Dravidian unity". In 1937, during the visit of Jawaharlal Nehru to Malaya, serious dissension among Tamils of Ceylonese and Indian origins obliged Nehru to state that Ceylonese Tamils could not claim to be Indians due to geographical and administrative distinctions (Tate 2008, p. 46). Part of the problem in promoting the use of the term "Indian" was the confusion about whether it was a political, geographical or a racial conception.

The charismatic leadership of Subhas Chandra Bose — in the context of the Japanese Occupation — did help to bring together the Indian community in Malaya. He managed to arouse a strong sense of anti-British nationalism in the community — a desire to free their motherland from colonialism — and drew large numbers into the Malaya-based Indian National Army (Tate 2008, pp. 66–70). But despite Bose, and the efforts of later leaders, it could still be said after decades of Malaysian independence that "if 'Indians' exist" then the grouping does so "as a set of people who temporarily suspend differences in order to engage in a political and economic struggle whose form is largely determined by the structures of the Malaysian nation state" (Mearns 1986, pp. 98–99).

Looking back over the colonial period we can see the racial structure of "Malay", "Chinese" and "Indian" emerging — authorized at numerous levels by the British administration. As discussed in the Introduction to this book, the category "race" began to be introduced into the official census in 1891: during the early colonial period, the basis of categorization appears to have been largely that of geographical origins — place of birth — supplemented by sub-categories based on dialects spoken (attributed as "tribes") (Hirschman 1987, p. 561). Stereotyped in popular writings (such as those of proconsul Swettenham), the "Malay", "Chinese" and "Indian" groupings related to one another increasingly in racial terms, perceiving interests and issues in that manner. Among other influences, the bitter Chinese-versus-Malay debates stirred up by the British Decentralization Policy during the 1930s contributed to this racialization process (Abraham 1997). A full account of the building of racial categorization would also examine the way local ideas entrepreneurs "localized" the idea of "race" to suit the social and political purposes of their own society (for the "Malay" case, see Milner 2011, chapters 5–8). Nevertheless, viewing this emerging race paradigm in historical context, the British influence seems profound — with the whole societal structure strikingly different from the world of kingdoms that had characterized the pre-colonial Archipelago.

THE RACE NARRATIVE FOR MODERN MALAYA/MALAYSIA

The history of the years leading up to Independence in 1957, and to the post-Independence state, can easily be — and is often — recounted through large, simplistic racial brushstrokes. The negative impact of the Japanese Occupation — so we are often told — was more severe for the "Chinese" than the "Malay" segment of the population. Following the war, there were severe clashes between "Chinese" and "Malay" groups — some "Malays" being accused of having collaborated with the Japanese administration, and some "Chinese" perceived to be seeking to take control of the country. Continuing the race-based narrative, on their return to Malaya the British administration attempted to impose the Malayan Union — a structure to replace the complex pre-War arrangement of British-protected Sultanates and Straits Settlements colony, along with the specific privileging of the "Malay" race. This change was immediately perceived in racial terms — viewed as a triumph for the "Chinese" and other non-Malay immigrants, and a devastating defeat for the "Malays". A "Malay" opposition movement began, the size of which astounded the British officials. In 1948 an alternative, federal scheme — the Federation of Malaya — was implemented, and it is seen to have restored the rulers' sovereignty and "Malays" rights, while the "non-Malay's status" was "considerably weakened". Citizenship regulations for the Federation included language requirements that "excluded a large number of non-Malays" (Cheah 2002, pp. 18–19).

In 1948 a "predominantly-Chinese", communist insurrection began (Cheah 2002, p. 23), and the British introduced measures to win support from the Chinese community, including far more liberal citizenship conditions. Apparently under British pressure, the Malay leader Dato' Onn bin Jaafar, attempted — without real success — to move his United Malays National Organisation (UMNO) away from its specifically racial base. He then began a new party — the Independence of Malaya Party — with the declared intention of moving beyond race politics. This party fared badly against the explicitly race-based parties in the important, pioneering Kuala Lumpur municipal elections of 1952. In 1954, Onn created another party, Party Negara, and now returned to racial appeals, attempting at times to outbid UMNO for the Malay vote (Smith 1995, pp. 180–81).

Attempts to move beyond race also took place on the political left. When (in 1947) the clearly non-Malay All-Malayan Council of

Joint Action (AMCJA) joined with the Malay Pusat Tenaga Raayat (PUTERA), to write a "People's Constitution", the two pledged their support for "equal political rights for all who regarded Malaya as their real home and as the object of their loyalty" (PUTERA-AMCJA 1947, p. 3). Nevertheless, as the new coalition also committed to paying "special attention" to the "advancement of the Malays" this was hardly a complete departure from the race paradigm. In any case, it was not the left but the more conservative "Alliance" comprising UMNO, the Malayan Chinese Association (MCA) and the Malayan Indian Congress (MIC) that assumed government in independent Malaya (1957) — and the Federal Constitution itself was shaped by a bargain between these three Alliance parties. UMNO agreed to recognize citizenship on the basis of *jus soli* (citizenship by right of birth), and on their part the non-Malay parties agreed to the inclusion in the Constitution of what is called "the special position of the Malays" (Fernando 2002, p. 85). This is the "historic bargain" between Malays and non-Malays, which Cheah Boon Kheng has identified as the basis of the new independent Malayan state: a "political framework within which the ethnic groups were to operate in Malaya" (2002, p. 235). Cheah says it remains "the basis of the country's nation-building efforts" (p. 39), and he devotes much of his influential study of that process to analysing the four Prime Ministers as "nation builders" — referring back frequently to the "bargain", and to the problem of "juggl(ing) between 'pro-Malay' and 'pro-Chinese' policies" (p. 112).

The formation in 1963 of Malaysia — bringing Malaya together with Singapore and the Bornean states — was based on the desire to strengthen Singapore against possible Communist takeover and also achieve a balanced racial composition (Simandjuntak 1969, pp. 127–28). In the deliberations preceding the expansion of "Malaya" the term sometimes used for the proposed state was "Melayu Raya" (Greater Malaydom), rather than "Malaysia" (Milner 1992), and Prime Minister Tunku Abdul Rahman insisted that the Iban of Borneo were of "the same stock as the Malays" (Soda 2000, p. 190).

Over the following decades there were numerous attempts to transcend the race paradigm — an aspiration which the Malayan Union concept, Onn's Independence of Malaya Party, the AMCJA/PUTERA alliance and the Malayan Communist Party, in their different ways, had all expressed. The post-Independence attempts include the Singapore leader, Lee Kuan Yew's call for a "Malaysian Malaysia", the introduction of a code of national ideological principles (the "*Rukun Negara*"), the emergence of "rakyat" socialism, the advocacy of other concepts such as "*Bangsa Malaysia*", "multiculturalism", and "1Malaysia" and — some would argue — the campaigns for an "Islamic state" (*Negara Islam*). In the next section of this chapter we turn to a closer examination of these "ideological episodes" — as they might be called. First, however, what of the *kerajaan* paradigm? In some respects monarchy was overwhelmed by the race paradigm — but certain ingredients in this institution continue to have a potential for resistance. To examine the role of the *kerajaan* has the further advantage that it provides an opportunity to assess whether pre-colonial experience is still relevant to Malaysia — or must we accept that for "identity formation" and other areas in the modern state, "colonial knowledge" is the real "baseline knowledge"? (Shamsul 1998, p. 49; Milner 2011*a*, pp. 26–27).

MONARCHY

Although initially resisting the advocates of a specifically "Malay" identity and loyalty, the Rulers later claimed a leadership role with respect to the Malay community, and portrayed themselves in "Malay" as well as royal terms. With respect to royal resistance, Ibrahim Yaacob's account of British Malaya on the eve of the Japanese invasion reports that members of royal courts were prominent among those who held "firmly to the old feeling and strongly oppose the new desire to unify the Malay people". In several states those seeking to establish Malay associations faced determined royal opposition (Milner 2002, pp. 269–70; Roff 1968, p. 119; Smith 2006, p. 128). Beyond the Peninsula, similar confrontation took place in Brunei and East Sumatra (Brown 1970, pp. 4, 9; Ariffin Omar 1993, pp. 23–24, 71, 77–78). The idea of a trans-Archipelago Malay race presumably caused discomfort to royal courts not just because loyalty to race had the potential to reach beyond any individual sultanate, but it carried as well an egalitarian ethos. Tension between monarchy and race activism was also sharpened because some proponents of the Malay race — such as the pioneer of "Malay" racial thinking, Abdullah bin Abdul Kadir, (1797–1854) and Ibrahim Yaacob himself — frequently criticized Malay rulers (Milner 2002, p. 15).

The *kerajaan* of the period before British and Dutch domination of the Archipelago could be described as race blind. The term "Malay", as suggested already, was not actually used by the Archipelago people to describe the wide range of Archipelago polities which were to be given that name in the nineteenth and twentieth centuries. The use of the expression "Malay world" is therefore misleading for this period, and it might be more accurate to speak of a "*kerajaan*" or "sultanate world" (Milner 2011, chapter 4). People of many backgrounds participated in a *kerajaan*. Rulers themselves claimed descent from Alexander the Great as well as from dignitaries of Indian and Arab origin (Milner 1982; Leyden 1968, pp. 101, 105), and even in their clothing displayed a flexibility regarding ethnic identification. In the early nineteenth century, Johor ruler Husain dressed his sons in "Tamil fashion, wearing wide trousers and Indian gowns" (Abdullah 2009, p. 275). Sultan Abdul Hamid of Kedah (1882–1943) "almost invariably wore western-style suites in preference to Malay dress"; on ceremonial occasions he tended to dress in a Siamese-style uniform (Sheppard 2007, pp. 4; 8–9). With respect to high officials in the *kerajaan*, at the opening of the seventeenth century a Peguan (from present-day Burma) was one of "the highest councilors" to the ruler of Kedah (Commelin 1969, p. 46). A mid-nineteenth century Kedah ruler gave a high title to a Hakka leader, who was "accorded a high place on State Functions" (Gullick 1992, pp. 372–73); and a little later in Pahang a "Tamil Indian" was the "treasurer and tax collector" (Gullick 1965, p. 52).

Commoner subjects, as discussed above, do not appear to have considered themselves members of a trans-sultanate race — but tended to identify with a particular geographic location (*orang Kelantan*, *orang Kemaman*) or as subjects of a ruler (*rakyat*) (Milner 2011, chapters 4 and 5). Well into the British period people who would eventually call themselves "Malay" continued to identify as "Minangkabau", "Bugis", "Baweyan" or "Javanese". Chinese could also be subjects of a ruler, and in the colonial period continued to be so (Ratnam 1965, p. 72; Mohamed Suffian 1972, p. 207; Emerson 1964, p. 509). In a 1931 legal case involving a Chinese man (Ho Chick Kwan), whom the British wanted the Sultan of Selangor to banish, Ho was described as a "natural born subject of the Ruler of the State of Negri Sembilan", and his adopted mother (Lui Ho) described herself as owing "true allegiance to His Highness the Sultan of Selangor" (Ho Chick Kwan v The Hon'ble British Resident Selangor, criminal appeal no. 11 of 1931).

Anxious as they may have been about the advocates of race, the Rulers were themselves conceptualized in racial terms by the British. Even in the foundation document for British engagement in the Peninsular States — the Pangkor Engagement — their "Malayness" was insisted upon when giving them a special role regarding "Malay Religion and Custom". Some early twentieth-century writings from the royal courts — particularly those courts most committed to modernization — also took a more positive approach to Malay racial sentiment. The "Hikayat Johor and the History of the Late Sultan Abu Bakar" [r. 1885–95] expresses a concern about "races" (not found in traditional court literature) and also makes direct reference to "subjects who are of the Malay race" (Milner 2002, p. 202). A coronation memento of the 1930s issued in association with the coronation of Sultan Abdul Aziz of Perak (r. 1938–48) presents the new Ruler as having a specific administrative concern for the Malay people (p. 242).

Although some courts tackled the new "Malay" movement in creative ways, in general Rulers continued to conceptualize their people as "subjects" (*rakyat*) rather than members of "races" (*bangsa*) — and also went on expressing concern for their "non-Malay" as well as "Malay" subjects. Even the Johor text cited above praises the Ruler for bringing outsiders (including Chinese) to Johor to develop plantations — and also for "looking after the Chinese subjects living in the state" (Milner 2002, pp. 208, 214). The later Perak document notes the new Ruler was "friends with many of the other races in the state" and had "not forgotten the help these races have given in making Perak wealthy and prosperous". At the coronation itself, not only Malays but also Chinese, Ceylonese, Indians and Japanese made formal declarations of loyalty to the new ruler — who, the text declares, "does not distinguish between his subjects" (Milner 2002, pp. 243–44). This relationship between rulers and non-Malays was confirmed in contemporary accounts. Rulers were reported as bestowing prestigious titles on Chinese subjects, and the Johor state council building was said to look like a Chinese audience hall — decorated with a record (in Chinese writing) of the personal service of wealthy Chinese people to the ruler (Milner 2002, p. 261). Rulers were certainly known to engage closely with Chinese in business (Gullick 1992, pp. 213–14; 131 n.125; Lim 2002).

In the immediate post-war years, in the struggle against the Malayan Union, the Rulers were pressed to identify more strongly with the Malay movement. They now became more explicitly "Malay rulers": monarchy was more sharply racialized. They had been bullied by the British into accepting the Malayan Union — and then protesting crowds (led in particular by Onn bin Jaafar) called on them to resist the change. The cry was "*Daulat Tuanku*" ("Power to the Ruler") — but as Ariffin Omar has pointed out, for many people "the interests of the rajas" were now "subordinated to the demands of Malayism" (1993, p. 53). Significantly, Onn bin Jaafar began to speak of the "*bangsa Melayu*" (Malay race) in the language once reserved for expressions of loyalty toward a Ruler, and the potent term *derhaka* (traitor) — once used with reference to the heinous crime of disloyalty to a ruler — was now employed to warn rulers against "disloyalty" to their Malay subjects (Ariffin 1993, p. 53; Milner 2011, p. 153; Smith 1995, p. 169; Kobkua 2011, p. 169). Seeing the need for change, the Sultan of Pahang now talked of "we Malays" and the Sultan of Perak declaring that he spoke "as a Malay not as a Sultan" (Ariffin 1993, p. 104).

TRANS-RACIAL RESIDUE?

Looking at the post-Independence period, how much survives of the old racially inclusive *kerajaan* ideology? Turning first to the Federal Constitution of 1957, the Rulers have the responsibility of both safeguarding the special position of the Malays, and the legitimate interests of the other communities (Mohd. Salleh 1986, p. 4) — a role of balancing both groups' interests that had been assigned to the British High Commissioner in the 1948 Federation of Malaya Agreement (Ratnam 1965, p. 104). The responsibility might look essentially even-handed, but public focus tends to be on the Malay dimension — probably because the entrenching of these special privileges is usually seen as "the most unusual feature of the Malaysian Constitution" (Harding 2007, p. 120). Amendments made to the Constitution in 1971 reinforced the impression of a Ruler-Malay community linkage, in that any change to Malay (and natives of Sarawak and Sabah) privileges now required "the consent of the Conference of Rulers, as well as the required two-third's parliamentary majority" (Harding 2007, p. 121).

Further racializing of the rulers can be seen in the way they have been increasingly described as the "symbol" or "cement" assisting to hold the Malay race or racial feeling together (Ariffin 1993, pp. 53, 102): in the 1980s the senior Malaysian legal official, Tun Haji Mohd. Salleh bin Abas wrote of "Malay rulership" as "the nub of Malay custom" (1986, p. 13). In a coronation document of 1971 from the royal court of Pahang, the Pahang monarchy's customs and ceremonial — which once would have been of vital importance merely because they were royal customs and ceremonial — are presented as significant because they are a "branch of Malay culture" and a reflection of the "national characteristics of the Malay people (*bangsa Melayu*)" (Anon 1971; see also Milner 2003, pp. 188–89). In public pronouncements, Rulers have also been deliberate in identifying themselves with issues of core importance to the Malay community. When the Sultan of Kedah told Malaysian soldiers to "hold on to your faith for the sake of defending our race, religion and country" (NST, 30 March 2011), he could only have been speaking to Malays — and was invoking his own special role in relation to the Malay community. Also, it should be noted that announcements from the Conference of Rulers employ the terminology "Malay Rulers" (Kobkua 2011, p. 424) — although in the Federal Constitution itself the Conference is called just "Majlis Raja-Raja (Conference of Rulers)".

Despite such profiling of "Malay Ruler", however, the residue of an earlier trans-racial substance has survived. Looking back over the last half century, we see an indication of this when the Sultan of Pahang has been described as a "symbol of the unity of the people (*rakyat*)" (and not just the Malay race, or *bangsa*) (Shariff Ahmad 1983, pp. xvii, 32; see also M. Hamzah Jamaludin, "Dynamic and caring ruler", NST, 24 October 2010); or when the last Sultan of Kelantan has been referred to as the "umbrella sheltering" the people (*rakyat*) (Mohd. Zain Saleh 1987, p. 14). There is a suggestion of such residue as well when Chinese people have recalled that in May 1969 — at a time of acute inter-racial crisis — the Sultan of Terengganu and other rulers took steps to protect their non-Malay subjects, warning headmen (*penghulu*) and other leaders in the Malay community not to allow the violence in Kuala Lumpur to spread to other regions.

A special press statement from the Conference of Rulers in October 2008 is an example of a royal attempt to find a balance between a specifically Malay and a strongly inclusive role. The Rulers explained that "the institution of the Ruler" had been "retained and legally enshrined in the Constitution of an independent Malaysia". The "institution of the Rulers" was "accorded eminence", positioned "at the apex of government as the head of the country and the states," and viewed as a "protective umbrella ensuring impartiality among the citizens". The institution of the Rulers "takes on the role of being a check-and-balance to untangle complications, if any". The statement points to the Rulers' "constitutional role" respecting the so-called "Social Contract" between Malays and non-Malays, and assured "non-Malays" that there was no need to "harbour any apprehension or worry over their genuine rights ..." (Kobkua 2011, pp. 425–26).

The birthday celebrations of the different rulers are a time when the continued trans-racial character of monarchy is evident. At the Perak 2011 Celebration the recipients of honours included a leading businessman whose father was Goanese and a wide range of Chinese and Indian people (P. Chandra Sagaran, "Sultan heads Perak honours list", NST,

19 April 2011). The Sultan stressed that "historically, Malaysia has long housed those from different races and religions" (NST, 20 April 2011). At the Johor 2010 celebration, the Sultan urged his people "to respect one another without regard to race". "The people", he said, "regardless of whether they are Malays, Indians or Chinese, are all citizens of my state. The rights of everyone will be protected" (*Bernama*, "Sultan calls for new bridge to Singapore", NST, 23 November 2010).

To conclude: with the rise of Malay racial sentiment in the middle decades of the twentieth century, the Rulers were increasingly defined in Malay terms. Yet the subjection of monarchy to race has not been complete. Elements of an older, inclusive *kerajaan* paradigm still exercise a degree of influence. The Rulers continue to make a claim to provide an umbrella sheltering all the people (*rakyat*), and the fact that politicians of various persuasions use the old word "*rakyat*" to refer to "the people" can itself be interpreted as an inheritance from *kerajaan* ideology.

THE MALAYAN UNION

The Malayan Union Plan, introduced following the Second World War, was intended to create a united Malaya and clarify the political status of the non-Malays (Lau 1991). With a "single united authority" at the state's helm (Lau 1991, pp. 83–90), political rights were to be given to all those regarding Malaya as their real home and the object of their loyalty. Citizenship was extended to people born in Malaya and relatively lenient residence conditions were set for foreign-born residents to acquire citizenship. The Malayan Union, in the first instance, was expected to "replace the confused loyalties of the pre-war period with a direct allegiance to the colonial state" (Harper 1999, p. 57), but the larger objective was to create a "multi-racial 'Malayan' national entity" (pp. 308, 358). "Consolidation of communal identity" was to be countered by "advancing a Malayan sensibility" — but the outcome was dramatically different. Malayan Union "inadvertently" contributed to the "consolidation of communal identity" (pp. 11–12).

As noted already, it was described by its opponents as a threat to the entire Malay race of British Malaya. Their protest demonstrations featured the cry "*Hidup Melayu*" ("Long live the Malays") — and the Malayan Union struggle has often been portrayed as a period when Malay solidarity was promoted, even over loyalty to the Rulers. Those who proposed the new scheme with hopes of transcending racial divisions could hardly have chosen a worse time. In the sharp racial friction of the immediate post-

War period the Malayan Union was almost inevitably perceived in race terms. Even those opposing the Malayan Union for non-race-based reasons — for instance, senior government officials anxious about a likely loss of the freedom they had once enjoyed in one of the Unfederated Malay States — could exploit community racial anxieties (Stockwell 1979). Opponents of the scheme saw it as a reversal of the inter-war, ostentatiously pro-Malay policy of the British administration — even though it did not in fact change substantively the pre-war legal status of the non-Malays. UMNO emerged from the struggle as the champion and protector of the Malay race, and a new plan to replace the Malayan Union was reached in the tripartite negotiations among the British administration, UMNO leaders and the state rulers in December 1946.

CREATING THE FEDERAL STATE AND THE CHALLENGE OF THE "PEOPLE'S CONSTITUTION"

What was called the Anglo-Malay Working Committee Report gave birth to the Federation of Malaya in February 1948. Besides preserving the individuality and identity of the nine existing states, the new Federation maintained a commitment to a "common form of citizenship" for the residents of the Federation who regarded it as "their real home and the object of their loyalty" (quoted in Vasil 1980, p. 24). British subjects and "any subject ... of His Highness the Ruler of any State" were eligible for this new form of citizenship, termed the "Federal citizen" (Federation of Malaya Agreement 1948, p. 223). Nonetheless, a new definition of a "subject of His Highness the Ruler of any State" was stipulated specifically for this purpose: the person had either to belong to an aboriginal tribe or be a Malay born in any of the States. In order to qualify, non-Malays had to be naturalized according to the respective state legislation (Federation of Malaya Agreement 1948, p. 224). In other words, the criteria for the admission of residents to the Federal citizenship by virtue of being a "subject of His Highness the Ruler of any State" were differentiated according to race: by *jus soli* for a Malay and by naturalization for a non-Malay. With the 1948 Constitution of the Federation giving the "Malay" subjects of a Ruler an advantage over non-Malay subjects with respect to federal citizenship, a racial connotation was given to the status of royal subject (Carnell 1952, Sinnadurai 1978).

In response to the Working Committee Constitution process — including the evidence of Malay bias — a consortium of social groups formed the Pan-Malayan Council of Joint Action (PMCJA, later changed to AMCJA, replacing "Pan" with "All") to raise objections. Its predominantly non-Malay platform was led by the Malayan Democratic Union (MDU), a leftist party of English-educated professionals and middle class intellectuals. The PMCJA was soon joined by the left wing Malay-based coalition group PUTERA (Pusat Tenaga Rakyat), under the leadership of the Malay Nationalist Party (MNP). The AMCJA-PUTERA coalition then came out with an alternative proposal to the Federation: the People's Constitutional Proposal for Malaya (abbreviated as "People's Constitution" herein). Did this Constitution transcend race? The coalition itself was based on ten commonly agreed principles. Three of these principles were articulated at the inauguration of the PMCJA, namely, to have a united Malaya inclusive of Singapore, a fully-elected central legislative body for Malaya and equal political rights for all who regard Malaya as their "real home and as the object of their loyalty". The Malay Nationalist Party (MNP) asked that three more principles be included, i.e. that the rulers would assume the position of fully sovereign and constitutional rulers, that matters related to Islam and Malay customs be under full control of the Malays, and that special attention was to be paid to the advancement of the Malays. Four more points were added when PUTERA joined PMCJA — these included the demands that the Malay language be made the official language of the country, that "Melayu" be made the name for the citizenship or national status in Malaya, and that the national flag should have the Indonesian white and red colours (Yeo 1973, p. 38).

Most of the points introduced by MNP and PUTERA were of course based on perceived Malay interests — and might well have been intended to garner Malay popular support. The call for a white and red flag could be interpreted as expressing the Malay leaders' commitment to the vision of Melayu Raya — a concept that regarded the natives of the whole of the Malay Archipelago as part and parcel of a Malay nation/race.

The People's Constitutional Proposal for Malaya used the rhetoric of democracy, claiming the AMCJA-PUTERA to be the proper representative of the people of Malaya who "regard Malaya as their real home and as the object of their loyalty". Equality "regardless of race, creed, colour or sex", and the principle of *jus soli* for citizenship, were affirmed. Although — as a product of inter-racial compromise — the document is obviously not devoid of racial consideration, it nonetheless attempts to draw out a road map whereby racial distinction could be minimized in the long run. Hence the People's Constitution proposed that only for the first three Federal Legislative Assemblies would there be a provision that no less than 55 per cent of members be citizens of the Malay race (PUTERA-AMCJA 1947, p. 33). In addition, a racially apportioned "Council of Races" would be elected by the Assembly to (a) ensure that no bill passed by the Assembly was racially or religiously discriminatory (PUTERA-AMCJA 1947, p. 39), and (b) recommend measures for the advancement or protection of not one but any section of the people (PUTERA-AMCJA 1947, p. 43).

A controversial issue in compiling the People's Constitution was the suggestion that to preserve the "historic name of the indigenous people", the name "Melayu" be used for the new nationality that is for Chinese and Indians as well as Malays. This PUTERA proposal, it should be noted, was only agreed to by the AMCJA leaders as a last resort — and as a compromise linked to PUTERA acceptance of the principle of *jus soli* citizenship (Ahmad Boestamam 1972, pp. 26–30). The proposal met strong resistance from the AMCJA representatives as well as from the wider public later — but it need not be understood in terms of the resilience of the race paradigm. The term "Melayu" had been given a very broad definition — in fact, an assurance was given that no religious or assimilative implications would be attached to the "Melayu" nationality, except for the effort to learn simple conversational Malay.

Although the "Melayu" proposal was opposed by influential sectors of the Malay as well as the non-Malay communities (Yeo 1973, p. 48), in the ideological — if not the political — context of the time it need not be seen as having been completely unrealistic. Recall here, for instance, how elastic a term "Thai" has been — for instance in the pre-Pacific War decades under the leadership of Phibun Songkhram (Baker and Pasuk 2010, pp. 132–33). "Melayu" too has been elastic in being defined in different ways over time, and in different locations. It was more narrowly defined in Sumatra than in British Malaya — and, at the other extreme, the left wing of Malayan politics advocated "Melayu Raya" as a concept that might automatically encompass peoples from across the Archipelago, even the Javanese (Milner 2011). The idea of a "Melayu" incorporating Chinese was even more ambitious — especially in light of the Malay-Chinese contest in the Malayan Union period, and not surprisingly aroused strong opposition. Despite this, however, the fact that such an inclusive "Melayu" proposal was made at all is a reminder that the term carries a history of openness, and one that may just possibly be relevant again in future societal planning in Malaysia.

THE MALAYAN COMMUNIST PARTY

The Malayan Communist Party, like the People's Constitution, became entangled in race — though it again might be credited with aspiring to a racially-inclusive vision of Malayan society. Even though the leadership and membership of the Malayan Communist Party (MCP) were predominantly Chinese, their programme was based on class struggle and anti-colonialism. For a brief period in the early 1930s they were anti-religion but abandoned this as well as their anti-propertied class position by the end of the same decade (Cheah 1992, pp. 95–98, Ting 2007, p. 227). During the post-war period, they envisaged joining potential allies in a "Malayan Democratic United Front" aimed at achieving self-rule, democracy, and the improvement of workers' rights and working conditions for both men and women. The vision of society fought for by the MCP was characterized also by a stated concern to enlarge democratic space. Interestingly, the armed wing the Party organized when the State of Emergency was declared was named "The Malayan Races Liberation Army". There is sufficient documented evidence to describe the MCP as an anti-colonial and anti-capitalist nationalist movement (Ting 2007), and the insurgency it led could well be designated an anti-colonial armed struggle (Khong 2003, Stenson 1970, Cheah 2002).

On its part, the British administration was determined to exploit the dynamics of Malayan racial rivalry and portray the MCP struggle as a "Chinese struggle". The British, as Cheah Boon Kheng has put it, strategically racialized the conflict in their psychological propaganda war against the MCP (Cheah 1979, p. 63). Even during the inter-war period, the British intelligence had sought to destroy Malay cells established by communist cadres (Chin et al. 2004, p. 72). Around the time when the State of Emergency was declared in June 1948, there were also mass (and secret) arrests of Malay activists associated with left-wing organizations, trade unions and parties. In an interview with a *Sin Chew Jit Poh* journalist in 1998, former Secretary-General of the Party, Chin Peng, claimed that 5,000 Malay activists were taken.

There is a case, therefore, for understanding the Communist movement in non-racial terms — although it has certainly been appropriated (or captured) by the proponents of the race paradigm. It has been formulated in the dominant historical discourse — for instance, in the school history curriculum — in a manner that profiles the inter-race dimension. The official school history textbook stresses that the Malays as opponents of atheism and violence were not interested in Communist ideology.

Also, three pictures chosen to accompany the text convey that those fighting the Communists — the Home Guards — happened to be Malay (Form 3 History Text pp. 93–94, Ting 2009).

THE SOCIALIST STRAND

Different attempts to promote various shades of class-based or socialist ideology took place in parallel with the failed Communist project. The earliest came from the short-lived Malayan Democratic Union (MDU) and the MNP-led PUTERA — both involved in putting forward the "People's Constitution". The Singapore-based People's Action Party (PAP) and its subsequent Malaysian version, the Democratic Action Party (DAP) — to be discussed shortly — also professed their belief in "socialist democracy". The decade of the 1950s saw as well the formation of the left-leaning Labour Party and the Partai Ra'ayat Malaya (PRM, literally the "Malayan People's Party") — which joined forces after Independence as the Malayan People's Socialist Front. In the Singapore and Kuala Lumpur campuses of the University of Malaya, the Socialist Club also existed on and off during the early years, and then thrived for nearly a decade in campus politics till it was closed down by the government in 1974.

These left-wing groups introduced, in greater or lesser degree, a class perspective into their political programme or social analysis. The Labour Party in its ten-point electoral manifesto in 1955 called for "a planned economy directed towards meeting the needs of the Malayan people"; it also pledged to "prevent the further exploitation of labour for private profit by ensuring public ownership and control of monopolies and inefficient industries" and promising the "granting of lands to peasants, establishment of an agricultural producers' cooperative, opening of agricultural banks, formation of collective farming on a voluntary basis" (Vasil 1971, pp. 108–09). Similarly, the predominantly Malay PRM proclaimed its anti-colonial struggle as "based on common sufferings of the people of Malaya". There was, said the party, "no question of race or colour" (Vasil 1971, pp. 167–69). Taking its inspiration from the Indonesian nationalist struggle, the PRM constitution adopted the *marhaenism* of Sukarno. *Marhaen* referred to "all workers, peasants, fishermen, students and small businessmen" — as distinct from the "proletariat" which denoted only those who did not own the means of production, and hence made a living through their labour. The PRM's economic programmes proposed state control of all sectors of production and distribution "important for the people", as well as the promotion of business and agriculture run on the basis of cooperatives (Vasil 1971, pp. 169–70). At its inception, the Socialist Front proclaimed that it sought the "establishment of a democratic socialist State of Malaya" — a State that would favour the peasants and workers, insisting on "common ownership of the means of production, distribution, and exchange" (p. 185).

While the leaders of both the Labour Party and the PRM in the Socialist Front sought to steer clear of communalism, they did not succeed in reaching a common ground on ethnically contentious issues such as multilingualism, the special position of the Malays, education and citizenship. Believing in the instrumental role of the Malay language in uniting all races, PRM leader Ahmad Boestamam was opposed to having Mandarin and Tamil also as official languages (Vasil 1971, p. 177). The Labour Party with its predominantly non-Malay base and constituency, on the other hand, was supportive of "linguistic cultural autonomy" (p. 129). The government's 1960 Rahman Talib Report — which effectively excluded Chinese-medium secondary schools from the national education system — was one of the difficult issues the socialist parties confronted, and resulted in Ahmad Boestamam resigning temporarily as the Chairman of the Socialist Front due to differences in opinion with the Labour Party (Vasil 1971, p. 139). Despite reaching a compromise in favour of PRM's position, the Chinese-educated faction of the Labour Party persisted in upholding their original position among their Chinese-speaking grassroots, but refrained from being publicly vocal about it. After suffering heavy losses in the 1964 general elections, the Front fell apart — with the two parties, the Malay-dominated PRM and the Chinese-dominated Labour Party, going their separate ways. Socialist ambitions, it would seem, had to struggle hard then — and still do — to escape the clutches of the race paradigm (Kahn and Loh 1992, p. 14).

MAKING THE INDEPENDENCE CONSTITUTION

In considering the drafting of the Federal Constitution, the question needs to be asked whether there was any attempt on the part of the Alliance political elites or the constitutional framers (particularly the Reid Commission) at offering an alternative paradigm, moving away from racial considerations. Joseph Fernando, in his history of the constitution-making process, argues that the Reid Commission sought to strike a compromise between competing communal demands, "with a view to creating a 'balanced polity'" — at least within the limits circumscribed by the Commission's terms of reference (Fernando 2002, p. 131). The latter included the need to safeguard the special position of the Malays and the legitimate interests of the other communities (Fernando 2002, pp. 107, 116).

Out of the 131 memoranda received by the Commission and the more than 100 hearings it held throughout Malaya, it was the submissions of the Alliance leaders — written and oral — that constituted the foremost reference in the way the commission dealt with contentious issues such as nationality and the special position of the Malays (Fernando 2002, pp. 124, 131). It is well-known also that the Alliance contribution to the Commission was a product of intense inter-racial, elite bargaining. In accordance with the position of the Alliance, the Commission report included an elaborate section of fundamental rights, "clearly intended to provide adequate constitutional guarantees for the rights of the citizens until such a time that communalism became insignificant" (p. 132). The Federal Constitution as a result provided that "all persons are equal before the law" and stipulated against discrimination toward citizens on the ground only of religion, race, descent or place of birth. It is true that this stipulation is qualified in that it does not apply to the provisions for the special position for the Malays, yet the importance of affirming this equality as a fundamental principle of the nation should not be overlooked. The commission also decided not to recommend Islam as the official religion of the Federation as they perceived this to be in direct contradiction with the Alliance leaders' expressed intention for the Federation to be a secular state (Fernando 2002, pp. 129–30).

The drafter commission of the Constitution expressed its misgivings regarding the special position of the Malays, because this seemed incompatible with democracy and could be seen as eroding the "legitimate interests" of non-Malay communities (Fernando 2002, p. 126). The Commission attempted to reconcile this anxiety by, on the one hand, authorizing reservations of quotas being made for Malays (in such areas as positions in the public service, federal scholarships, and the issuance of permits); and, on the other, including clauses that circumscribe the reach of this provision. In particular the Commission was careful not to deprive non-Malay citizens of what they might normally and reasonably expect to enjoy. Most importantly, in response to the oral requests by UMNO leaders during the closed-door meeting between the Alliance representatives and the Commission members, the Commission provided that the "Malay" provision would be a temporary measure to be reviewed after fifteen years (Fernando 2002, pp. 127–28, Stockwell 1995, pp. 321, 323).

When the Commission recommendations were announced, much dispute took place along communal lines: in particular, there was discontent in the Malay community over the fifteen-year time limit for the review of the Malay special position and the decision not to declare Islam the official religion; on the other side, there was non-Malay dissatisfaction regarding the refusal to provide retrospective application for the principle of *jus soli* for citizenship, and also the failure to give official status to the Chinese language. In the inter-party negotiations that followed up the Commission report, UMNO leaders succeeded eventually in making the Malay special position a permanent section of the constitution, and also in obtaining a clause making Islam the "religion of the Federation" (Fernando 2002, p. 157). Succumbing to pressure from Malay groups, therefore, various modifications were made to the Reid Commission's draft — modifications that "altered the inter-communal balance" in the finalized version of the constitution, making it "more favourably disposed towards Malay interests" (Fernando 2002, p. 165). This imbalance in its way sharpened the influence of the societal race paradigm — helping to insure that it shaped the politics of the country for decades to come.

MALAYSIAN MALAYSIA

In 1965 Singapore's Lee Kuan Yew presented his People's Action Party (PAP) as a proponent of "democratic socialism" struggle against an Alliance leadership that was making "highly charged communal appeals" (Lee 1965, p. 2): he looked forward to a time when the country had "an alternative multi-racial leadership" (p. 8). He denied his party was "anti-Malay" (p. 6), but stressed that his opponents were "communally segregated political parties, organized along exclusive racial lines" (p. 12). He said that even the Pan-Malayan Islamic Party (the future PAS), which was in opposition at that time, "stands for a Malay nation" (p. 26). Despite his claim to a socialistic perspective, it should be noted, race came time and again into Lee's speeches. "There is a logic to communal politics", he observed at one point, and at times his own political statements became entangled in that "logic" (Lee 1965*a*, p. 33).

In 1963, when Malaysia was in the process of formation, Lee had looked forward to a time when the country would have "political loyalties rallying around competing economic policies and competing political ideologies", and he argued that his own party, the PAP, was "a forerunner of this new order of things". Nevertheless, he admitted that in the existing context "if the Chinese were in a majority in Malaya" then they would "probably choose a Chinese leader", just as they "have done in Singapore where the Chinese are in the majority" (Lee 1963, pp. 7–8). In expanding on his party's policies over the next two years, Lee himself would invoke the standard communal/race categories, even promising special assistance to "the Malays". In the "multi-racial integration" which the PAP was promising, he said "the non-Malays" would help the "12 per cent Malays to raise their standards of education and life to that of the others as quickly as possible" (1965, p. 4). Furthermore, when Lee discussed his political rivals he seemed to focus most of all on the Malay "Ultras" — whom he regarded as "irrational and obscurantist" — and he warned that because of them, Malaysia might have the task of proving that it was a country in which "all communities must have a place" (p. 26). Such statements, of course, reached out specifically to the non-Malay communities. At one point Lee expressed concern even for the Chinese in the rival Malayan Chinese Association (MCA, UMNO's partner in the Alliance Government). When the MCA Minister of Commerce and Industry spoke of the problems of achieving progress in the Malay community, a Malay-language newspaper headlined: "Minister of Commerce insults the Malay language and the Malay people". Lee defended the Minister — saying he had been misquoted — and declared that "Hatred of the Chinese is in the air" (1965*a*, pp. 33–35).

RUKUN NEGARA

In the aftermath of the race riots of May 1969, the Malaysian Government sought both to reassure the Malay community that Malay anxieties had been heard, and to build a greater sense of national community incorporating all races. A National Consultative Council was set up in 1970, including most Parliamentary parties — and the Council participated in the formulation of the *Rukun Negara* (literally the "basic principles of the state"), which has been described as affirming "the multi-racial and liberal-democratic nature of Malaysian society, and the Constitution and rule of law as its bases ..." (Harding 2007, p. 118; Funston 1980, pp. 219–21). The Rukun Negara — which contains five beliefs and principles of "Our Nation", and a commentary on each principle — was stressed in Government speeches and taught in schools. By early twenty-first century, however, it was observed to be "seemingly forgotten" — though interest seemed to revive somewhat in the lead-up to the celebrations of the country's fifty years of independence in 2007 (Harding 2007, p. 118).

It is true that the *Rukun Negara* in some respects conveys an intent to move beyond race — stressing a "greater unity" of "all (Malaysia's) peoples", a "just society", a "liberal approach", and a "progressive society" oriented toward "modern science and technology" (Harding 2007, pp. 131–32). According to Abdul Rahman Embong, it represented a "form of thinking" that stressed "a new national consensus" that might "serve as a glue to hold the diverse nation together". It was to be a new "'development-oriented nationalism' in which the non-Malays would have a place in the scheme of things" (2008, p. 41). Nevertheless, the Rukun Negara document is also frank about the fact that "Malaysia is a multi-racial society with all its complexities" (Harding 2007, p. 131) — and proceeds (in language that would appear in later years, even in the Najib Government's rhetoric about "1Malaysia") to suggest that the country's "unique" diversity of "cultural traditions and practices" can be "an asset and a source of strength" (Harding 2007, p. 132). For some Malay leaders, such statements indicated a refusal not a commitment to promote "a strong common feeling of national identity" (Funston 1980, p. 220).

The other problem with the *Rukun Negara* was its association with a government that was perceived by many to be pro-Malay, and was responsible for a number of potent constitutional amendments and the so-called New Economic Policy (NEP) which were especially designed to assist the Malay community. As noted in our discussion of the Rulers' role, one 1971 amendment to the Constitution (Article 153) actually entrenched the Malay (and natives of Sarawak and Sabah) privileges by requiring both the consent of the Conference of Rulers and a two-third's parliamentary majority to make any future change. A further amendment strengthened restrictions on freedom of expression, including (and many would think, especially) in relation to the issue of the special position of the Malays (Harding 2007, pp. 121–22). Under the NEP, race-based sponsorship of Malays for socio-economic mobility was further expanded in all areas of the national economy and tertiary education. The National Culture Policy, also formulated in 1971, privileged "indigenous" culture and Islam as the core of national culture (and allowed selective inclusion of cultures of non-Bumiputera deemed appropriate) (Tan 1992, p. 283).

In the early 1970s — following race riots — two widely-read books, both associated (though in very different ways) with UMNO, reinforced the race paradigm. Mahathir Mohamad's *The Malay Dilemma* (1970) and *Revolusi Mental* (edited by UMNO Secretary-General, Senu Abdul Rahman in 1973) sought to privilege and also to challenge Malay society — and in doing so presented essentialized formulations of "the Malay" and other races, and juxtaposed these races in a structure of competition and threat.

A defense of such a focus on race in government policies and public commentary might well be that only by lifting economically the Malay community and the natives of Sabah and Sarawak — together increasingly called the "Bumiputra", or "Sons of the Soil" — would Malaysia achieve a true "just society" (to use the words of the *Rukun Negara*). But the policies and commentary also reinforced the race paradigm at a time when the *Rukun Negara* seemed to be reaching out to something different.

VISION 2020 AND BANGSA MALAYSIA

In a landmark speech on 28 February 1991 to the Malaysian Business Council, Prime Minister Mahathir announced what was later called Vision 2020. To achieve the "ultimate objective" of "a Malaysia that is a fully developed country by the year 2020", Dr Mahathir outlined nine challenges to be overcome by the nation (Ahmad Sarji 1993, p. 403). The first, which he described as the "most fundamental, the most basic" (p. 405), was to establish "a united Malaysian nation with a sense of common and shared destiny". Such a nation, he continued, "must be a nation at peace with itself, territorially and ethnically integrated, living in harmony and full and fair partnership, made up of one *Bangsa Malaysia* with political loyalty and dedication to the nation" (p. 404).

Much discussion took place about what such a *Bangsa Malaysia* might entail — whether it meant total equality among all Malaysians, whether the Malay special position would be affected, and whether it implied the assimilation of all the different races into a single race. The last suggestion seemed improbable, given that Mahathir's fifth Vision 2020 challenge referred to achieving a "society in which all colours and creeds are free to practice and profess their customs, cultures and religious beliefs and yet feeling that they belong to one nation" (p. 405). Also, when he spoke about "economic justice" (in the eighth challenge) he referred to eradicating the "identification of race with economic function, and the identification of economic backwardness with race" (p. 405) — an aspiration that immediately invokes the race-focused New Economic Policy, put in place in the 1970s. Mahathir then went on to affirm his commitment to the "healthy development of a viable and robust Bumiputera commercial and industrial community" (p. 407), and hoped that by 2020 no particular ethnic group would be perceived as "inherently economically backward" (p. 407).

A non-race-based ideal, therefore, was stated here — a "Malaysian Malaysia" — but the process of achieving this ideal was clearly envisaged in specifically race terms. Mahathir was obviously seeking to reassure members of the Malay community — anxious about their capacity to compete economically — by suggesting continuity in the years ahead with the NEP. In his 2011 memoirs the former Prime Minister explained that "*Bangsa Malaysia*" "basically means that people should regard themselves, first and above all, as Malaysians". He observed that "you cannot be totally Chinese or wholly Indian and still be Malaysian. Even the Malays will have to lose some of their Malayness". He admitted that "ideally of course we should all forget the country of origin of our ancestors and be just Malaysians", but added that what is ideal "is not always possible". Here he pointed to the embedded nature of the race paradigm — embedded, it might be commented, partly as a result of the political structure which his party helped to put in place. In Malaysia, he observed, "much has always been made of racial issues", and he predicted that "for a long time, there will still be a number of different ways of being Malaysian, including the Chinese, the Indian, the Iban, the Kadazan and others, and of course, the Malay way" (Mahathir 2011, pp. 602–03).

The MCA, on its part, claimed credit for a special role in the formulation of Vision 2020, and the related National Development Plan (Ling 1995, pp. 31–48) — and did so in a manner that asserted again the primacy of race. They interpreted the plan in hopeful and self-congratulatory (and race-based) terms — as benefiting the Chinese community by doing away with ethnic identification in favour of the emergence of "one single race: Bangsa Malaysia" (p. 37); by lifting the time frame for achieving the 30 per cent Bumiputera target for corporate ownership (pp. 37–38); by gaining greater educational opportunities for the Chinese (p. 38); and by promoting the idea of "eradication of poverty … irrespective of race" (p. 40). They tailored their message to the Chinese constituency in such a way as to convince them of the specific advantages of the "*Bangsa Malaysia*" vision to the Chinese community.

1MALAYSIA

The latest governmental attempt to counter the race paradigm has been the "1Malaysia" policy which, according to Prime Minister Najib, takes "into account the spirit enshrined in the Federal Constitution and the principles of Rukun Negara" (NST, 18 March 2011). In his speech to the 2010 UMNO General Assembly, Prime Minister Najib Razak drew other links between his "1Malaysia" concept and past UMNO efforts to promote "national unity", referring even to Onn's efforts to open UMNO to non-Malays, and stressing that Onn's successor (Tunku Abdul Rahman) had been "aware of the importance of multi-ethnic cooperation to achieve independence" and had adopted the strategy of "pioneering an Alliance among the various races". In arguing for "1Malaysia", Najib pointed out that he had "decided not to reinvent the wheel" — but to "take the examples of the wisdom and foresight of the past leadership". "1Malaysia", he concluded, is therefore a "pragmatic continuation of the vision of our forefathers" (NST, 22 October 2010).

The Prime Minister was not attempting to reject the race paradigm but to reconcile it with a commitment to "national unity". True, "1Malaysia" suggests a united rather than a racially-divided Malaysia, and the government's persistent focus on the needs of "the people" or *rakyat* — a term which, as we have seen, harks back to the relatively race-blind *kerajaan* polity — conveys the hope of transcending race divisions. The focus on race, however, continued in both the execution and the formulation of "1Malaysia" — and this has helped to convey a degree of ambiguity that has caused anxiety (Ong 2009, p. 463).

The race-blind dimension of "1Malaysia" has been present, for instance, in some aspects of the Administration's Government Transformation Programme (GTP). In the words of the Prime Minister, the GTP stresses "improving service delivery to the people" — the "*rakyat*" — and the need to "deliver quickly tangible outcomes that can be felt and experienced by all Malaysians". Based on public feedback, the *rakyat*'s concerns have included the reduction of crime, the improvement of living standards, public transport and student outcomes — and the race-blind spirit of the GTP has been apparent in the combating of poverty, where it is a declared concern to help the poor, no matter which ethnic group they come from (NST, 28 March 2011). A *New Straits Times* opinion essay of 2011 adopts a similar "1Malaysia" tone when it applauds the Chief Secretary to the Government for saying that "the harsh reality of competitiveness" is that it is "blind to race, colour, creed or gender". The essay goes on to praise him as "one of the true champions of 1Malaysia" — though it invokes the race paradigm in doing so, noting he has brought about "greater representation of non-Malays in top civil service posts" (G. Ganalingam, "For his dynamism, Sidek is 'Malaysian of the Year'", NST, 6 March 2011).

That "1Malaysia" did not mean displacing the race paradigm is evident in numerous policy pronouncements. "1Malaysia" proponents would deny the observation (made, for instance, by Ong) that "1Malaysia" must "remain an illusion so long as ethnic identity continues to be a factor in the lives of [Malaysia's] citizens" (2009, p. 465). The Prime Minister, by contrast, has declared that he "appreciates and respects the ethnic identity of all communities" (NST 18 March 2011). When the government has insisted that "the future of all" will be "championed" (NST, 18 March 2011) — when stress has been placed on "the people" (*rakyat*) rather than one race or another — this does not seem to deny that different races have different needs. What it certainly means is that the government wanted non-Malays to know that their anxieties were being addressed — although the results of the 2013 general elections suggest that this aspiration failed.

The Prime Minister has contrived to reach out to non-Malays, for instance in his speech to the 2010 Barisan Nasional Convention, where he opened with "Salam 1Malaysia", and then formulated "1Malaysia" as "*yige* Malaysia (Mandarin), *oray* Malaysia (Tamil), *ndi* Malaysia (Bidayuh), *ji* Malaysia (Orang Ulu), *ise* Malaysia (Kadazan/Dusun), *saumi* Malaysia (Murut) and *sato* Malaysia (Iban)". Referring to Malaysia's rejection of the "melting pot" approach, he lauded the fact that "there is no need to change the name Samy Vellu to Suhaimi or Sazali; or Chua Soi Lek to Salleh, So'ud or Ayoub". It was a matter for pride too, Najib said, that Malaysia is "the only country in the world which allows the existence of Chinese and Tamil schools which use their mother tongue as the medium of instruction" ("PM: Each free to retain identity", NST, 6 December 2010).

The difficulty of satisfying all racial or ethnic groups, however, is underlined by the determined opposition "1Malaysia" has met from sections of the Malay community, particularly the right-wing advocacy group, Perkasa (Ong 2009, p. 463) — opposition that has stimulated powerful reassurances. The Prime Minister, for instance, spoke of the need "to strengthen the race", and reminded his audience that the "position of the Malays and the Bumiputras and other races" is "enshrined" in the nation's Constitution (NST, 22 October 2010). Despite the call for "1Malaysia", it would seem the juggling of one race interest against another goes on and on.

In this respect, a difficult development in the pre-2013 election political context in which "1Malaysia" was promulgated was the emergence of a demand for "1Melayu". Here we see in stark detail how the race paradigm is able to subvert an ideological alternative. In the April 2011 Sarawak election the governing party — the Barisan Nasional, the then champion of "1Malaysia" — lost six seats to the Opposition DAP. In some quarters, this result was immediately interpreted in racial terms — as a major political shift on the part of the Chinese community (R. Sittamparam, "Dr M: BN is more multiracial", NST, 24 April 2011). The assistant editor of the newspaper *Utusan Malaysia*, Zaini Hassan, then argued that as the DAP was uniting the Chinese it made sense to launch a "1Melayu, 1Bumi" movement to promote Malay unity. In response, Prime Minister Najib told "the Malays" that "if you want to be united politically, support UMNO" (NST, 23 April 2011). Although this answer made political sense, it was also a further reminder that the Government did not see the promotion of "1Malaysia" as contradicting the continued authorization of a race-based politics.

RELIGIOUS AND OTHER CHALLENGES

A comprehensive discussion of the different challenges to the race paradigm would demand a consideration of the role of Islam. It is true that in the past some analysts argued strongly that Islam is "too integral a part of Malay culture for it to be a force for change and new involvement" (Wilson 1967, pp. 64–65). Even in the case of the "revitalized Islam" of the 1980s Judith Nagata suggested it was being used by Malays as the "chief symbol and guiding spirit of a new form of Malay distinctiveness" (1984, p. 72). Shamsul has argued that the *dakwah* movement "redefined Malay ethnicity", moving Islam to centre stage as a "pillar of Malayness" (1997, pp. 210, 222). Some have taken a different tack, suggesting that Islamic allegiance could conceivably compete with Malayness — could rival race as a focus of loyalty, and thus counter the race paradigm. In Sri Lanka, to take a distant example, the religious revival has led certain Malays — especially those who have sought employment in the Middle East or undertaken the Haj — to see "the Islamic ummah" as more important than "ethnic identity". With the "Malays" making up only one twentieth of the total Muslim population, the fear has been expressed that the idea of the "indivisibility of Islam" will be "used for the purpose of hurrying the Malays in their journey to extinction as has happened in South Africa" (Saldin 1996, pp. 45–46; Milner 2011, chapter 6).

In Malaysia the *ulama* (religious scholars) who took over the leadership of the Islamic Party (PAS) in the early 1980s were seen by some to be primarily concerned to compete with the governing UMNO party for the Malay nationalist vote: but they can also be said to have offered a policy to transform Malay society. They have been encouraging Malays to think of themselves as members of the international Islamic community — the *Umat Islam* — and not primarily as members of a race (Milner 2011, pp. 215–22; Zainal Kling 2006). Although opinion surveys are notoriously difficult to assess, a 2005 survey in Malaysia might be interpreted as suggesting that a growing number of Malays are beginning to consider their Islamic identity to be more important than their racial identity (Martinez 2006).

Two issues require highlighting in the Malaysian ideological context when we consider the subject of religion. The first concerns just how successful has the Islamic campaign been among the Malay ethnic community — and some have argued that it has been strongly resisted (Wazir Jahan 1992; Peletz 2002). The second concerns how non-Malays view increased religiosity among the Malays. Many non-Malays perceive Islam primarily as a badge of Malayness (in the manner suggested by Judith Nagata), and from that perspective the Islamic or Islamist movement of recent decades simply sharpens the ethnic divide. Thus, even if it is the case that the movement is driven by specifically religious objectives, its unintended impact might well be to strengthen not weaken the race-based paradigm. Moves to moderate religious extremism, it must be added, can face a similar race-based interpretation. Thus, when former Prime Minister Abdullah Badawi introduced his moderate doctrine of *Islam Hadhari* (civilizational Islam) his initiative was perceived in certain quarters as just a "move in the direction of deeper ethnocentrism" (Ooi 2009, p. 461).

Turning to other ideological resources that might counter the race paradigm, a number of scholars (Loh 2002, Lee 2004) have noted a government switch towards ethnically more inclusive policies in the 1990s (in tandem with the "*bangsa Malaysia*" concept), and an increased emphasis on the discourse of developmentalism. It was argued that developmentalism — which stresses the importance of political and economic stability in ensuring that the emerging multi-ethnic middle class continues to enjoy the fruits of development — has displaced the politics of ethnicism prevalent during the 1970s and 1980s (Loh 2002). With closer analysis the situation seems more complex. As Abdul Rahman Embong has pointed out, the Malaysian version of the "developmentalist state" is not understood only in economic and community-inclusive terms. It is shaped by the race paradigm. In the Malaysian context, a distinctive feature is that "state intervention in the economy was affirmative in nature in favour of the Malay majority while in Japan and Korea, no such distinctions among ethnic groups were necessary" (2008, p. 33). The middle class itself also has a tendency toward internal division on ethnic grounds (Derichs 2004), though since the 1980s it has established some cause-specific NGOs that "are usually multi-ethnic in orientation" and "consciously avoid racial bating ..." (Loh 2010*a*, p. 21). Some years ago, Shamsul detected a shift in Malaysian political culture from race and religion toward "interest-based" concerns — though he admitted that "the most obvious vehicle for articulating interests may still be ethnic-based organizations ..." (2001, p. 209).

The Reformasi era — the sustained political mobilization commencing with the abrupt sacking of Anwar Ibrahim as Deputy Prime Minister in 1998 — has been called "the end of ethnic politics" (Fenton 2003, p. 141). As leader of the *Parti Keadilan Rakyat* (Peoples's Justice Party), which made significant gains in the 2008 and 2013 general elections, Anwar has called for the replacement of the ideology of *ketuanan Melayu* (Malay supremacy) with *ketuanan rakyat* (people's supremacy). Given the way "*rakyat*" — the term for "people" which we have noted was central in the *kerajaan* ideology, but in a "feudal" context — can denote all citizens regardless of race, the expression "*ketuanan rakyat*" would seem to possess the potential to operate as a racially-inclusive concept in political mobilization. (Chapter 3 explores in detail the historical and genealogical development of the idea of *rakyat*.)

Democratic action — including the struggle for social justice and human rights — has also been portrayed as having the potential to transcend race/ethnic division and race/ethnic thinking. Through the advocacy of democracy and participatory NGO activity, Loh Kok Wah has argued, people come to work together — crossing the ethnic and religious divide (2010, p. 4). In 2011, BERSIH 2.0 — a multiethnic popular movement demanding electoral reform and free and fair elections — was arguably an example of this. Indeed, in April 2012, when BERSIH 3.0 came to the fore again with a much bigger ethnically-mixed crowd, the movement's multiethnic appeal and support became much more obvious. While their popular mobilization has been met by the strong will of the government — determined to thwart their initiatives — the transethnic nature of the public confrontation that has taken place suggests a political divide rather than a racial one.

With respect to the political (the practice of politics), although it is often said that politics in Malaysia is divisive — and there is a case for characterizing Malaysia as a highly political (though perhaps not highly democratic) country — in one sense political activity may actually have a unifying impact. The terms of political contest are what matter. Even when contest entails a clash of race-based interests and perspectives, the way these interests are argued may promote a degree of unity — at least of discursive unity. When both sides put their case in a similar manner — for instance, expressing similar objectives and invoking similar standards in determining what is a legitimate argument — the contest itself, probably quite unintentionally, can stimulate the growth of a unifying "public sphere". The operations of the Westminster system in Malaysia — with a parliament in which representatives of a range of seemingly incompatible ethnic and religious interests are pressed into dialogue — could be seen as an example of how political activity, on occasion, seems to foster a sense of sharing space (and even some ground rules) in a national arena (Milner 1991; Harper 1999). Also, Shamsul and Anis (2011, p. 22) appear to touch on this surprisingly constructive role of politics in their argument that "tongue wagging" can have a moderating rather than simply divisive impact in Malaysia (Shamsul and Anis 2011, p. 22).

CONCLUSION: ENTANGLED IN THE RACE PARADIGM

Looking back over the different types of challenge to the race paradigm — monarchy as a "symbol of the unity" of all the people; the recovery in the current era of the race-blind "subject" — the "*rakyat*" or "people"; the aspiration of a "multi-racial 'Malayan' national entity" with Malayan Union; the all-inclusive concept of "*Melayu*"; the AMCJA/PUTERA People's Constitution promising equality of all "regardless of race, creed, colour or sex"; the importance of equality before the law in the official Federal Constitution; the hope for a "Malaysian Malaysia" in which debates would be about "economic policies" and "political ideologies" not race interests; the attempt to structure society on a class basis; the stress on greater unity in the *Rukun Negara*; the possibility that "Bangsa Malaysia" might refer to a united national people; the various projects for social justice which have the potential to transcend race barriers as well as correct damaging inequalities; the imperative of a society constructed around religious not racial allegiance — all these ambitions allude in some manner to a world beyond the race paradigm, as does that illusive banner, "1Malaysia". Yet time and again these programmes and ideals become entangled in the race paradigm. Often what appears to be a rejection of that paradigm, so it turns out on closer examination, is in reality an attempt to work around or through it. The explanations of former Prime Minister Mahathir reflect the paradoxical way Malaysians reconcile with race — for instance, when he argues that "race-based parties like UMNO, MCA and MIC are not truly racial because they have decided they will work together in a multiracial coalition". They are, in fact, "more multiracial in practical terms than the so-called multiracial parties like DAP and PAS" — who "are not really working together" (R. Sittamparam, "Dr M: BN is more multiracial", NST, 24 April 2011).

Reading such observations the sense of entanglement with race grows and grows; and, as discussed in the Introduction to this volume, the majority of Malaysians still seem relatively comfortable thinking in racial or ethnic terms. It appears to be the case, too, that although opposition groups in the country tend to oppose governmental discrimination based on ethnicity they are nevertheless not inclined to "believe a radical critique of the very notion of 'race' and its primordial associations is necessary" (Mandal 2004, p. 70). Such a standpoint could well be grounded in faulty logic. Without a critique of the race paradigm, it might be asked, will it ever be possible — in the Malaysian context — to bring discrimination of one type or another to an end? So long as policy is couched in terms of race, will there not always be an insistence by "the Malays" that they are both "Sons of the Soil" and historically disadvantaged as a community — and therefore require special consideration?

Setting aside the race paradigm to advance Malaysia into a new era will not be easy. Even loosening or problematizing the paradigm, however, may be helpful. The historical review of the race paradigm presented here serves to remind us that although the racial architecture within which Malaysians operate has become an embedded, dialectical social dynamic, it is not to be understood as a demographic reality but rather as a construct. Man-made, it is therefore open to modification and adjustment. Also, despite the fact that the race paradigm has proved ferocious in its tenacity it has by no means been the only way of thinking about Malaysia as a national community. Examining the history of ideas in Malaysia with a degree of analytical distance — standing back from the emotion that drove contest in the past — may help promote today a degree of flexibility. Concepts from the past which have been discussed in this essay — a broader, more inclusive definition of the concept of "Malay"; an understanding of the trans-ethnic potential of the old concept of "*rakyat*", and of monarchy; a loose conceptualization of "*Bangsa Malaysia*" or "1Malaysia" (which at least seeks to harmonize if not to deny ethnic affiliations); and so forth — may in some form or another make a contribution to future national imagining. As noted in the Introduction to this book, there has also been the suggestion that a re-examination of the process of forging the "social contract" (that underpinned Malaysia's Independence Constitution) might provide support for a more relaxed approach today to communal relations — one that stresses interethnic interdependence.

The mere reminder that there has been a contest of ideas as well as of interests in the making of modern Malaysia can offer a degree of ideological elbow-room — a measure of encouragement for those concerned about how best to equip Malaysia to escape the middle rungs of national development. Invoking a history of ideas broadens the context in which planning is carried out — and has the potential to enrich current discussions. Looking beyond Malaysia, real structural transformation has often been carried out in dialogue with a heritage of thoughts from the past. The history of the Renaissance in Europe reminds us dramatically of this, with its emphasis on recovering the learning of ancient Rome and Greece. The Meiji Restoration of 1868, which transformed Japan, drew not only on Western political and constitutional ideas but also on an earlier centralized system in Japan dating back to the seventh century, and influenced by Chinese political thought at that time.

Some would put the view that structural change only takes place as a consequence of dramatic economic or security challenges, and that ideological deliberation makes no serious independent contribution. As argued in the Introduction to this book, however, the historical record can be read differently: there is room for human agency. The narrative presented in this chapter is intended to foster such agency — to assist the ideological work that is likely to be an element in any attempt to bring about paradigmatic change in Malaysia.

Note

1. Acknowledgements: A number of people have contributed directly or indirectly to the unpacking of ideas in this chapter. We would like to thank in particular Lee Poh Ping and Philip Koh for their views and suggestion. The usual disclaimer applies.

References

Abdul Rahman Embong. "The Culture and Practice of Pluralism in Postcolonial Malaysia". In *The Politics of Multiculturalism: Pluralism and Citizenship in Malaysia, Singapore and Indonesia*, edited by Robert W. Hefner. Honolulu: University of Hawai'i Press, 2001.

———. "Developmentalist State in Malaysia: Its Origins, Nature and Contemporary Transformation". In *Globalization and National Autonomy: The Experience of Malaysia*, edited by Joan M. Nelson, Jacob Meerman and Abdul Rahman Embong. Singapore: Institute of Southeast Asian Studies, 2008.

Abdullah bin Abdul Kadir. *The Hikayat Abdullah*. Kuala Lumpur: Malaysian Branch of the Royal Asiatic Society, 2009.

Abraham, Collin E.R. *Divide and Rule: The Roots of Race Relations in Malaysia.* Kuala Lumpur: INSAN, 1997.

Ahmad Boestamam. *Dr Burhanuddin: Putera Setia Melayu Raya.* Kuala Lumpur: Penerbitan Pustaka Kejora, 1972.

Ahmad Sarji Abdul Hamid, ed. *Malaysia's Vision 2020: Understanding the Concept, Implications and Challenges.* Petaling Jaya: Pelanduk Publications, 1993.

Ahmat Adam. *Letters of Sincerity: The Raffles Collection of Malay Letters (1780–1824).* Kuala Lumpur: Malaysian Branch of the Royal Asiatic Society, 2009.

Anon. *Peraturan Adat Istiadat Raja Negeri Pahang.* Pekan: Pejabat Adat Istiadat Pahang, 1971.

Arasaratnam, S. "Malaysian Indians: The Formation of Incipient Society". In *Indian Communities in Southeast Asia*, edited by K.S. Sandhu and A. Mani. Singapore: Institute of Southeast Asian Studies and Times Academic Press, 1993.

Ariffin Omar. *Bangsa Melayu: Malay Concepts of Democracy and Community 1945–1950.* Kuala Lumpur: Oxford University Press, 1993.

Baker, Chris and Pasuk Phongpaichit. *A History of Thailand.* Cambridge: Cambridge University Press, 2010.

Brown, D.E. *Brunei: The Structure and History of a Bornean Malay Sultanate.* Brunei: Brunei Museum, 1970.

Brown, Rajeswary Ampalavanar. "The Indian Political Elite in Malaysia". In *Indian Communities in Southeast Asia*, edited by K.S. Sandhu and A. Mani. Singapore: Institute of Southeast Asian Studies and Times Academic Press, 1993.

Carnell, F.G. "Malayan Citizenship Legislation". *The International and Comparative Law Quarterly* 1, no. 4 (1952): 504–18.

Cheah Boon Kheng. *The Masked Comrades: A Study of the Communist United Front in Malaya, 1945–48*. Singapore: Times Book International, 1979.

———. *From PKI to Comintern, 1924–1941: The Apprenticeship of the Malayan Communist Party — Selected Documents and Discussions*. Ithaca, New York: Southeast Asia Program, Cornell University, 1992.

———. *Malaysia: The Making of a Nation.* Singapore: Institute of Southeast Asian Studies, 2002.

Chin, C.C. and Karl Hack. *Dialogues with Chin Peng: New Light on the Malayan Communist Party*. Singapore: Singapore University Press, 2004.

Commelin, I. *BeginendeVoortgang VandeVereenigdeNeerlandscheGeoctroyeerdeOost-IndischeCompagnie*, vol. 3 (facsimile reproduction of the original printed in Amsterdam in 1646). Amsterdam: Facsimile Uitgaven Nederland, 1969.

Derichs, Claudia. "Political Crisis and Reform in Malaysia". In *The State of Malaysia: Ethnicity, Equity and Reform*, by Edmund Terence Gomez. London and New York: RoutledgeCurzon, 2004.

Emerson, Rupert. *Malaysia: A Study in Direct and Indirect Rule.* Kuala Lumpur: University of Malaya Press, orig. pub. 1937, 1964.

Fernando, Joseph M. *The Making of the Malayan Constitution.* MBRAS Monograph No. 31. Kuala Lumpur, 2002.

Fenton, Steve. "Malaysia and Capitalist Modernisation: Plural and Multicultural Models". *International Journal on Multicultural Societies* 5, no. 2 (2003): 135–47.

Funston, John. *Malay Politics in Malaysia: A Study of UMNO and PAS.* Kuala Lumpur: Heinemann, 1980.

Gomez, Edmund Terence. *The State of Malaysia: Ethnicity, Equity and Reform.* London and New York: RoutledgeCurzon, 2004.

Government of Malaysia. *Federation of Malaya Agreement, 1948* (*Citizenship provisions*) in Federal Constitution Malaysia. Kuala Lumpur: Government of Malaysia, 1982.

Gullick, J.M. *Indigenous Political Systems of Western Malaya.* London: Athlone Press, 1965.

———. *Rulers and Residents: Influence and Power in the Malay States 1870–1920.* Singapore: Oxford University Press, 1992.

Harding, Andrew. "The Rukunegara Amendments of 1971". In *Constitutional Landmarks in Malaysia: The First 50 Years, 1957–2007*, edited by Andrew Harding and H.P. Lee. Kuala Lumpur: Malayan Law Journal Sdn. Bhd., 2007.

Harper, T.N. *The End of Empire and the Making of Malaya.* Cambridge: Cambridge University Press, 1999.

Hefner, Robert W. *The Politics of Multiculturalism: Pluralism and Citizenship in Malaysia, Singapore, and Indonesia.* Honolulu: University of Hawai'i Press, 2001.

Hirschman, Charles. "The Meaning and Measurement of Ethnicity in Malaysia: An Analysis of Census Classifications". *JAS* 42, no. 3 (1987): 555–82.

Kahn, Joel S. and Francis Loh Kok Wah. "Introduction: Fragmented Vision". In *Fragmented Vision: Culture and Politics in Contemporary Malaysia*, edited by Joel S. Kahn and Francis Loh Kok Wah. North Sydney: Allen and Unwin, 1992.

Kassim Ahmad. *Hikayat Hang Tuah.* Kuala Lumpur: Dewan Bahasa dan Pustaka, 1968.

Khong Kim Hoong. *Merdeka!* Petaling Jaya: Strategic Information Research Development, 2003.

Khoo Kay Kim. "Sino-Malay Relations in Peninsular Malaysia before 1942". *Journal of Southeast Asian Studies* 12, no. 1 (1981): 93–107.

———. "The Emergence of Plural Communities in the Malay Peninsula before 1874". In *Multiethnic Malaysia: Past, Present and Future*, edited by Lim Teck Ghee, Albert Gomes and Azly Rahman. Petaling Jaya: Strategic Information and Research Development Centre, 2009.

Kobkua Suwannathat-Pian. *Palace, Political Party and Power: A Story of the Socio-Political Development of Malay Kingship*. Singapore: National University Press, 2011.

Lau, Albert. *The Malayan Union Controversy 1942–1948*. Singapore: Oxford University Press, 1991.

Lee Kuan Yew. *Malaysia Comes of Age*. Singapore: Ministry of Culture, 1963.

———. *Towards a Malaysian Malaysia*. Singapore: Ministry of Culture, 1965.

———. *The Battle for a Malaysian Malaysia*. Singapore: Ministry of Culture, 1965*a*.

Lee Poh Ping. *Chinese Society in Nineteenth Century Singapore*. Kuala Lumpur: Oxford University Press, 1978.

Lee, Raymond L.M. "The Transformation of Race Relations in Malaysia: From Ethnic Discourse to National Imagery, 1993–2003". *African and Asian Studies* 3, no. 2 (2004): 119–43.

Leyden, John. "Sketch of Borneo". In *Notices of the Indian Archipelago*, edited by J.H. Moor. The University of Michigan, 1968.

Lim, P.P.H. *Wong Ah Fook: Immigrant, Builder and Entrepreneur*. Singapore: Times Editions, 2002.

Ling Liong Sik. *The Malaysian Chinese: Towards Vision 2020*. Petaling Jaya: Pelanduk Publications, 1995.

Loh Kok Wah, Francis. "Developmentalism and the Limits of Democratic Discourse". In *Democracy in Malaysia: Discourses and Practices*, edited by Francis Loh Kok Wah and Khoo Boo Teik. Surrey: Curzon Press, 2002.

———. "Introduction". In *Building Bridges, Crossing Boundaries: Everyday Forms of Inter-Ethnic Peace Building in Malaysia*, edited by Francis Loh Kok Wah. Jakarta: Ford Foundation, 2010.

———. "Where Has All the Violence Gone? Mapping Old and New Conflicts". In *Building Bridges, Crossing Boundaries: Everyday Forms of Inter-Ethnic Peace Building in Malaysia*, edited by Francis Loh Kok Wah. Jakarta: Ford Foundation, 2010*a*.

Mahathir Mohamed. *The Malay Dilemma*. Singapore: Times, 1979 (reprint from 1970).

———. *A Doctor in the House: The Memoirs of Tun Dr Mahathir Mohamad*. Petaling Jaya: MPH Publishing, 2011.

Mandal, Sumit K. "Transethnic Solidarities, Racialisation and Social Equality". In *The State of Malaysia: Ethnicity, Equity and Reform*, edited by Edmund Terence Gomez. London and New York: RoutledgeCurzon, 2004.

Martinez, Patricia. "Malaysian Muslims: Living with Diversity". NST, 10 August 2006.

Mearns, David. "Do 'Indians' Exist? The Politics and Culture of Ethnicity". In *Ethnicity and Ethnic Relations in Malaysia*, edited by Raymond Lee. DeKalb: Center for Southeast Asian Studies, Northern Illinois University, 1986.

Milner, Anthony. *Kerajaan: Malay Political Culture on the Eve of Colonial Rule.* Tucson: University of Arizona Press for the Association for Asian Studies, 1982.

———. "Inventing Politics: The Case of Malaysia". *Past and Present* 132, 1991.

———. "'Malayness': Confrontation, Innovation and Discourse". In *Looking in Odd Mirrors: The Java Sea,* edited by V.J.H. Houben, H.M.J. Maier and W. van der Molen. Leiden: Rijksuniversiteit, 1992.

———. *The Invention of Politics: Expanding the Public Sphere in Colonial Malaya.* Cambridge, New York and Melbourne: Cambridge University Press, 2002.

———. "How 'Traditional' is the Malaysian Monarchy?" In *Malaysia: Islam, Society and Politics,* edited by Virginia Hooker and Norani Othman. Singapore: Institute of Southeast Asian Studies, 2003.

———. *The Malays.* Oxford: Wiley-Blackwell, 2011.

———. *Malaysia's Dominant Societal Paradigm: Invented, Embedded, Contested.* Bangi: Penerbit Universiti Kebangsaan Malaysia, 2011*a*.

Mohd. Salleh bin Abas. "Traditional Elements of the Malaysian Constitution". In *The Constitution of Malaysia: Further Perspectives and Developments,* edited by F.A. Trindade and H.P. Lee. Singapore: Oxford University Press, 1986.

Mohamed Suffian Hashim. *Introduction to the Constitution of Malaysia.* Kuala Lumpur: Government Printer, 1972.

Mohd. Zain Saleh. *Keluarga Kelantan Darulnaim.* Kota Bharu: Perbadanan Muzium Negeri Kelantan, 1987.

Nagata, Judith. *The Reflowering of Malaysian Islam.* Vancouver: University of British Columbia Press, 1984.

Ong Puay Liu. "Identity Matters: Ethnic Perceptions and Concerns". In *Multiethnic Malaysia: Past, Present and Future,* edited by Lim Teck Ghee, Albert Gomes and Azly Rahman. Petaling Jaya: Strategic Information and Research Development Centre, 2009.

Ooi Kee Beng. "Beyond Ethnocentrism: Malaysia and the Affirmation of Hybridization". In *Multiethnic Malaysia: Past, Present and Future,* edited by Lim Teck Ghee, Albert Gomes and Azly Rahman. Petaling Jaya: Strategic Information and Research Development Centre, 2009.

Peletz, Michael G. *Islamic Modern: Religious Courts and Cultural Politics in Malaysia.* Princeton and Oxford: Princeton University Press, 2002.

Purcell, Victor. *The Chinese in Southeast Asia.* Kuala Lumpur: Oxford University Press, 1980.

PUTERA-AMCJA (Pusat Tenaga Ra'ayat & All-Malaya Council of Joint Action). *The People's Constitutional Proposals for Malaya,* 1947 (mimeography).

Ramlah bt. Adam, Abdul Hakim bin Samuri and Muslimin bin Fadzil. *Buku Teks Sejarah Tingkatan 3* (Form 3 History Textbook). Kuala Lumpur: Dewan Bahasa dan Pustaka, 2004.

Ratnam K.J. *Communalism and the Political Process in Malaya*. Kuala Lumpur: University of Malaya Press, 1965.

Roff, W.R. "The Persatuan Melayu Selangor: An Early Malay Political Association". *Journal of Southeast Asian History* 9 (1968): 117–46.

———. *The Origins of Malay Nationalism*. Kuala Lumpur: Oxford University Press, 1994.

Saldin, B.D.K. *The Sri Lankan Malays and their Language*. Dehiwala: Sridevi, 1996.

Senu Abdul Rahman et al. *Revolusi Mental*. Kuala Lumpur: Penerbitan Utusan Melayu, 1973.

Shamsul, A.B. "Identity Construction, Nation Formation, and Islamic Revivalism in Malaysia". In *Islam in an Era of Nation-States*, edited by Robert W. Hefner and Patricia Horvatich. Honolulu: University of Hawai'i Press, 1997.

———. "Ethnicity, Class, Culture or Identity? Competing Paradigms in Malaysian Studies". *Akademika* 53 (July 1998): 33–59.

———. "The Redefinition of Politics and the Transformation of Malaysian Pluralism". In *The Politics of Multiculturalism: Pluralism and Citizenship in Malaysia, Singapore and Indonesia*, edited by Robert W. Hefner. Honolulu: University of Hawai'i Press, 2001.

Shamsul A.B. and Anis Y. Yusoff. *Managing Peace in Malaysia: A Case Study*. Bangi: Institute of Ethnic Studies, 2011.

Shariff Ahmad. *Menjunjung Kasih*. Kuala Lumpur: Berita, 1983.

Shen Sung-chiao and Chien Sechin Y.S. "Turning Slaves into Citizens: Discourses of Guomin and the Constitution of Chinese National Identity in the Late Qing Period". In *The Dignity of Nations: Equality, Competition and Honour in East Asian Nationalism*, edited by S.Y.S. Chien and J. Fitzgerald. Hong Kong: Hong Kong University Press, 2006.

Sheppard, M.C. *Tunku: His Life and Times*. Subang Jaya: Pelanduk, 2007.

Simandjuntak B. *Malayan Federalism 1945–1963: A Study of Federal Problems in a Plural Society*. Kuala Lumpur: Oxford University Press, 1969.

Sinnadurai, Visu. "The Citizenship Laws of Malaysia". In *The Constitution of Malaysia: Its Development, 1957–1977*, edited by Tun Mohamed Suffian, H.P. Lee and F.A. Trindade. Kuala Lumpur: Oxford University Press, 1978.

Smith, Simon C. *British Relations with the Malay Rulers from Decentralization to Malayan Independence 1930–1957*. Kuala Lumpur: Oxford University Press, 1995.

———. "'Moving a Little with the Tide': Malay Monarchy and the Development of Modern Malay Nationalism". *Journal of Imperial and Commonwealth History* 34, no. 1 (2006): 123–38.

Soda Naoki. "Melayu Raya and Malaysia: Exploring Greater Malay Concepts in Malaya". Setsutaro Kobayashi Memorial Fund Research Paper, Kyoto, 2000.

Stenson, M.R. *Industrial Conflict in Malaya: Prelude to the Communist Revolt of 1948*. London: Oxford University Press, 1970.

Stockwell, A.J. *British Policy and Malay Politics during the Malayan Union Experiment 1945–1948*. Kuala Lumpur: The Malaysian Branch of the Royal Asiatic Society, 1979.

———. "[Constitutional Commission and the Alliance Submission]: Transcript of Hearing [Extract], 27 September 1956". In *Malaya — Part III: The Alliance Route to Independence 1953–1957*. London: HMSO (Document no. 427, CO 889/6, ff 281–90) (1995): 317–23.

Swettenham, Sir Frank. *Malaya: An Account of the Origin and Progress of British Influence in Malaya*. London: John Lane and Bodley Head, 1907.

Tan Chee-Beng. "Socio-cultural Diversities and Identities". In *The Chinese in Malaysia*, edited by Lee Kam Hing and Tan Chee-Beng. Shah Alam: Oxford University Press, 2000.

Tan Liok Ee. *The Rhetoric of Bangsa and Minzu: Community and Nation in Tension, the Malay Peninsula, 1900–1955*. Clayton: Monash University Centre of Southeast Asian Studies, 1988.

Tan Sooi Beng. "Counterpoints in the Performing Arts of Malaysia". In *Fragmented Vision: Culture and Politics in Contemporary Malaysia*, edited by Kahn Joel S. and Loh Kok Wah Francis. Sydney: Asian Studies Association of Australia in association with Allen and Unwin, 1992.

Tate, Muzafar Desmond. *The Malaysian Indians: History, Problems and Future.* Petaling Jaya: Strategic Information and Research Development Centre, 2008.

Ting, Helen. "From Ketuanan Melayu to Bangsa Malaysia? A Study of National Integration and Identity in West Malaysia". Ph.D. thesis submitted to Institute of Political Studies of Paris [Sciences Po] and defended in November 2007.

———. "Malaysian History Textbooks and the Discourse of *Ketuanan Melayu*". In *Race and Multiculturalism in Malaysia and Singapore*, edited by Daniel Goh, Philip Holden, Matilda Gabriel Pillai and Khoo Gaik Cheng. London and New York: Routledge, 2009.

Vasil, R.K. *Politics in a Plural Society: A Study of Non-Communal Political Parties in West Malaysia*. Kuala Lumpur/Singapore: Oxford University Press, 1971.

———. *Ethnic Politics in Malaysia*. New Delhi: Radiant Publishers, 1980.

Wazir Jahan Karim. *Women and Culture: Between Malay Adat and Islam*. Boulder: Westview Press, 1992.

Wilson, Peter J. *A Malay Village in Malaysia*. New Haven: HRAF Press, 1967.

Yao Souchou. "After the Malay Dilemma: The Modern Malay Subject and Cultural Logics of 'National Cosmopolitanism' in Malaysia". *Sojourn* 18, no. 2 (October 2003): 201–29.

Yen Ching-hwang. "Historical Background". In *The Chinese in Malaysia*, edited by Lee Kam Hing and Tan Chee-Beng. Shah Alam: Oxford University Press, 2000.

Yeo Kim Wah. "The Anti-Federation Movement in Malaya, 1946–48". *Journal of Southeast Asian Studies* 4, no. 1 (1973): 31–51.

Zainal Kling. "UMNO and BN in the 2004 Election: The Political Culture of Complex Identities". In *Malaysia: Recent Trends and Challenges*, edited by Saw Swee-Hock and K. Kesavapany. Singapore: Institute of Southeast Asian Studies, 2006.

3

KNOWLEDGE CONSTRUCTION, THE *RAKYAT* PARADIGM AND MALAYSIA'S SOCIAL COHESION

Abdul Rahman Embong

INTRODUCTION

This chapter proposes that the *rakyat* paradigm is an inclusive paradigm that has the potential to break through the dominant race-based societal paradigm that has dominated Malaysian history of nation-building in the last five decades or so. This inclusive paradigm can be creatively tapped for the purpose of building and maintaining social cohesion in a diverse multiethnic society like Malaysia. To understand the progressive content of the *rakyat* paradigm, a historical sociology approach by examining, in particular, the history of ideas and their social forces in different periods of Malaysian society is necessary.

The chapter argues that while the concept *rakyat* already gained extant usage during the pre-colonial feudal era of *kerajaan* or the *raja*-centred polity in the Malay states, it did not have the racial or communal overtones because the *rakyat* were subjects of a ruler, irrespective of their racial or ethnic origin. Nevertheless during the feudal era, *rakyat* was always the subject class, subservient to the ruler, and in terms of social status, they occupied the lowest rung in the social hierarchy. When the idea of the nation and nationalism was invented during the early decades of the twentieth century in colonial Malaya — the era of "the invention of politics" as

Milner (2002) puts it — the imagined nation had to reside or had to be located not only within a territory, but also and very importantly within the womb of a people. It was during this period spanning several decades before the Second World War and the subsequent post-war decade that the *rakyat* paradigm dramatically changed; the semantic permutation took place whereby the *rakyat* who was the subject class subservient to the ruler, was transformed to embody the yet to-be-born nation, the imagined community (Anderson 2006 [1983]).

With the spread and deepening of the anti-colonial movement that relied on the mobilization of the people, the notion of *daulat* also underwent a transformation whereby we saw the emerging notion of *kedaulatan*, or sovereignty — from raja's *daulat* to *kedaulatan rakyat* or sovereignty of the people in whose imagination the nation is embedded. Nevertheless, the long historically constituted symbiotic relationship between the *raja* and *rakyat* had to be addressed in a way that accommodated not only the new political awakening and democratic impulses of the people but also the institution of the *kerajaan* and *raja* itself. Over and above that, both the *raja* and the *rakyat* had to engage the British colonial power so that the process of gaining self-rule and independence could be facilitated in an orderly way.

With the attainment of independence in 1957, Malaya — then Malaysia since September 1963 — had to grapple with the *kerajaan* and *rakyat* paradigm in a more concerted and creative way. The *kerajaan* system evolved and had been transformed into a constitutional monarchy; the nine rulers in the nine Malay states that formed the Federation together with the former Straits Settlements of Malacca and Penang as well as Sabah and Sarawak, retained their position. At the same time, a new institution, the *Yang di-Pertuan Agong*, was invented to symbolically represent the newly unified independent state as its head of state or supreme ruler, adopting a system of rotation every five years among the nine brother rulers.

Nevertheless, while the *kerajaan* of the traditional Malay society had a ruler, a position which was hereditary,[1] and the subjects or people belonging to the ruler, a modern nation state as a new political invention is differently conceived. Instead of having *subjects*, it has *citizens* who belong not to the ruler, but to the modern state embodying the country and the whole populace. Thus while the issue of *kerajaan* was settled by having a constitutional monarchy, i.e., monarchs who reign in accordance with the country's constitution, the question of governing the country and that of citizenship had to be settled. For this purpose, parliamentary democracy based on the Westminster model was instituted, with a bicameral parliament whose lower house consists of members who are elected by citizens, the electorate. The party with the majority of elected members forms the government to address the business of ruling or governing the country, while the constitution also enshrines relevant clauses on citizenship as well as rights and responsibilities of citizens. Under such a system, the concepts of citizens and people or *rakyat* should converge, though it is not always the case in all situations. Theoretically, it is the people or *rakyat* as citizens, with their constitutional rights who should define the affairs of the state, through elections and other constitutional means, while state officials should be held accountable to the people. In short, the citizenry, the modern term to mean the *rakyat* of a country with their constitutional rights, is an inclusive term, a term that includes everyone who are citizens irrespective of their ethnic, religious and socio-economic backgrounds, to partake in sharing and building the nation together.

However, what appears viable and neat in theory is not always feasible and implementable in practice. The *rakyat* paradigm and the embedded racial paradigm exist side by side in a state of continuous negotiation, contestation and oftentimes tension in contemporary Malaysia. This is very much related to the socio-political dynamics of the country generated and enacted by the various contending politico-social forces that are involved in a continuing tussle over the country's political economy, political domination and ideological hegemony.

This chapter takes note that in contemporary Malaysia, the raging public discourse regarding the *rakyat*, citizenry and the race paradigm with strong ethno-religious overtones has reached a new feverish level, and a decisive turning point. The various slogans that have been dominating or that have entered the discourse such as "1Malaysia, Rakyat Didahulukan, Pencapaian Diutamakan" (1Malaysia, People First, Performance Now) put forward by Prime Minister Najib Razak upon assuming office in April 2009 to be catchphrase and rallying point of his Barisan Nasional government under his leadership; "ketuanan Melayu" (Malay supremacy) which is the battlecry of UMNO, the dominant partner in BN; "ketuanan rakyat" (people's supremacy), the slogan of Pakatan Rakyat to reflect its ideology and multiethnic political platform as a challenge to the UMNO-led BN; "1Melayu, 1Bumi" (1Malay, 1Bumiputera) put forward in April 2011 by the right wing *Utusan Malaysia* and Perkasa; and the statement by the Deputy Prime Minister Muhyiddin Mohd. Yassin that he is "Malay first, Malaysia second" (*The Star Online,* 1 April 2012) to reflect his preferred identity when asked about his position regarding Najib's *1Malaysia*, are but expressions of a set of convoluted politico-cultural debates along the road of Malaysia's socio-cultural and political modernization under the present domestic and international conditions. All these show in stark terms the divides between the *rakyat* paradigm and the dominant race paradigm, and that sometimes, even the non-communal *rakyat* paradigm is infected or coloured by the race paradigm.

To discuss in greater detail based on the framework above, this chapter is divided into five parts. It will first examine the "competing paradigms" in Malaysian studies as part and parcel of the process of knowledge construction, and consider if other paradigms namely the *rakyat* paradigm can be offered not only as a discourse in the policy and public domains, but also as an analytical framework to contribute to the corpus of knowledge; second, a brief discussion on the *rakyat* paradigm within the *kerajaan* polity in pre-colonial Malay society; third, the semantic permutation due to socio-economic and political changes namely the impulses of modernization and democracy, from *rakyat* to *bangsa*, and the shift in the location of *daulat* from the king's or raja's *daulat* (the mystical power supposedly possessed by the sovereign) to that of *kedaulatan rakyat* or people's sovereignty in an emerging modern state; and fourth, the post-Merdeka evolution of the *rakyat* paradigm in public discourses. And, finally, it will offer some reflections on two issues, viz., the usefulness of the *rakyat* paradigm as an analytical construct, a contribution of local ideas and concepts towards social science knowledge, in particular the corpus of Malaysian studies, and whether the *rakyat* paradigm is a viable answer towards realizing Malaysia's dream of social cohesion and unity. As the focus of this chapter deals with the history of ideas, namely the evolution of the concept of *rakyat* from the feudal era until today and the significance of the concept to social science, it will not discuss in any detail the political contestations, the unity and splits within the ruling elite and the contending forces, and so on.

ARE THERE COMPETING PARADIGMS?

In his essay on competing paradigms in Malaysian studies, Shamsul (1998) outlines four analytical paradigms — ethnicity, class, culture and identity — that according to him, have been competing with one another to inform our studies and have served to frame or organize knowledge about various aspects of Malaysian society. At the same time, Shamsul in this essay and elsewhere considers colonialism not only had invaded and conquered the physical space of a country, but also conquered its epistemological space, i.e., its realm of knowledge construction. In the process, it did not produce Western knowledge *per se*, but colonial knowledge, that is knowledge constructed and developed by colonial scholar-administrators about the colonized society, written and codified to enable these administrators and the authorities in the "mother" country to have a detailed understanding of the colonized subjects and their habitat, thus enabling them to administer the colony accordingly. The codification of such knowledge takes place through the use of "scientific" terminologies, concepts, theories and methodologies, transmitted through institutions, published in reports, articles, books, and other forms, and subsequently became enduring and consumed by users from one generation to another. Showing that Malaysian social science had its origins in colonial knowledge, Shamsul argues that colonial knowledge constituted the "baseline knowledge" for Malaysian social science, and it is on the basis of this colonial knowledge that Malaysian social science has since developed. He also reiterates that "each of these paradigms [ethnicity, class, culture or identity] began as a form of public advocacy and eventually developed, expanded and entered the realm of academic analysis framed during the colonial period and within the colonized epistemological space." Although this originated during the colonial period, it continued into "independent Malaysia ... [which] had to come to terms with nation-building" (Shamsul 1998, p. 41), a point which we shall return to later.

Shamsul's attempt at examining the history of ideas in Malaysian social science as part of the knowledge construction exercise is definitely noteworthy and useful. Studying the history of ideas helps us to sieve through and identify not only ideas, namely the dominant ideas, as they were used in the past, and how knowledge was constructed and perpetuated, but also how the dominant societal ideas or paradigms that served as the framework of thinking or for organizing some kind of order for society and the polity became institutionalized, and also how certain ideas became ideologies. Through this study, one can investigate the meaning, usefulness and durability of certain paradigms, and see how they have persisted in modified form in the present.

The question of whether colonial knowledge is the baseline knowledge in Malaysian studies has also been addressed — albeit obliquely — by other scholars, namely Anthony Milner, in his trilogy, namely, *Kerajaan: Malay Political Culture on the Eve of Colonial Rule* (1982), *The Invention of Politics in Colonial Malaya* (2002 [1995]) and *The Malays*

(2011 [2008]). In these three volumes and other works, Milner suggests that the baseline knowledge about Malay society can be found in the traditional Malay texts about the Malay world and its polity, that such knowledge was defined by the *kerajaan* paradigm centring around the *raja* or *sultan*, and that this polity which developed for centuries well before colonial rule, was legitimated and strengthened by the *kerajaan* ideology and economy. An understanding of such a polity, economy and society, and knowledge about this Malay world could be found through a close reading of the Malay texts or *hikayat*, or the court chronicles. Underlining the value of using Malay texts as sources of historical study, Milner argues that by doing so, "scholars will encourage comparative research" (1982, p. 115). Furthermore, what is important is that "Malay concepts" can be discovered, and "in doing so will convey a message for the modern man" that "categories such as "political institution", "real power" and "individualism" are no less culture-bound than the *kerajaan* and *nama* which defined Malay "political experience" (Milner 1982, p. 116).

What should be emphasized here perhaps is that the colonial knowledge baseline articulated by Shamsul is about the origin of the construction of modern social science in Malaysia, while the pre-colonial Malay texts and Malay concepts constitute the primary materials embodying knowledge about the Malay society in the past, as understood and put together by the court chroniclers about the *ancien regime*, including the ideas and thinking of the rulers, members of the nobility and the *rakyat* about their world and their place and role in such a world. It is not the intention of this chapter to enter the debate about the baseline or baselines as the case maybe. Rather this chapter intends to underscore the fact that certain paradigms — the "Malay concepts" such as the *kerajaan* and *rakyat* found in Malay texts that Milner suggests — not only have sociological significance in the traditional Malay society, but these constructs maybe employed as useful analytical tools to dissect the society, politics, economy and ideology of the time as well as to understand in varying degrees some important aspects of the modern Malaysian society today. In short, besides class, ethnicity, culture and identity, certain other paradigms emerging from the pre-colonial Malay society can also be used thanks to their analytical value to help us understand the society of the past and its historical evolution to the present, a point that will be discussed in the section below. While they may appear to be competing — for example, between class and ethnicity — they are also complimentary depending on situations.

KERAJAAN SYSTEM AND THE *RAKYAT* PARADIGM IN PRE-COLONIAL MALAY SOCIETY

There are several approaches in the study on the *kerajaan* and *rakyat.* Sociologist Syed Husin Ali, in his book *The Malays: Their Problems and Future* (2008, p. 31) saw the *kerajaan* as exemplified by Melaka — calling it as "the zenith of the old Malay kingdoms" — as a class society.

> It can be said that, in the hierarchy of that time, the Sultan of Melaka, the various rulers under him, the chiefs and their relatives, constituted the upper class of society. Their respective positions were determined by tradition. They were acknowledged leaders in whose hands all political, economic and military power was concentrated. Obviously at the apex of all power was the Sultan himself. The chiefs were in a slightly different role. Although they exercised authority in their own area as middlemen between the ruler and the people, they also served as a kind of cog in the administrative machinery.

While Syed Husin looks at the *kerajaan* system from a class perspective, Milner examines it from the perspective of the history of ideas. Noting the European observation regarding the dearth of political institutions in the Malay world and relying on Malay texts, such as *Hikayat Deli* as evidence, Milner has this to say on the *kerajaan* system:

> The Malay "working system" in the *Hikayat Deli* entails an understanding of political experience which does not fit comfortably into Western categories .... The Raja is not only the "key institution" but **the only institution**, and the role he plays in the lives of his subjects is as much moral and religious as political. Malays believed service to the ruler offered the opportunity for social and spiritual advancement. They understood that their position in this life and the next depended on the Raja; he was the bond holding men together, and the idiom through which the community experienced the world. ... Political life [of the Malays] could be subsumed under one term: men constituted themselves to be living not in states or under governments, but in a *kerajaan*, in the "condition of having a Raja" (Milner 1982, pp. 113–14; emphasis added).

In a later book, Milner explains the *kerajaan* thus:

> The sultan or raja was the lynchpin of this system — as the term *kerajaan* would suggest. Rank (and the associated "reputation", *nama*)

> was determined in relation to him; it issued from him. The royal court offered opportunities to display rank, and making sure that this was done properly — that all the subjects of the ruler were treated appropriately, according to rank — was an aspect of the ruler's "work". The ruler himself had reason to satisfy his subjects' needs, because he needed subjects. The more *rakyat* he had ... the higher his own status (Milner 2011, p. 66)

Looking at it critically, it is clear the *kerajaan* paradigm is a top-down ruler-centred paradigm that sees the world from the vantage point of the ruler. It is a necessary analytical paradigm to help us understand and analyse the workings of a ruler-centred system and its maintenance and perpetuation itself over centuries. This chapter would like to look at the ruler-subject relationship from the other side, from the people's perspective. What would the picture be like if we were to look at the system from below, from the point of view of the ruled, the subjects or *rakyat*?

To begin with, we need to clarify what we mean by the *rakyat.* The Malay dictionary, *Kamus Dewan* (1989, p. 1017) gives several meanings to the term *rakyat,* four of which will be highlighted here. First, *rakyat* refers to *seluruh penduduk sesebuah negara (sebagai syarat mendirikan sebuah pemerintah)* — meaning the whole population residing in a country (as condition to establish a government); second, it means *anak buah, orang-orang bawahan* — meaning followers, those in the lower stratum; third, *orang kebanyakan, orang ramai, orang biasa* — meaning lay people, lay public, ordinary people; and fourth, *pasukan perang, bala tentera* — meaning a fighting force, an armed force; an example of its usage is: *maka baginda pun berangkat diiringi oleh seluruh rakyat lengkap dengan senjatanya* — meaning, the ruler then set forth on the journey accompanied by the whole people who were armed to the teeth. *Kamus Dewan* also notes that as *rakyat* refers to *orang kebanyakan* (ordinary people), it differentiates itself from *orang bangsawan* (nobility). *Kamus Dewan* (3rd edition 2002, p. 1091) also defines the term *kerakyatan* — a term of modern usage — to mean three things: *perihal rakyat* (about the people), *demokrasi* (democracy), and *kewarganegaraan* or citizenship.

While there are different shades of meaning and nuances of the term *rakyat* as stated in the *Kamus Dewan,* which gives us not only the contemporary meaning but also its usage during the time of the sultanate, what is clear is that *rakyat* exists in a dialectical relationship to those holding power be it then or now. From the meaning given in the dictionary, let us now examine directly the meaning of *rakyat* in Malay manuscripts, e.g., in *Sejarah Melayu*, and other *hikayat* produced during the era of the *kerajaan.* As there are many Malay manuscripts,[2] what we shall do here is to refer to one of the most well-known and important, that is, *Sulalus-Salatin*, or *Sejarah Melayu*,[3] a Malay text which originated from the Melaka Sultanate and edited in the beginning of the seventeenth century. *Sejarah Melayu* always talks of the symbiotic relationship between the ruler and the *rakyat,* that the latter was always seen or positioned in relation to the *raja* and *kerajaan*, as an integral, necessary and indispensable part of it — meaning that without the *rakyat*, there would be no *raja*. Using the analogy of the tree and its roots, *Sejarah Melayu* quotes Sultan Muzaffar Shah, one of the sultans of Melaka, thus: "the *rakyat* is like the roots, the ruler like the tree; without the roots the tree won't be able to stand upright, that's how the ruler is with the *rakyat*" (*Sejarah Melayu* p. 127, author's translation),[4] so the ruler is enjoined to treat the *rakyat* well, with justice and fairness. Sultan Muzaffar Shah is portrayed in the text as "just and generous, treating all his *rakyat* with fairness".

In another part of *Sejarah Melayu*, Sultan Mahmud Shah was quoted as advising his son to be forgiving and meticulous in handling his *rakyat*, because the latter always seeks the ruler's justice and generosity, only then his *kerajaan* would be peaceful and prosperous.[5]

It has been pointed out above that the more *rakyat* a ruler had, the greater his prestige and status would be. However, in *Sejarah Melayu*, the binding and crucial role of the *rakyat* in the *kerajaan* system can be discerned from the *wa'ad* (covenant or pact) between the Sang Sapurba (representing the *raja*) and Demang Lebar Daun (representing the *rakyat*) which was made at Bukit Siguntang Maha Meru. While the ruler could demand allegiance and loyalty from the *rakyat*, such loyalty is not absolute, but conditioned upon the *raja* acting with justice towards the *rakyat*. This is clear from the *wa'ad* in which Demang Lebar Daun pledged his loyalty and placed in the hands of the sultan and his descendants the fate of his children, grandchildren, great grandchildren and so on [meaning the people], and requested that the ruler should forever be just and never abuse them or treat them inhumanely. In his words, "*Dan jika ia berdosa, sebesar-besar dosanya pun, jangan difadhihatkan, dinista dengan kata-kata jahat; jikalau besar dosanya dibunuh, itupun kalau berlaku pada hukum Syarak*" (*Sejarah Melayu*, p. 19). The gist of the text states Demang Lebar Daun's request to the *raja* that should the *rakyat* commit the gravest of crime, the ruler could mete the punishment of death (if that was in accordance with *Syariah*), but on no account should the person be reviled or humiliated with evil words, a condition which Sang Sapurba agreed.

Here, the issue of honour and dignity (or *nama baik* or the good name) of the *rakyat* to be protected and respected by the ruler is of supreme importance, a condition for loyalty and allegiance.

Another part of the *wa'ad* which deals with the question of the conditions under which the covenant could be broken is also telling regarding the relationship between the *raja* and *rakyat*. Quoting the relevant part in *Sejarah Melayu* (p. 19) again, it reads:

> *Maka titah Sang Sapurba, "Hendaklah pada akhir zaman kelak anak cucu bapa hamba jangan durhaka pada anak cucu kita, jikalau ia zalim dan jahat pekerti sekalipun." Maka sembah Demang Lebar Daun, "Baiklah Tuanku. Tetapi jikalau anak buah Tuanku dahulu mengubahkan dia, maka anak cucu patik pun mengubahlah." Maka titah Sang Sapurba, "Baiklah, kabullah hamba akan waadat itu."*

In this excerpt, the Ruler gave the condition to Demang Lebar Daun that the latter's descendants should never be disloyal to his descendants even if they were oppressive and evil in character. To that, Demang Lebar Daun replied in agreement, but insisted that if the Ruler's descendants were the first to break the pact, then his descendants would do likewise, to which the Ruler replied in the affirmative agreeing to the undertaking. What it means here is that from the perspective of the *rakyat*, while the latter was bound to the loyalty pact to the ruler, it was imperative for the ruler to rule with justice and fairness, protecting the honour and dignity of the *rakyat*, by not disgracing or shaming them even if they committed the worst of crimes, failing which, the *rakyat*, by the letter and spirit of the covenant, could dishonour the pledge.

However, as has been aptly pointed out by Chandra (1979, p. 5), "is rebellion justified if the subject is put to shame?" Does it mean the *rakyat* "can break his contract by acting disloyally?" Chandra goes on to say that his reading of the *wa'ad* shows that there is nothing in it to sanctify rebellion and disloyalty on the part of the *rakyat* even if they were put to shame. "All that we can say is that if a subject is disgraced or put to shame he may withdraw his loyalty from the ruler *which is not the same as acting disloyally*" (1979, p. 5; emphasis added), citing that while the pact itself implicitly did not condone disloyalty, "there is hardly a single instance in Malay society of "withdrawal of loyalty" brought about by disgrace suffered at the hands of an oppressive ruler which had won moral [societal] approval on the ground that it was justified because the covenant had been broken by the king" (1979, p. 5).

However, while there maybe no single instance of moral approval of disloyalty as stated by Chandra, it does mean there had never been acts of fighting back against any of the ruler's unjust and oppressive behaviour and actions. Hang Jebat rebelled against the injustice meted out by the sultan of Melaka to his bosom friend, Hang Tuah; and Laksamana Bentan assassinated Sultan Mahmud of Johor — known in history as *Sultan Mahmud Mangkat Dijulang* (Sultan Mahmud assassinated while on a carriage) — for killing his pregnant wife over a slice of the jackfruit from the king's garden. Hang Jebat is known to have said *Raja adil raja disembah, raja zalim disanggah* (a just ruler is hailed, a cruel ruler is opposed), implying that the disloyalty or opposition is to the acts of injustice and cruelty of individual rulers, not to the institution of kingship or *kerajaan*. As I have shown elsewhere (Abdul Rahman 2006, p. 72), *Sejarah Melayu* makes a clear distinction between *raja* as an individual, and *raja* (or *kerajaan*) as an institution, and that while there were rulers who were just, there were also those wayward and unjust rulers, and those who caused the downfall of the *kerajaan*. Nevertheless, taken as a whole, "*kerajaan* as an institution and the *raja*-based political system remains intact although it might have gone through several changes with changing times. However, the behaviour of an individual ruler and the power wielded by him is subject to scrutiny by his officials and the *rakyat*" (Abdul Rahman 2006, p. 72; translated by the author).

FROM *RAKYAT* TO *BANGSA*: MODERNIST IMPULSE AND *KERAJAAN* REDEFINED

As shown above, while the *kerajaan* and *rakyat* paradigm originated and was absolutely crucial in the traditional Malay polity, it is important to underline here that these concepts — *kerajaan* and *rakyat* — reverberated into subsequent stages of history, and have tremendous relevance in the present and future. This section will show that while there were maybe no overt criticisms and opposition to the ruler and *kerajaan* in the past, the subsequent period following British colonial rule since their occupation of Penang in 1786 and Singapore in 1819, and subsequently the Treaty of Pangkor in 1874, a new era had been ushered in that saw the emergence of a different discourse which openly challenged the unquestioning loyalty of the past.

With the advent of Western colonialism namely the introduction of colonial capitalism by the British especially after the signing of the Treaty of Pangkor in 1874, far-reaching political, economic, demographic and social changes took place in the Malay society. These changes transformed the once vibrant maritime-based trading society of the *kerajaan* to a plural society (consisting of different races besides Malays due to immigration) whose economy was characterized by dualism, i.e., the modern economic sector made up of tin-mining, rubber plantation as well as commerce, while the rural sector consisted of subsistence agriculture and fishing. However, in the Straits Settlements, particularly Singapore, new Malay social groups began to emerge, who subsequently became the articulators of Malay political views and aspirations. The introduction of the colonial civil service which absorbed sons of Malay aristocrats in the lower rungs of the administrative ladder since the first decade of the twentieth century, together with the introduction of Islamic and Malay education that had been responsible for the emergence of the Islamic and Malay educated intelligentsia since the early decades of the last century played important sociopolitical roles in the nationalist movement of the 1930s and 1940s, representing the impulse of modernization and democracy and the fight for the country's independence. With the rise of these new social groups, we saw the semantic permutation namely the shift from the *rakyat* to *bangsa*, and the shift in the location of *daulat* from the king's or raja's *daulat* (the mystical power supposedly possessed by the sovereign) to that of *kedaulatan rakyat* or people's sovereignty in an emerging new modern state yet to be born.

As shown by various researchers, the open criticisms and challenge to the *kerajaan* came from two sources. First, they came from British officials and historians who highlighted the injustices, wastage, maladministration and the mistreatment of the rulers towards their subjects, and even used these as excuses for them to force their way in various forms including gunboat diplomacy into the Malay states. This can be seen clearly in how Perak was annexed via the Treaty of Pangkor signed on 24 January 1974. An example of British officials' report containing stinging criticisms of the sultan was the one penned by Hugh Clifford in 1899 which reads thus: "The old native rulers had been oppressive, with hearts like flint and hands of crushing weight, but they always had a personal motive for their acts, a motive which their people recognized and understood" (quoted in Chandra 1979, p. 17).

The internal critique came from several sources, the first from Abdullah Munshi who severely criticized the sultan and princes, and spoke for the *rakyat*. In *Pelayaran Abdullah ke Kelantan* (1838, p. 55), Abdullah wrote that the reason for the *rakyat*'s lack of motivation to produce more was because of the "raja's cruelty and misrule" leading to their dissatisfaction.

Abdullah asserted that due to this, the thinking among the people then was "it's better for us to remain poor" than to have our produce taken by the *raja*. Writing on his dialogue with a Kelantan prince, Abdullah noted thus:

> Maka jawab sahaya: "Ingat2, Tengku; lagi akan ditanyai Allah Ta`ala pada hari kemudian akan segala hal **ra`yat** itu kepada rajanya. Dan lagi, Tengku, bermula2 yang masuk neraka itu segala raja2 yang zalim ia atas ra`yatnya. Dan lagi, yang bermula2 masuk syurga itu, segala raja2 yang [adil]. (*Pelayaran Abdullah ke Kelantan* (1838, p. 129)).

In this excerpt, Abdullah unreservedly condemned the cruel raja, invoking Allah's wrath in the afterworld towards them, and that "the first to enter Hell are all such cruel rulers, who oppress their rakyat. And that the first to enter Heaven are the rulers [who are just to their subjects]".

The psychological liberation from the ideology of unquestioning loyalty towards the *kerajaan* and *raja* as expressed by Abdullah could not have occurred in a *raja*-centred polity, but could only take place in a new environment created by the British in Singapore and Melaka. While there has been a fierce debate among scholars on Abdullah's political and ideological stance, we are not entering here into the debate of whether Abdullah was an anti-feudal revolutionary as claimed by scholars such as Kassim Ahmad or on the contrary a British sycophant. What we want to stress is the fact that the *rakyat* paradigm has now been raised to the fore, and the *kerajaan* paradigm has come under severe criticisms. This assertion of the *rakyat* paradigm continued into the early twentieth century during the polemics of *Kaum Tua-Kaum Muda* and subsequently in the stirrings of nationalism from the 1930s onwards. From then on, we witnessed the elevation of the *rakyat* from a lowly status at the bottom of the social hierarchy to the grand status of the makers of history, and motive forces in the struggle against colonialism and for an independent nation.

What we see here is the semantic permutation in the history of the concept *rakyat* that began to take place with the rise of political consciousness and the nationalist movement. In this regard it is worth digressing briefly by referring to such permutation in the English case from *people* to *nation*. In an interesting book on nationalism, Greenfeld suggests that "to understand the idea of the 'nation', it might be useful to examine the semantic permutations which eventually resulted in it, as we follow the history of the word" (1992, p. 4). Referring to English history as her case in point, she argues that before the term "nation" came into being, the term "people" was used to mean the population of a region, and "specifically it applied to the lower classes and was most frequently used in the sense of rabble or plebs (1992, p. 6). In other words in the context of the English political culture of the period before the rise of capitalism and the nation-state, the term "people" was somewhat derogatory compared to nobles or elite. However, with the emergence of nation and nationalism, the term "people" underwent a semantic permutation, it became a respectable category. As argued further by Greenfeld (1992, p. 7), with the identification of "nation" — an elite — with "people", the latter term "lost its derogatory connotation and, now denoting an eminently positive entity, acquired the meaning of the bearer of sovereignty, the basis of political solidarity, and the supreme object of loyalty" (1992, p. 7). As the term "nation" means a population and a country, it therefore also means "a sovereign people" (1992, p. 8). She states further that:

> [T]he specificity of nationalism, that which distinguishes nationality from other types of identity, derives from the fact that nationalism locates the source of individual identity within a "people", which is seen as the bearer of sovereignty, the central object of loyalty, and the basis of collective solidarity. The "people" is the mass of a population whose boundaries and nature are defined in various ways, but which is usually perceived as larger than any concrete community and always as fundamentally homogeneous, and only superficially divided by the lines of status, class, locality, and in some cases even ethnicity (Greenfeld 1992, p. 3).

In the context of British Malaya, we could discern a similar dramatic change beginning in the early twentieth century. We could see the elevation of the *rakyat* to a dignified status with whom the emerging *bangsa* identified itself, when we study the emergence and role of the anti-colonial and nationalist Kesatuan Melayu Muda formed in 1938 which already put forward the idea of independence from the British, and its successor Parti Kebangsaan Melayu Malaya which was formed after World War II on 17 October 1945 which adopted five principles, which are: Belief in God; Nationalism; Sovereignty of the people (*kedaulatan rakyat*); Universal brotherhood; Social justice (Ariffin Omar 1993, p. 43). In an interesting study by Ariffin (1993) on *Bangsa Melayu* and nationalism, he notes further that "PKMM felt that it could enhance Malay unity in the Peninsula and was inclined to press for *kedaulatan rakyat* as a means of countering the feudal monarchies in the Malay states. It can be surmised that *kerakyatan* and *kedaulatan rakyat* were simply two ways of expressing democracy, but the latter was more radical than the former" (Ariffin 1993, p. 44). Unlike in Indonesia, PKMM's "call for *kedaulatan rakyat* had no qualifications attached to it, while the Indonesian Pancasila in their fourth principle qualified it by cautioning that it should be wisely guided and led by close contact with the people through consultation" (Ariffin 1993, p. 44). The term *rakyat* is significant for PKMM which even used it for its party organ, *Suara Rakyat* (People's Voice).

UMNO was formed six months later than PKMM in May 1946. The term *rakyat* also entered UMNO's discourse briefly in the beginning. A brief disconnect seemed to have occurred between the sultan and the *rakyat* during the early stages of the Malayan Union controversy, when the sultans were perceived as not standing up to the British colonial machinations. Nevertheless the disconnect was quickly overcome by at least two political developments. The major contenders for power during that period, UMNO and other parties saw the crucial role of the sultans as a rallying point to mobilize the *rakyat*. The leader of UMNO, Onn Jaafar took a position on this. As shown by Ariffin (1993, p. 102) during the Malayan Union controversy, "[in order] to bring about *rapprochement* between the rulers and the subjects, Onn coined a new slogan — Raja Jadi Rakyat; Rakyat Jadi Raja (lit: The Ruler becomes the Subject and the Subject becomes the Ruler) — at a meeting of the Malay Congress at the Istana Besar Sultan Johor." Actually, a close reading of the statement indicates the elevation of the status of the *rakyat* to the metaphorical position of the Raja, symbolizing the emergence of the *rakyat* as embodiment of the nation. But as history has shown, UMNO quickly abandoned the slogan of *rakyat*, and changed it to *bangsa* by raising the battle cry *Hidup Melayu* (Long Live the Malays).

It was the PKMM that pursued the *rakyat* paradigm but with a proper place and role for the sultans. In opposition to the Federation of Malaya proposals that were put forward by the British and UMNO following the collapse of the Malayan Union, PKKM formed a coalition of Malay-based political organizations into what was known as Pusat Tenaga Rakyat (Centre for People's Forces) while the non-Malay-based anti-colonial organizations formed the All-Malaya Council of Joint Action (AMCJA). Both PUTERA and AMCJA established an anti-colonial united front called PUTERA-AMCJA, which held two conferences on 4–7 July and 10 August 1947, and came forward with their People's Constitution or *Perlembagaan Rakyat* (Ariffin 1993, p. 113) containing ten principles.

On the position of the sultan, the People's Constitution states that: "The Malay Sultans [are] to assume the position of full sovereign and constitutional rulers, accepting the advice, not of British 'adviser' but of the people through democratic institutions" (PUTERA-AMCJA 2005, p. 4). There would also be a conference of rulers being envisaged. It is clear from this document that the will and position of the *rakyat* were being asserted while simultaneously recognizing the historical role of the sultan from the traditional *kerajaan* polity.

Although this anti-colonial united front was crushed by the British with the declaration of the Emergency in June 1948, leading to the demise of *Perlembagaan Rakyat*, the idea of independence and *kedaulatan rakyat* (sovereignty of the people) had become part and parcel of the people's psyche and public discourse that fed into the Independence struggle. The concept of *rakyat* had been elevated to a very central position in the political discourse to represent the new *bangsa* (nation) with the birth of a new independent state of the Federation of Malaya on 31 August 1957, and subsequently the Federation of Malaysia on 16 September 1963.

POST-MERDEKA EVOLUTION OF THE *RAKYAT* PARADIGM

Machiavelli (1469–1527), a political theorist and political sociologist, born in Florence (Italy) who wrote *The Prince* and *The Discourses* in the early sixteenth century, made a sharp observation that "A people accustomed to live under a Prince, should they by some eventuality become free, will with difficulty maintain their freedom" (1970, p. 78). It is this so in the context of a people fighting for independence from colonial rule? What Machiavelli said may be true for people who might have had no political education and who did not understand the value of freedom. However, for people who have been resisting colonialism, oppression and injustice and fighting for the birth of a new nation, the country's independence means a reaffirmation of their birth right, their dignity and honour for they would not have to continue to live in servitude and shame as colonized subjects. This was true in postcolonial Malaysia during the early Independence years. However, the people have to fight new realities, the legacy of the colonial days and the resulting new awakening.

This section will discuss the contestations, tension and compromises between ethnonationalism and populism in post-independence Malaysia, and how the *rakyat* paradigm evolved under these conditions. Under conditions of *Merdeka* with the establishment of parliamentary rule which stipulates the government to be elected by the people through regularly held elections, and constitutional monarchy, the rules of the game have changed. With the promulgation of the Federal Constitution, emerged a new concept in both the political and legal discourses, that is, citizenship and citizens, which differ markedly from the concept of *rakyat*. While the *rakyat* in the traditional *kerajaan*-centred polity had their relationship bound up with a ruler, with their allegiance given to the latter, any dissenting *rakyat* could disavow his loyalty to one ruler and could become subject of another ruler. In a modern society, however, one becomes citizens of a state by virtue of the operation of certain laws enshrined in the constitution. Thus with the emergence of independent statehood comes the issue of citizenship as well as the rights and responsibilities of citizens.

Nevertheless, in Malaysia given the specifically Malay *kerajaan*-centred character for a long part of its history as well as the emergence of a heterogeneous population of Malays and non-Malays since the British colonial period, the society in post-independence Malaysia has two distinct characteristics, i.e., a *raja*-defined Malay polity and society, and also a plural society with ethnic, linguistic, religious and cultural diversity (cf. Milner 2011*a*). The new state enshrined in the constitution the nine rulers as heads of their respective *negeri*, while a new head of state for the whole of the federation was created, called the Yang di-Pertuan Agong or King of Malaysia, elected every five years from among brother rulers. What is important to note is that while we have citizenship and citizens of Malaysia on one hand, we also have subjects or *rakyat* of a ruler as head of *negeri* and of Yang di-Pertuan Agong for Malaysia as a whole on the other. So it is not uncommon to find on different occasions such as royal birthdays, the sultans of various states talk of the *rakyat* as their majesties' subjects irrespective of their race, colour, and creed, urging them to unite and work hard for the country's prosperity.

At the federal level, the king as head of state is supposed to be neutral and above partisan politics because he is the constitutional protector of the citizens, and the hope of the *rakyat*. For example, in the recent controversy and confrontation between the BN-led government of Prime Minister Najib Tun Razak on the one hand, and BERSIH 2.0, the coalition of over sixty NGOs who came together to fight for free and fair elections on the other, the king on 3 July 2011, intervened in the name of the country and *rakyat* as a whole urging for restraint, dialogue and compromise. In his royal decree, while expressing his disapproval of street demonstrations to be held by BERSIH 2.0 on 9 July 2011, the King had this to say to the government:

> I also urge the government to carry out everything that is entrusted to it by the people in a just and wise manner, and it is important that I as the Yang di-Pertuan Agong do not want to see this country with a plural society in a situation where there is animosity among them or a section of the people being enemies with the government, on whatever grounds.

While the sultan or the king speaks as protector of the *rakyat*, the government and political leaders of various persuasions view the *rakyat* as crucial for political mobilization because of their voting power in a democratic polity. As such we hear promises of serving the *rakyat* and of various programmes being proclaimed to have the *rakyat* as the ultimate beneficiary. For example, in Prime Minister Najib's *1Malaysia* discourse, we find attempts to address at least two things: the plural nature of the society on one hand, and the people as political constituency and source of political support and legitimacy on the other. Thus we hear of the slogan of moving beyond "mere tolerance" of ethnic diversity to "acceptance", and the call for unity in diversity. At the same time to appeal to the *rakyat* as political constituency, we have the slogan of "Rakyat Didahulukan Prestasi diutamakan" (People first, performance now), indicating the appeal to populism. Nevertheless, since UMNO and BN are parties that operate within the race- or ethnic-based paradigm, they often oscillate between the multiethnic and populist paradigm of *1Malaysia* to one that appeals to ethnic identity and chauvinist sentiments, even to the extent of shouting "ketuanan Melayu" (Malay supremacy) depending on the circumstances and occasions. Thus, this *1Malaysia* espousal — while having a powerful progressive content, appeal and potential — is often reduced to political expediency and sloganeering when partisan party politics comes in the way.

In the same way, we have the coalition of opposition parties — Pakatan Rakyat — which espouses "Ketuanan Rakyat" or "people as masters" whom the politicians should serve. They too appeal to the *rakyat* as the motive force and the harbinger for change, with the promise that development will have to be people-centred, or people-oriented as articulated in their "Buku Jingga", their economic blueprint for change. While the political overtures are clear, the difference is that Pakatan Rakyat — upholding the *rakyat* paradigm in their discourse and political machinations — attempts to project and maintain a multiracial image and strives to go beyond the race-based paradigm.

THE *RAKYAT* PARADIGM AS AN ANALYTICAL CONSTRUCT

What then can be drawn from the discussion above? How useful is the *rakyat* paradigm as an analytical construct, as a contribution of local ideas and concepts towards social science knowledge, in particular the corpus of Malaysian studies? Also, can the *rakyat* paradigm be the answer to push Malaysia beyond the current impasse? These last two sections will attempt to answer these questions briefly.

By way of revisiting or reconsidering whether the *rakyat* paradigm as a set of core assumptions about the relationship between members of society, the ruled, and members of the ruling class who wield the levers of power, is a useful contribution to social science, it maybe instructive to recall the arguments put forward by Shamsul and Milner in the beginning of this chapter. As shown earlier, Shamsul highlights four competing paradigms — ethnicity, class, culture and identity — taken from the social science arsenal that have been introduced or constructed initially by colonial knowledge and subsequently developed in Malaysian studies; and the point made by Milner (1982, p. 116) upon studying Malay texts of pre-colonial Malay society that there are local ideas or "Malay concepts" that are useful contributions to Malaysian studies.

In this regard, it is useful to reflect on the following quote from Chakrabarty (2000, p. 29) who states thus:

> For generations now, philosophers and thinkers who shape the nature of social science have produced theories that embrace the entirety of humanity. As we well know, these statements have been produced in relative, and sometimes absolute, ignorance of the majority of humankind — that is, those living in non-Western cultures .... The everyday paradox of third-world social science is that *we* find these theories, in spite of their ignorance of "*us*", eminently useful in understanding our societies.

As implied in the quote above, one major criticism against Western social science is that its theories and concepts about non-Western cultures have been generated and developed based on Western experience, and that knowledge construction regarding non-Western societies has been very much shaped by Eurocentric lenses and prejudices. In the words of Chakrabarty, the knowledge construction has been undertaken "in relative, and sometimes absolute, ignorance of ... those living in non-Western cultures".

Lately much discussion has taken place about the need for decentering knowledge so that Western centrism can be critically evaluated and refuted, while at the same time, the contribution of local knowledge should be acknowledged so that it reflects more accurately local cultures. In this regard, just as much as the *kerajaan* can be accepted as a concept encapsulating a *raja*-centred traditional Malay polity, the same should apply to the concept of *rakyat*. The *rakyat* paradigm which emanated from the time of the *kerajaan* and which has metamorphosed into a powerful dynamic concept embodying both the physical and inner being of the multiethnic nation of Malaysia, has its own distinct local contribution in enriching Malaysian studies.

CONCLUSION: TRANSCENDING THE RACE PARADIGM

Our discussion of the *rakyat* paradigm and knowledge construction above goes beyond academic imperatives, as it has direct implications for the sociopolitical life of citizens of Malaysia. Such discussion leads us to one crucial question: In what way can the bottom up *rakyat* paradigm serve as a viable answer towards realizing Malaysia's dream of social cohesion? What is the relevance of the discussion of the *rakyat* to the present day conditions and the future?

It is instructive to remind ourselves that history is not something about the dead past, but it is about the past that lives in the present. While the concept of *rakyat* originated from the time of *kerajaan* as shown in Malay *hikayat* many centuries ago, the discussion of the concept *rakyat* conjures historical memory and actually resonates well into the present, and would most likely be so in the future. Indeed our studies of history, of historical episodes, concepts and institutions always have a bearing on the present. Historian Benedetto Croce puts it succinctly when he writes: "The practical requirements which underlie every historical judgment give to all history the character of 'contemporary history' because, however remote in time events there recounted may seem to be, the history in reality refers to the present needs and present situations wherein those events vibrate" (1970, p. 19). In the same vein, Malaysian historian Cheah Boon Kheng (2005, pp. 91–92) argues that, "All history [is] … written, consciously or unconsciously, from the perspective of the present … All history thus has a present-day purpose and inspiration", meaning that the historical discussion of the concept *rakyat* reverberates with the concerns of today and tomorrow.

It is indeed its relevance to the present that we are particularly interested in the historically evolved concept of *rakyat*. Two dimensions are of special significance here. First, while historically the *rakyat* was a subject class in a highly hierarchical kerajaan-centred society, it was elevated to the dignified status of *bangsa* (nation) during the modern period that saw the rise of nationalism and of independence struggle and also during the post-Independence era. Because *rakyat* has been identified with the nation, it has become the exalted symbol and bearer of sovereignty, the central object of loyalty, and a source of reference for legitimacy whose name has always been invoked to justify whatever actions to be taken. The slogan "*Rakyat Didahulukan, Prestasi Diutamakan*" (People First, Performance Now) which has been used as the rallying call by Prime Minister Najib's administration is a manifestation of this, just as much as the slogan "*Ketuanan Rakyat*" (loosely translated as People's Sovereignty) advanced by the opposition, Pakatan Rakyat. Whether the political leaders really serve the *rakyat* or use it as political expediency is up for debate. Nevertheless, all power contenders clearly understand that for them to rise to the position of power and to retain it in their hands, they have to appeal to the *rakyat* for support and to always speak in their name. This shows clearly that the term *rakyat* has metamorphosed from one of being the lowly subject class to that of an exalted position of respect and as source of power and legitimacy.

Second, in the wake of the dominance of the race-based paradigm in public discourse in Malaysia for many decades until today, the trans-racial perspective of the *rakyat* paradigm and its inclusiveness embracing Malays and non-Malays, appears to be a viable answer for uniting the various multiethnic communities and realizing Malaysia's dream of national unity and social cohesion. This power of trans-ethnic inclusion is a profound one that has long historical roots. We have inherited the concept of *rakyat* as an organizing idea or paradigm, and as a mobilizing force which can be the most bonding and enduring. As the saying goes, ideas particularly those that reflect "the spirit of the age", have consequences. Given its inclusiveness and unifying role, as well as its historic significance that provides the basis of legitimacy, the infectious potency of the *rakyat* paradigm for transforming Malaysia is indeed compelling. It is here we see humanity's optimism and hope for Malaysia's future.

Notes

1. A slightly different system is practised in Negeri Sembilan where the *rakyat* elect the territorial chiefs or *undang*, then the four *undang* elect the Yam Dipertuan (the supreme ruler) to be the ruler of the state.
2. Based on existing research, Malay manuscripts are estimated to number some 10,000 titles, kept in 151 institutions in 28 countries scattered in various parts of the world. To date only about 30 per cent of the manuscripts have been studied (Ding Choo Ming 2009, p. 25). Renowned colonial scholar-administrator, Richard Winstedt during his time studied only 100 manuscripts and wrote definitive works on Malay history, culture and literature.
3. According to some sources, *Sejarah Melayu* was believed to have been written in Melaka and brought along when Sultan Mahmud Shah retreated from Melaka in 1511 following Portuguese attack and conquest of the city. According to this version, the text was edited again in 1612 by Tun Seri Lanang. It is also stated that there are 29 versions of the manuscript, the most well-known is the Shellabear's edition which is used for this chapter. However, other sources such as Winstedt stated that *Sejarah Melayu* was written by Tun Sri Lanang in February 1614 and completed in January 1615, well over a century after the fall of Melaka. Furthermore, Tun Seri Lanang wrote it while in captivity in Acheh, and died there, thus it is believed that the text contained Acheh's influence.
4. The Malay text reads: "Dan lagi tiada akan sentosa kerajaannya, kerana raja-raja itu umpama api, akan segala menteri itu umpama kayu; jikalau tiada kayu, di manakah api bernyala? … [Rakyat] itu umpama akar, yang raja itu umpama pohon; jikalau tiada akar nescaya pohon tiada akan dapat berdiri, demikian raja itu dengan segala rakyatnya" (*Sejarah Melayu* halaman 127).
5. In the Malay text, it reads thus: "Sangat-sangat ampun periksamu akan mereka itu sekalian, akan ia bernaung kepada keadilan dan kemurahanmu; dan jangan engkau taksir daripada menafahus dan memeriksai atas *rakyatmu*, supaya sentosa kerajaanmu" (*Sejarah Melayu* 272, p. 18).

References

Abdul Rahman Embong. *Negara-bangsa: Proses dan Perbahasan*. 2nd ed. Bangi: Penerbit Universiti Kebangsaan Malaysia, 2006 [2000].

Anderson, B. *Imagined Communities: Reflections of the Origin and Spread of Nationalism*. 7th impression. London: Verso, 2006 (1996 [1983]).

Ariffin Omar. *Bangsa Melayu: Malay Concepts of Democracy and Community 1945–1950*. Kuala Lumpur: Oxford University Press, 1993.

Chakrabarty, Dipesh. *Provincialising Europe: Postcolonial Thought and Historical Difference*. Princeton, NJ: Princeton University Press, 2000.

Chandra Muzaffar. *Protector? An Analysis of the Concept and Practice of Loyalty in Leader-Led Relationships within Malay Society*. Penang: Aliran, 1979.

Cheah Boon Kheng. "Ethnicity in the Making of Malaysia". In *Nation-building: Five Southeast Asian Histories*, edited by Wung Gungwu. Singapore: Institute of Southeast Asian Studies, 2005.

Croce, Benedetto. *History as the Study of Liberty*. Chicago: Heny Regnery Company, 1970.

Ding Choo Ming. *Manuskrip Melayu: Sumber Maklumat Peribumi Melayu*. (Siri Syarahan Perdana). Bangi: Penerbit UKM, 2009.

Eisenstadt, S.N. *Comparative Civilization and Multiple Modernities*. Leiden: Brill, 2003.

Greenfeld, L. *Nationalism: Five Roads to Modernity*. Cambridge, Mass: Harvard University Press, 1992.

Kamus Dewan Edisi Baru. Kuala Lumpur: Dewan Bahasa dan Pustaka, 1989.

Kamus Dewan (Edisi Ke-3). Kuala Lumpur: Dewan Bahasa dan Pustaka, 2002.

Machiavelli, N. (edited with an Introduction by Bernard Crick for the Penguin Classics Series). *The Discourses*. London: Penguin Books, 1970.

Milner, A.C. *Kerajaan: Malay Political Culture on the Eve of Colonial Rule*. Arizona: The University of Arizona Press, 1982.

———. *The Invention of Politics in Colonial Malaya*. Cambridge: Cambridge University Press, 2002 [1995].

———. *The Malays*. Oxford: Wiley-Blackwell, 2011 [2008].

———. *Malaysian Monarchy and the Bonding of the Nation*. 8th Pok Rafeah Chair Public Lecture. Bangi: Penerbit UKM, 2011*a*.

Pelayaran Abdullah Ke Kelantan (edited by Amin Sweeney, 2005. *Karya Lengkap Abdullah bin Abdullah Munsyi*, Jilid 1). Jakarta: Kepustakaan Populer Gramedia, 1838.

PUTERA-AMCJA. *The People's Constitutional Proposals for Malaya 1947*. Kajang: Ban Ah Kam Pusat Bahan Kajian Sejarah Tempatan, 2005.

Shamsul A.B. Ethnicity, Class, Culture or Identity?: Competing Paradigms in Malaysian Studies. *Akademika* 53 (July 1998): 33–59.

Syed Husin Ali. *The Malays: Their Problems and Future*. Kuala Lumpur: The Other Press, 2008.

4

RACE PARADIGM AND NATION-BUILDING IN MALAYSIA

Helen Ting

INTRODUCTION

In Malaysia, usage of the term "race" is widespread, and is mixed with some form of uncritical, stereotypical cultural explanation of racial differences. In this sense, as argued in the Introduction, it is apt to describe the functioning of the Malaysian society as dominated by the paradigm of race. In scholarly works, the term "ethnicity" is often preferred, due to the awareness of the inherent conceptual fallacy of the biological basis of "racial differences". In addition, the concept of ethnic identity could easily integrate the religious dimension, while it would be a misnomer to speak about the religious dimensions of a "race". Nonetheless, simply replacing the word "race" with "ethnicity" does not necessarily mean that the user of the term "ethnicity" may view ethnic phenomenon with a more critical, theoretically informed perspective, as what many so-called "plural society theorists" are accused of. It is equally easy to fall into the trap of "essentialising" ethnicity, to regard it as immutable or given. For instance, referring to the emergence of "ethnic paradigm", Shamsul (1998) was critical of academic knowledge and discourse which is "trapped in the ethnic-oriented plural society frame" (p. 41).

Is the prevalence of race paradigm in a society necessarily a hindrance to nation building? Eriksen (1998) who examined the multiethnic Mauritius society did not think so. Perspective on Malaysia, on the other hand, is mitigated. On the one hand, Malaysia is perceived internationally as a country which has successfully maintained political stability and peace. The government highlighted the fact that among Asian countries, Malaysia ranks only second to Japan in 2011 in terms of the Global Peace Index which assesses the degree of peacefulness, security and presence/absence of internal violent conflicts among nation-states ("National unity: 'M'sia ranks second after Japan", *Malaysiakini*, 18 June 2011). At a constitution-drafting conference in Khartoum, Sudan in May 2011, Malaysia was reportedly highlighted as a model, a moderate, progressive and ethnically harmonious Muslim-majority country (Shad Saleem Faruqi, "Spirit of Moderation Animated", *The Star*, 1 June 2011). On the other hand, there is a general recognition among many scholars that ethnic division constitutes a formidable force in shaping national policies and was disruptive of forging national consensus.

This chapter is interested in how the state and nation-building policies have contributed to the shaping of the race paradigm, in particular the role of "state-making" (Verdery 1996) in rendering increased political significance to ethnic practices as well as the constitution and maintenance of ethnic boundaries. Race paradigm does not function merely at the ideational level but is constitutive of actions, practices and social processes, including policy-making and its implementation. Nation-building policies which institutionalize and heighten the political significance of racial/ethnic belonging may contribute to more tension and division within the nation rather than forging a greater sense of national unity. In recent times, the phenomenon of Islamic resurgence and decades of Islamization policies have added a religious edge to the "race" paradigm, in particular for the Malay community. While for Dr Mahathir, resolving the Malay dilemma and the Muslim dilemma may be dealing with different facets of the same problem, the growing importance of religious identity and political Islam, and the inter-religious contentions which are becoming more frequent have added a religious twist to the racial problematic of nation-building.

ETHNICITY AND NATION-BUILDING

Even though the usage of the term "ethnic" is not new, the word "ethnicity" was first included in an English dictionary only in 1972 (Glazer and Moynihan 1976, p. 1), indicating its relative novelty as a concept. Increased interest in ethnicity as a social phenomenon was in tandem with the unprecedented augmentation in the number of new nation-states after the Second World War which stirred up concerns over the creation of political cohesion and national identity in these countries.

In a well-known article, Clifford Geertz (1973) described the nation-building efforts of new states as an "integrative revolution" aiming to "domesticate primordial strifes". Ethnic belonging was perceived as a competitor for national loyalty and a destabilizing factor to the state authority. The "ethnic phenomenon", termed as "tribalism" in Africa, was initially dismissed as a transient symptom of maladjustment to modernization, even a residual or epiphenomenal feature of class conflicts. Many social theorists in particular Marxists had predicted during early twentieth century that ethnicity would be replaced by class consciousness as a consequence of modernization, industrialization and individualism (Eriksen 1993, p. 2). Yet with passing time it refused to go away.[1] The capacity and credibility of the state to be a mediator of ethnic conflicts or even to forestall ethnic tension was put on the line.

Academic studies of the "ethnic phenomenon" and nationalism mushroomed during the last few decades of the twentieth century, in part shaken by the conflictive or socially destructive nature of their manifestation. There has since been an emerging perspective, albeit articulated in different directions, among scholars who saw ethnic problems in terms of the inherent bias or blind spot of the ideology of nation-state to deal in an appropriate way the notion of local or ethnic communities (Williams 1989, Verdery 1993, 1996, Chatterjee 1993, Duara 1995, 1996, Kaufmann 2008*a*). The idea of nation forms the basis of political legitimacy and rights in this age of nation-state, rendering it "an essentially contested concept" (Calhoun 1997, p. 98). Nation-building programmes formulated by the governing elites often reflect in one way or another the strengthening or institutionalization of sectional interests of the dominant political forces rather than a neutral effort in forging national cohesion or a balanced compromise sought among conflictive groups (Kaufmann 2008*b*). Depending on the situation, the implementation of nation-building programme may contribute to the appeasement of interethnic strife, or become the very source of interethnic contention.

MALAYSIANISTS' PERSPECTIVES ON ETHNICITY AND NATION-BUILDING

Generally, nation-building is understood as fostering national cohesiveness and unity among citizens. In the West, this often refers to class differences and the need to integrate economically marginal groups into the mainstream society (Varshney 2005). In Malaysia as in the case of many developing nations, socio-economic dimensions have always been there, but the division is aligned ethnically.[2] For instance, the primary concerns of the race-based affirmative action programme known as the New Economic Policy (NEP) are poverty and socio-economic mobility but cast in ethnic terms. Ethnic bargaining leading to the independence of the Federation of Malaya was intense, and racial arithmetic was fundamental to the Prime Minister Tunku Abdul Rahman's proposal to form the Federation of Malaysia. Unsurprisingly, the efforts of nation-building that ensued after independence and upon the formation of Malaysia were beset by ethnic contestations. The *Rukun Negara* formulated in 1970, the idea of fostering a *Bangsa Malaysia* announced in 1991, the slogan of *Malaysia Boleh* during the 1990s, as well as *1Malaysia* popularized since 2010 are successive attempts by the government to patch up perceived ethnic divisions and to foster a common sense of belonging, unity and national destiny. Unfortunately, manoeuvring between competing socio-political demands often resulted in policy-makers choosing political expediency over principled inclusivity and durable solution to interethnic contentions.

There are three broad approaches to analyse Malaysian politics. The first two are what Loh and Kahn (1992) called the "plural society" approach and "political economy" approach. A third is perhaps what could be called a deconstructionist approach.[3] In analysing the Malaysian society, the "plural society" approach takes existing ethnic categorization as immutable and as a function of cultural differentiation (Shamsul 1998, Loh and Kahn 1992, p. 10). Though inadequate for understanding ethnic phenomenon, plural society theorists rightly warn "against being too complacent about ethnic cleavages" and that "governments cannot wish primordial sentiments out of existence" (Loh and Kahn 1992, p. 10). Political economists, on the other hand, analyse ethnic phenomenon from the point of view of class. At the extreme end of the spectrum is the attribution of ethnic identity as "false consciousness". Deconstructionist approach, in its turn, tries to comprehend the ethnic phenomenon as a social construction, problematizing the conventional, uncritical way of looking at the social reality in ethnic terms.[4]

Both plural society theorists and political economists generally perceive the period 1957–69 as a "consociational, liberal consensus" forged by multiethnic Western-educated political elites who successfully maintained peace and social stability over "culturally fragmented" masses. Plural society theorists approve of government efforts to construct a Malay-dominated "national identity" through the development of a national language, national educational system and national culture while catering for the political and economic interests of ethnic minorities (Loh and Kahn 1992, p. 9). The political economists characterize these elites as dominant classes with a shared interest to preserve their social and capitalist privileges, hence duping the masses with their "ideology of domination" while implementing pro-capitalist policies (pp. 10–11).

Both approaches differ in their explanations of 1969 political crisis of the Alliance of UMNO-MCA-MIC. Plural society theorists blamed it on the "pressures of ethnicity", "an eruption of mass cultural particularism into the politics of the elite"; while political economists contended that it was a matter of "class conflict" and that the breakdown of the liberal consensus was inevitable "given that it was a thinly veiled ideology to prop up the ruling class" (Loh and Kahn 1992, pp. 11–12). Increased authoritarian rule from the 1970s was thus regarded by plural society theorists as necessary given the deep ethnic division and the lack of social consensus (p. 12).

Crouch (1996), on the contrary, credited ethnically organized communities as providing for "a solid foundation for the checks and balances of democracy", provided communal violence is banished (p. 10). Leaders of the majority community felt constraint to be responsive, albeit in limited ways, to grievances aired by the sizeable minorities to ensure political stability (pp. 175–76). He saw the communal structure in the Malaysian society as "a built-in obstacle to the establishment of authoritarian rule exclusively in the hands of the ethnic majority" (p. 10).

Shamsul (2005) who consistently took a deconstructionist approach in his ethnic analysis, adopted a pragmatic perspective in looking at interethnic relations in Malaysia, that he called the "break-out" perspective. The "break-out" perspective recognizes and accepts realistically that "we cannot agree on everything". In order to coexist peacefully and tolerate mutual differences, Malaysians strive to negotiate their differences and find viable common ground (p. 5). Horowitz seems to share this "break-out" perspective, preferring to talk about "interethnic accommodation" (Horowitz 2007) instead of the more ambitious term, "nation-building" in attaining the "imagined unity". Despite describing Malaysia as a country in a state of "stable tension", Shamsul distances himself from the alarmist "break-down" perspective, which perceives Malaysians as living and surviving from one ethnic conflict after another, in anticipation of things getting out of control (Shamsul 2005, p. 4).

Over the years, Malaysia seems to have survived numerous conflicts far better than many other countries, avoiding the occurrence of the more treacherous consequences of widespread interethnic violence.[5] Based on his study of Hindu-Muslim violence in India, Varshney (2005) argues that the existence of interethnic civic engagement may hold the key to the absence of ethnic tension and violence, while the presence of monocommunal organizations appears to be otherwise. He nonetheless found Malaysia to be a counterexample of his thesis, whereby "ethnic integration is clearly not the reason for its peace" (p. 23). Brubaker (2002), on the other hand, noted perceptively that the chief protagonists of ethnic conflicts and violence are organizations and not ethnic groups as such, and "the relationship between organizations and the groups they claim to represent is often deeply ambiguous" (p. 173). This corresponds with the findings of Horowitz (2001) from his cross country comparative study of ethnic riots. Dissecting the stages leading to racial riots, he noted that racial riot is usually a meditated, orchestrated process.[6] Racial tension could serve as a rich fodder for specific interest groups to encourage "precipitating events" which provoke such incidents, but a racial riot is **not** the inevitable development from racial polarization or tension. There needs to be other facilitating conditions such as a social climate which legitimizes ethnic killings as morally condonable; or the instigation by initiators through rumours;[7] or the perceived subsequent impunity of perpetrators which remove restraints on the expression of violence. In this sense, the perceived "neutrality" of the law-enforcement authorities, the demonstrated political will of the state to nip tensions in the bud and restrain trouble makers are all determinant in the prevention of violence.

REALMS OF ETHNIC RELATIONS

How does race paradigm operate in the Malaysian society, and how does politics come into the picture? This chapter proposes to distinguish between the realm of happenings in the public domain which may be reported in the mass media, and the realm of the more personal, micro-level of the day-to-day interethnic interaction and relationship among individuals. What is happening in the public sphere may or may not affect one's daily dealings with people around self in the neighbourhood, workplace or interpersonal network.[8] At times, the ethnic or religious impact of public incidents may only be felt at a delayed timing or over long term. At other times, it depends on the organizational skills of the group leaders in creating popular awareness and mobilizing grassroots support. A lot also depend on the effectiveness of the mass media and modern information technology to reach their potential audiences.[9] In this sense, the potential reach of influence of a leader intervening in the public domain, e.g., on an ethnic platform, is distinctively different from the limited impact of an individual's behaviour in his private sphere in terms of interethnic relations. Policy-making and the bureaucratic implementation of the policy, on the other hand, may have a more direct impact on the citizens or a section of the citizens, depending on the reach of the policy concerned, and for our case, with its intended or unintended consequences on the dynamics of interethnic relations such as the regulation of ethnic boundaries. This chapter limits itself to examining the impacts of nation-building policies on specific aspects of ethnic relations.

A public opinion poll of around 2,000 respondents conducted by Merdeka Centre in February and March 2006 found that 61 per cent of them described the ethnic relations in Malaysia as "good", and 17 per cent attributed as "very good". Some 64 per cent of them thought that Malaysians from different ethnic groups "are getting closer together". When asked how they think ethnic relations will evolve in the next ten years, 43 per cent thought there will be improvement while 26 per cent predicted that it will remain the same. In other words, the majority of the respondents seem to be rather positive about ethnic relations.

Yet just a few months before the poll, the highly publicized case of the failed legal struggle by the widow of Moorthy Maniam to claim his body for Hindu burial was causing dissension and indignation in the public sphere. She claimed that he ate pork and attended Hindu religious rites till his death. Based on evidence of conversion tendered by the Islamic officials, the civil court judge ruled that the civil court cannot challenge or review the Syariah court decision, without hearing Moorthy's widow. Anger over the issue and other social grievances led to the formation of Hindu Rights Action Force (HINDRAF) regrouping more than fifty Hindu associations to defend the rights of the community. Following the court decision, the Malaysian Consultative Council of Buddhism, Christianity, Hinduism and Sikhism (MCCBCHS) also expressed its concern for the perceived widening of jurisdiction of the Syariah court at the expense of the civil court, rendering non-Muslims without legal remedy for legitimate religious grievances. MCCBCHS launched a month-long candlelight vigil in front of a courthouse in Kuala Lumpur to create public awareness.

Political observers may validly argue that inter-religious relations had deteriorated based on what transpired during and after the Moorthy's case. Cohen (1976), as many other scholars who adopted the instrumentalist approach to ethnicity, saw the heightened salience of ethnicity as a consequence of political mobilization (p. 96). Some observers talked about "sudden flare-up" of ethnic/religious tension. Yet how do we explain the contradicting results of an opinion poll which was conducted less than two months after which affirmed the contrary? If we accept the poll results in good faith and set aside the issue of their reliability, the contradictory picture illustrates the importance of asking how an assessment on interethnic relation is made, and based on what criteria. All public incidents of ethnic contentions do not have the same impact on interethnic relations on the ground. Some historical events may have a long-lasting impact on popular perception of interethnic relations but it cannot be determined *a priori*. Interethnic violence such as racial riots, arguably, may have a wide social ramification in terms of interethnic relations.

As long noted by Edward Shils (1957), people are generally more concerned with what is concrete and near at hand, and more responsive to persons around him and justice in his own situation than what is remote and abstract.[10] The respondents of public opinion poll may report interethnic relations to be "good" because they did not perceive much interethnic conflicts in their daily lives. Interethnic contestations in the public domain may not affect their personal social networks or elicit deep personal concern. It is likely to be people who follow closely and are concerned with how current affairs unfold at the national level who would assess the interethnic relations based on what transpired in the public domain.[11] A non-representative sample among Malaysian public university students found that those who are more knowledgeable about ethnic politics were more likely to assess the role of politicians in national unity in a negative way (Ting 2007).[12]

Saliency of race paradigm in everyday life of Malaysians, while omnipresent, may be unevenly experienced and perceived at different times and by different people. Individuals may encounter specific circumstances whereby his ethnic identity becomes imperative in determining the nature of his interethnic encounter, e.g., a child being bullied in school, or not getting a place in university due to his ethnic belonging. A 1968 survey among more than 7,000 secondary school students found that interethnic mistrust was prevalent especially among Form 5 arts students in competitive, ethnically heterogeneous schools. Sentiment of mistrust was engendered by their anxiety over low career mobility inconsistent with their high occupational aspiration, compounded by active academic sponsorship of Malay students by the state (Bock 1970, pp. 400–06).

Collective memory may also be selective. Commentators of current affairs spoke about increased interethnic and religious tension since 2008 general elections. From time to time, casual references were made in the media to "our Golden Age of yesteryear", claiming that interethnic relations were far more relaxed then. Yet a review of past empirical studies contradicts this claim (Ting 2012). It could actually be argued that interethnic tensions in the public sphere were as frequent before, except perhaps during a larger part of the 1990s. At interpersonal level, the present ethnic pattern of mixing seems to have been around as far back as the 1960s (Ting 2012, Tey et al. 2009, Daniels 2010). The 1966/67 survey of Rabushka (1973) in Kuala Lumpur and Penang among more than 700 respondents confirmed that racially stereotyped views were commonplace, but found to have no detectable impact on either social interaction or political unity (p. 67).

Noting similarity with Sri Lanka, Rabushka (1973) concluded that "political polarization" (which led to racial riots in 1969) and social behaviour (with its accompanying racial attitudes) are independent of one another, and that "multiracial living experiences do not necessarily promote racial tolerance or political unity" (p. 101). He found politics and unwarranted government interventions the most potent cause for interethnic tension.[13] In the same light, Horowitz (1989) noted that increased interethnic business cooperation during the 1980s "did not translate into a general reduction of ethnic tension" (p. 276).

POLITICAL SIGNIFICANCE OF CULTURAL PRACTICES

Barth (1969) suggests that it is not the cultural forms that matter, but the social significance given to the cultural forms, hence the meaning we attribute to cultural practices. In this analysis, religious practices are also regarded as one form of "cultural/ethnic practices", in particular for the Malays who constitute the overwhelming majority of Muslims in West Malaysia, and whose Islamic faith is integral to their constitutional definition as Malays.

Katherine Verdery (1996) extends Barth's theory of ethnic boundary to "state-making". She contends that "aspects of state-making process tend to make identities more rather than less imperative, as identity categories become mandatory elements of people's existence within the state" (p. 39). Extending Barth's thesis to see ethnicity as a social organization of cultural difference, Verdery notes that state efforts to forge a national identity institutionalize a particular social frame in the generation of ethnic identities.

The national culture policy which was formulated in 1971 may be understood as an example of government policy which accorded particular cultural practices incremental political significance.[14] Daniels (2005), an anthropologist, observes that the visual and symbolic impact of Malay-dominated cultural representations in government-sponsored functions reproduced "a sense of cultural citizenship in which Malays are the default full belongers, the definitive national groups, and non-Malays are second-class citizens who should assimilate many aspects of the definitive Malay, written as national, culture" (p. 265).

In the name of the policy, government authorities particularly in the 1980s controlled and obstructed cultural activities carried out by the Chinese communities through the use of their prerogative to grant permits for activities, such as the performance of lion dance (Milne and Mauzy 1978, p. 367) and Chinese cultural performances (Tan 1992). In 1979, the then Home Minister, Ghazali Shafie, publicly chided the Chinese community for promoting the lion dance as an example of "hindrance" to the emergence of a national culture. He suggested modifying it into a tiger dance accompanied by indigenous music to enable it to be accepted as a Malaysian dance form and music (Kua 1990, pp. 10–12). Lim (1999) noted how the popular performance of lion dance which was on the decline was given a boost after Ghazali criticized it as "unMalaysian". Government restrictions imposed on the performance of lion dance were perceived as disrespectful of the Chinese community and elicited a reactionary response which rendered lion dance a popular cultural activity. In effect, by 1991, Malaysia became the world's biggest importer of tools and apparatus for lion dance performance from China (pp. 145–46). As noted by Brubaker (2002), high levels of "groupness" may be more the results of conflict rather than the cause (pp. 176–77).

In the name of national language policy and national culture policy, local authorities determined the size and proportion of Chinese characters on billboards of shops (Milne and Mauzy 1978, p. 370;

Horowitz 1989, p. 261; Kua 1990, p. 230) and at one point, issued directives on the type and number of songs and cultural activities to be taught in Chinese schools (DongZong 1987, pp. 666–71). Prime Minister Dr Mahathir announced in December 1982 that "unity and stability should be built and nurtured through one culture, that is the national culture based on the culture of the indigenous people of Malaysia" (Tan 2000, p. 328). The Chinese and Indian communities submitted in 1983 and 1984 respectively, memorandum to the Ministry of Culture to express their disagreement with the definition of National Culture and its implementation. They objected to existing government policies on language, education and culture as "heavily tainted with communalism and tend towards forced assimilation" (Kua 1990). Public debates on the policy surfaced from time to time throughout the 1980s, including a sustained discussion in English language newspaper, *The Star* in 1984 (Kua 1990).

Lim (1999) argued that the way the Chinese community defined Chinese culture and popularized annual cultural festivals took inspiration from the way culture was conceptualized in the national culture policy, while affirming equal right to their own cultural practices (pp. 146–61). In fact, Chinese performing arts experienced a revival in the 1970s and 1980s, thanks to the policies implemented by the government which led to a rise in ethnic consciousness (Tan 2000, p. 328). Tan (2000) observed that cultural groups with different political orientations began to stress commonalities and cooperate and share resources to "promote Chinese culture" (p. 329). The forging of "Chinese consciousness" did not signify Chinese unity in a primordial way but was a by-product of reactions to and rebellion against the oppression of Chinese community actors which occurred in the process of "nation-building" (Lim 1999, p. 169).[15]

Historical evolution of local cultural performances such as *bangsawan* provides instructive insights into how creative innovation and adaptation of cultural and artistic forms were reflective of the social and political development of their society. As a popular commercial endeavour, *bangsawan* was regarded as a "modern" form of cultural performance during the late nineteenth and early twentieth centuries, incorporating freely Malay, Western and other foreign elements to suit the changing tastes of the multi-ethnic audiences (Tan 1993, p. vii). It lost its popular appeal following the Japanese Occupation, socio-political unrest and the expansion of film industry. Some bangsawan performers switched their emphasis to Malay historical tales in accordance with changing popular mood associated with the struggle for independence and the assertion of Malay nationalism but could not reverse its declining popularity (pp. 166–75). Under the sponsorship of the National Culture Policy, *bangsawan* was revived as "traditional theatre". Tan (1993) lamented how the re-traditionalized and Malayised *bangsawan* from the 1970s was not able to attract non-Malay audiences or performers neither inspire resonance and interests in younger generation of Malays (p. 186).

In Sabah and Sarawak, notions of racial stereotypes and identities were not altogether absent. Attempts to assert political hegemony by Ibans, the largest native group in Sarawak, was unsuccessful due to inter- and intra-ethnic rivalry on top of federal political interference. Similar problems plagued Kadazan-Dusun leaders in their quest for ethnic assertion and resistance to federal intervention (Singh 2003). This relatively more fluid and heterogeneous nature of ethnic identities among the natives, in contrast with the Sino-Malay mobilization and confrontation as two major ethnic blocks in West Malaysia, arguably rendered the nature of ethnic identity incomparably less politicized in East Malaysia.

STATE REGULATION OF ETHNIC BOUNDARY

Government policies and legislation have direct or indirect implications on the institutional regulation of interethnic and interreligious boundaries. The use of racial categories and stereotypes in the day-to-day dealings of the people may or may not evolve over time, but state intervention and legal provisions may render racial boundaries more rigid, rendering the crossing of ethnic boundaries politically contentious. Though both processes may reinforce each other, the imperative nature of the latter may only become apparent when boundary transgression occurs.

In June 2011, controversies broke out over the determination of the "race" of a baby born of Hannah Yeoh, a Chinese mother (who happened to be a state assembly member of Selangor) and an Indian father. Officer in the National Registration Department (NRD) told the parents to register their newborn daughter's race as either parent's race rather than "anak Malaysia" or ticking both races ("Lawmaker fails to register child as 'anak Malaysia'", *Malaysiakini*, 7 June 2011). Subsequently, the couple were obliged to register their daughter as "Chinese" but filed an appeal to the Prime Minister. Yeoh declared that registering her daughter as a "Chinese" is inconsistent with her stand against racial distinction among Malaysians. Her anti-racial position drew huge public support across political divide among those who reject racial politics and those who believe in equal treatment regardless of race for all "Malaysians". There were also politicians from both sides who disagreed with or circumspect about removing the race column from identification papers and official forms. Kamaruddin Jaafar from the opposition Islamic party, PAS, for instance, noted that "race designation is part of the Constitution which has components or sections which refer to race, so it is therefore not the end of the matter by just deleting them in birth certificates." Those who are opposed to doing away with race column in official forms countered that there is nothing wrong with preserving one's ethnic identity or being proud of one's racial origins ("Kit Siang, Soi Lek agree race column outdated", *Malaysiakini*, 11 June 2011). The incident reflects the ironic effects of a new state policy which appear to increase the rigidity of the racial boundaries among Malaysians, in the face of 1Malaysia slogan of the government, purportedly to promote a greater national unity.

The crux of the matter is the constitutional provisions for "special position" of the Malays and natives of Sabah and Sarawak, collectively designated as Bumiputera (sons of the soil), authorizing the setting aside of racial quotas in the issuance of licences, public services and educational scholarships and training facilities for them. In 1971, under the NEP, the scope was broadened to access to government contracts, financial assistance, housing scheme, and special public educational institutions. In order to determine who qualify for the Bumiputera scheme, it is necessary to regulate who is in and who is out.

The Malaysian Federal Constitution provides for definitions of a Malay as well as natives of Sabah and Sarawak. Malays are defined culturally rather than racially as a Muslim, habitual speaker of the Malay language and practising Malay custom (Article 160). Due to the different ways "native" is defined, the status of a Sabahan native could be passed down through one of the parents whereas a Sarawakian only qualifies if both parents are designated "native" (Article 161A(6) and (7)). Regulation of ethnic boundaries among non-Bumiputera, on the other hand, is left to the informal social processes.

While who is a Malay is spelt out clearly in the Federal Constitution, its determination in practice could be more tricky. In the dispensation of government programmes meant for Bumiputera, the state administration in Peninsular Malaysia depended on the name of applicants in determining his eligibility. During the 1970s, there was reportedly a surge in the number of conversion to Islam,[16] due to the intention to benefit from the NEP allocations (Nagata 1984, p. 197). In order to stamp out abuses, a guideline in naming new converts was sent by the National

Registration Department (NRD) to various state religious departments, stipulating that the surname of the converts should appear in their newly registered Muslim name. Only if the male non-Bumiputera convert marries a Malay woman then his offspring may adopt a full Muslim (read, Malay) name if he so wishes, so that the latter may benefit from opportunities set aside for Bumiputera. No such requirement is imposed on East Malaysian Bumiputera who convert to Islam. A change in name upon conversion to Islam is more an administrative requirement rather than based on Islamic teachings. Hence a convert who adopts fully a Malay way of life but did not change his name may find himself ineligible for Bumiputera handouts, while another who adopts a full Muslim name without being culturally assimilated may be eligible (Hew 2005, pp. 126–36).

Recent decision of the NRD to state the racial origins of the child seems to have added an additional dimension to the determination of ethnic boundaries. Whereas NRD in West Malaysia used to habitually designate the racial descent of a child of intermarriage according to his father (Daniels 2005, p. 189), a choice of either parent's race is henceforth allowed, as is the case in Sabah ("One Malaysia, but three sets of registration rules", *Malaysiakini*, 10 June 2011). In Sarawak, the child is usually designated the father's race, which poses the question as to whether a Sarawak native father could pass on his native status to his offspring of mixed marriage against the constitutional stipulation. In practice, it used to be flexible, but in 2009, a girl of Iban father and Chinese mother was refused a place in matriculation programme for not being a native, which created public consternation in Sarawak. In response, the federal government issued a directive in November 2009 to recognize such children from Sabah and Sarawak as Bumiputera for the administrative purposes of accessing public education and scholarship. However, two similar cases of Sarawakian high achievers of O-level public examinations of mixed parentage were again refused admission to matriculation places recently ("Students of mixed parentage denied varsity admission", *Malaysiakini*, 1 June 2011). This had led to Sarawak assemblyman, Baru Bian, calling for amendment of state and federal constitutions to streamline criteria in determining the native status of Sarawakians with other parts of Malaysia. He noted that, "When children of mixed marriages are not recognized as bumiputera, they are denied the privileges that come with the status" ("Baru Bian demands clarity in mixed-race laws", *Malaysiakini*, 24 June 2011).

Interpretation of Special Position

More contentious than the regulation of ethnic boundaries for Special Position is the interpretation of the meaning of this provision and in tandem, the NEP. There has always been two parallel competing interpretations. The special position has generally been interpreted by some earlier scholars as some form of privileges or symbolically affirming Malay political primacy or feature of a "'Malay' nation-state" (cf. e.g., Cheah 2002, pp. 36–38; Funston 1980, pp. 4–5). Studies based on newly available information show that the Alliance leaders reached consensus on the special position based on the common understanding that they are temporary "protective measures" for the Malays (Fernando 2002, p. 85; Ooi 2007, p. 217). Despite so, this initial understanding of the independence leaders had been contested, steadily eroded and misrepresented over time, not less due to the politics of ambiguity practised by these same leaders for political expediency.

In subsequent political discourse, the grant of citizenship to the non-Malays based on the principle of *jus soli* was interpreted as a *quid pro quo* condition for the Special Position of the Malays (Vasil 1980), currently known controversially as the *social contract*. Over time, the meaning of the much legally circumscribed special position became understood by some as a privilege and entitlement (Ong 1990), and as symbolizing Malay supremacy. In 1986, Abdullah Ahmad, former political secretary of Premier Abdul Razak, resurrected a stormy controversy over his assertion that the political system of Malaysia was based on the principle of Malay hegemony and the perpetuation of the special position of the Malays. Subsequently, debates over special rights re-surfaced when *suqiu*, an electoral memorandum signed by over two thousand Chinese associations asking, among others, to abolish the distinction between Bumiputera (indigenous) and non-Bumiputera, was politicized by UMNO youth at the beginning of the millennium. Current official understanding of the "independence deal" as reflected controversially in the latest version of history textbooks emphasizes the immigrant origin of non-Malays, apparently to remind them that they were graciously granted citizenship in a Malay country (Ting 2009*b*).

In a survey conducted among more than 400 respondents in 1975 in Melaka town, 54 per cent of Chinese and 60 per cent Indian respondents actually agreed with the special rights accorded to the Malays, seeing it as a means to improve their standard of living and provided that it was a temporary measure. A majority of those who expressed their support were of higher socio-economic status, while the contrary was true among non-Malay respondents who disagreed with Malay special rights. The latter justified their objections by noting that rich Malays would also be helped and the government should instead have helped all the needy ones regardless of race. Among the 91 per cent Malay respondents who agreed with the special rights provisions, the majority of them saw it as an entitlement in a "Malay country" (*negeri Melayu*) (Sanusi 1979, pp. 60–61).

At the initial stage of NEP implementation, there was an understanding among political elites and policy-makers that non-Malay firms were to be left alone unless they sought to expand or make changes to their corporate structure, while the Malays were to be brought into modern economy through public enterprises and the expansion into new economic sectors (Horowitz 1989, p. 262). Nonetheless, from time to time, individual "policy innovation" by Malay officials which strayed from this "spirit of the New Economic Policy" raised tension and encountered resistance on the part of the non-Malays.

In the last couple of decades, the emergence of a sizeable Malay middle class, as well as an increased association of the affirmative measures with corruption and patronage politics may have contributed to growing opposition to the discourse of special rights for the Malays.[17] On the other hand, the discourse of special privileges attributed to the natives in Sabah and Sarawak, the majority of whom remain the poorest ethnic groups in Malaysia, elicit very different connotation and reactions. In effect, it could be argued that affirmative action in favour of rural-based native communities in East Malaysia remains inadequate. On top of that, many are currently fighting against the encroachment on their customary land by state-linked plantation operators. There are those who lamented that they remain in actual fact "second-class Bumiputera".[18]

Over time, the notion of "Malay special rights" becomes a reference point in the construction of Sino-Malay relations and ethnic identities in West Malaysia. An ethnographic study among secondary school girls in the Klang Valley reported that their construction of "Chineseness" and "Malayness" was intricately intertwined with the NEP, showing "a symbiotic relationship with the economic and political spheres". Resentment was vividly expressed by non-Malay teenage girls, while Malay schoolgirls in turn articulated their ethnic discourse around the affirmative action policy in the education sector, revealing "some of the tensions and contradictions in conceptualising ways of being and knowing in Malaysia" (Joseph 2006, p. 71).

Similar tendency was found in Daniels' ethnographic study of the practices and representations related to the Malaysian National Culture Policy in Melaka in 1998. Daniels examined how the prevalent notion of "Malay privilege" and the popular representations of Malaysia as a unified and harmonious diverse society "reflect tensions in the process of national formation" (Daniels 2005, p. 109). He noted how both his Chinese and Malay informants tried to reduce the "cognitive dissonance" between the two representations by introducing notions of Chinese superiority over the Malays, be it educational, economic or "cultural", which necessitates such institutional policy. Daniels noted that "many non-Malay people maintain commitment to these ideological formulations as, at least, a sense of hope that they will continue to be accepted as part of Malaysian society and that their differences will continue to be tolerated" (p. 261). His Malay informants, on the other hand, "preserve a strong commitment to ideals of establishing Islam more completely in Malaysian society and freeing themselves from Chinese and foreign domination in the private sector of the economy" (p. 261).

This vertical sense of hierarchical belonging to the nation reproduced in official functions and institutions is softened by the relative freedom of cultural expression in private and non-official public realms. Daniels proposed that participation in festive celebrations and open house visiting among non-Malays was not only a way to forge social solidarity but also to reclaim their sense of cultural citizenship and belonging in the broader society, through which the power structures and social orders could be resisted or subverted (pp. 155–77). Similarly, in a separate study of a multiethnic neighbourhood between 2006–09, Daniels (2010) observed how residents displayed freely a barrage of ethnic symbols around their homes and in the shop lots as "struggles over space" (p. 188) and "as an expression of their respective public presence and predominance in different parts of the neighborhood landscape" (p. 187).

On the other hand, in the same neighbourhood, Daniels (2010) noted that government policy ensured the ubiquitous presence of Muslim prayer space (even in buildings or area with a low presence of Muslims) and mosques. This reality was read by the residents as a "visible expressions of *Malay* 'special privileges'". Non-Malay residents expressed fears or concerns that these "special privileges" may "encroach upon their rights as 'equal' citizens of 'Malaysia's diverse society'" (p. 188). In popular perception, just as for the mastermind of Islamization policy, Dr Mahathir, religious and ethnic dimensions are often perceived as two sides of the same coin. This conflation of ethnic and religious identities is manifest in the use of the expressions "pure Chinese" or "pure Indian" by the residents as meaning that they were Buddhist-Taoist or Hindu (p. 187).

POLITICIZATION OF RELIGIOUS BOUNDARIES AND PRACTICES

Just as the ever-expanding scope of the NEP, the extent of increased social ramifications following progressive institutional changes introduced with the Islamization policy from the 1980s had become what a respected legal expert deemed as a "silent re-writing of the Constitution" (Ting 2009*a*). One of the most far reaching reforms during this period was the Syariah judicial reforms. The status of Syariah court was upgraded and expanded. In 1988, a constitutional amendment which inserted Article 121 (1A) stipulating that civil courts "shall have no jurisdiction in respect of any matter within the jurisdiction of the Syariah courts". The legislation increased the autonomy of the Syariah court *vis-a-vis* their civil counterparts.

Subsequent evolution in its interpretation had resulted in a situation whereby jurisdiction of the syariah court takes precedence in inter-religious disputes involving a Muslim party. Three decades down the road, many current inter-religious conflicts in Malaysia such as the Moorthy's case mentioned above, could arguably be traced back to this incremental process of Islamization. While public controversies used to be Malay (read, national) versus the other cultures, religion increasingly becomes a source of conflicts in the new millennium, with Islam versus other religions.

Incidents of Islamic religious authorities fighting with family members over the burial of the dead, as the case of Moorthy, appears to be a phenomenon of rather recent origins, due in part to the strengthening of Islamic bureaucratic machineries and its widening of legal sphere of competence. Religious conversion among Malays and Muslims used to be a personal affair and required a simple statutory declaration, but a change in the policy of the National Registration Department (NRD) in 2000 but backdated to October 1999 stipulated that the religion of Muslims be stated on the identity card. In addition, the NRD henceforth required formal documentation from the relevant Islamic authorities certifying renunciation of Islamic faith as a condition to remove "Islam" from the identity card of an apostate (Malaysian Court of Appeal 2005). Otherwise, the person concerned could be arrested for whatever inappropriate behaviour deemed prohibited for a Muslim as offences punishable under Syariah legislation.

In 2007, a Malay woman, Lina Joy, who was baptized into Christianity since 1998 lost her final appeal and was told by the Federal Court to seek formal validation from Syariah Court in order for her changed religious status to be recognized by the State. She first filed a suit against the NRD in 2000, seeking for declaration to confirm her status as a Christian. The High Court judge Faiza Thamby Chik, in his dismissal of her application in April 2001, argued that freedom of religion as enshrined in Article 11 of the Federal Constitution should be read together with Article 3 which declares Islam as the religion of the Federation, and hence Syariah court should be sought in matters related to Muslim religious conversion. He further argued that by virtue of the definition of Malay by Article 160(2) which stipulates Malay as "person who professes the religion of Islam, ...", he or she "remains in the Islamic faith until his or her dying days" (Thio 2006, p. 8). This statement technically precluded the conversion out of Islam of Malays. Pending the decision by the Federal Court, various Islamic organizations mobilized Muslims to put pressure on the judges. They feared that civil court might become an avenue for Muslims to opt out of Islam. Around fifty Muslim groups came together to form a platform named Pembela Islam in 2006. A forum organized by them to discuss apostasy was estimated to have attracted 10,000 participants. Within three months, they managed to collect 700,000 signatures to be presented together with their memorandum to the Prime Minister and the King (Ting 2007). The majority judgement of federal judges on Lina's case affirmed that getting approval from Islamic authorities for renunciation of religion may prevent non-practising Muslims from leaving the religion lightly to avoid punishment for religious offences (Malaysian Federal Court 2007). The argument of the high court judge against recognition of Lina's conversion and other anecdotal evidences (Azizah 2009) appear to indicate that exiting Islam seems easier for converts than a Malay like Lina Joy who was born into a Muslim family.

While some have argued that Islamization policy affects only Muslims, as only Muslims are subject to Syariah laws and Islamic bureaucracy, it appears more and more that this is not to be the case. The case of Lina Joy may be argued by some as an "internal affair" since it has something to do with leaving the Muslim faith. Issues over conversion of minors to Islam have been a concern from time to time. Cases involving conversion of a spouse to Islam, on the other hand, have demonstrated how the tussle over decision of the religion of their children could become bitter struggle. Given the rigid way exiting Islam has been regulated, non-Muslim spouses are commonly perceived as fighting a losing battle to challenge the conversion of their children without their prior knowledge.

In January 2010, violence erupted over the use of the word *Allah* by Malay-speaking Christians. Eleven churches were firebombed when *Herald*, a Catholic weekly newspaper, won the challenge against government prohibition to use the word *Allah* in its publication, a problem which despite repeated mediation, provided only temporary respite since 1998. Police moved quickly to arrest some of the troublemakers, while more than a hundred NGOs, including a handful of Muslim NGOs, signed a joint declaration condemning the acts of violence. The Muslim Professionals Forum, in particular, made a strong public stand quoting Quran verses, asserting that the attacks on churches are "un-Islamic", attributing them as "cowardly and utterly senseless act of a group of misguided, chauvinistic bigots" ("Attack on churches un-Islamic", *The Nutgraph*, 8 January 2010). Prompt actions of civil society actors, including some Muslim NGO leaders, and the police may have successfully stopped the violence from spreading, the source of conflict remains unresolved. Home Ministry has appealed against the High Court decision while an injunction has been obtained for the Christians not to use the word pending the deliberation of its appeal.

The problem originated in a 1981 ruling whereby the Malay-language bible, Alkitab, was banned by the government in the name of national security. After negotiation, it was decreed that while the ruling stayed, an exception was made for it to be used in church and by Christians. Apparently, the ban was motivated by the perception that Alkitab was used to carry out proselytization activities by Christian missionaries. In 1986, the Publication Control Division of the Home Ministry issued circular letter to all Christian publishers prohibiting the use of four Malay words in Christian publications: Allah, Kaabah, Baitullah and Solat (Ng 2010). During 1980s, various state assemblies also enacted laws prohibiting non-Islamic religions to use various Malay words in the context of proselytizing Muslims. Over time, the context of usage of these terms was overlooked, while the use of these words by Christians is interpreted as having an ulterior motive ("Pembela: Christianity biggest 'threat' to Islam", *Malaysiakini*, 7 May 2011). Subsequently, the argument against the use of the word Allah is henceforth articulated in terms of Allah being the proper name of the God referred to in Islam ("Mufti says Islamic law bars release of Alkitab", *The Malaysian Insider*, 23 March 2011). Some Malay-Muslim leaders even argued that Christian usage of Allah to refer to their god understood in the Trinity concept amounts to "a grave offence and a serious affront to Islam" ("In bibles" release, Perak Mufti sees Muslim fury", *The Malaysian Insider*, 18 March 2011).

The Herald court case was but one of a number of other consequences following the prohibition of the use of the word Allah. Importation of Alkitab and other Malay-language Christian materials from Indonesia has also been subject to repeated harassment and deterrence at the ports, requiring quiet political mediation, but only with temporary respites. The problem grabbed the headlines again in January 2011, when 30,000 copies of shipment of Alkitab to Kuching, Sarawak, were disallowed for release by the authorities over the use of the word Allah. Church leaders highlighted that another consignment of 5,000 copies was stopped at Port Klang in 20 March 2009, and had remained at the warehouse since ("'Defaced' Bible collected from Port Klang", *Malaysiakini*, 13 March 2011). In view of approaching state elections in Sarawak with sizeable Christian voters, the federal government moved quickly to get them released, but only after stamping ministry's order and serial numbers on them. Following objections and pressure from the Christian churches, the government made concessions in the form of a ten-point formula through a Christian minister. The formula effectively reduced the regulation of Alkitab to the requirement of displaying the words "Christian publication" and a cross sign on the front cover, and in Peninsular Malaysia only ("Statement from the Office of Datuk Seri Idris Jala", *The Malaysian Insider*, 2 April 2011). The Churches welcomed the promised freedom to print and import Malay-language bibles, but sought permanent solution to the prohibition of publications containing the word *Allah*. Muftis of Selangor and Perak as well as an Islamic pressure group, Pembela Islam, weighed in, making public their objections to the ten-point formula, seen as the government backing down in the face of Christian political pressure ("Muslim NGOs say Putrajaya bowing to Christians", *The Malaysian Insider*, 4 April 2011). Yusri Mohamad, spokesperson for Pembela, claimed that Islam's position is "under siege" in Malaysia, as the concession was made through a Christian minister without consultation with the Fatwa Council, religious scholars and Muslim NGOs ("Islam's position under siege in Malaysia, warns Pembela", *Malaysiakini*, 4 May 2011).

Incidents of firebombing and vandalization of churches and ban on the importation of Alkitab demonstrated how politicization of a particular religious practice which was innocuous over centuries had turned it into an issue of major interreligious impasse in the present. It seems all the more surreal that while the majority of Malay-speaking Christians reside in East Malaysia, major acts of vandalism and violence against churches occurred in Peninsular Malaysia.

CONCLUSIONS

Malaysia as a multiethnic, multireligious and polyglot country has its ups and downs in interethnic relations. The increased intensity and frequency of public debates and confrontations over ethnic and religious issues over the last decade or so are not disputed. While some political commentators sounded alarm over the frequent public outbursts and exchange of diatribes over ethnic and religious issues,[19] others saw it as a normal development following the more open flow of information and free expressions thanks to increased internet access and online newspapers and blogs serving as alternative avenues of exchange. This chapter directs its attention to the role of state policies and nation-building programmes which inadvertently became the cause of public controversies and tension in a dialectical relation with the race paradigm. While the more visible interethnic and interreligious contestations in the public sphere should not be the only yardstick in the assessment of the state of interethnic relations of the country, it is a cause for concern. A single isolated incident may be pacified, but more will crop up if the systemic source of the problem is not addressed judiciously. Repeated occurrence of ethnic or religious disputes will sooner or later erode pockets of interethnic or interreligious goodwill; even provoke the emergence of social groups aiming at defending what is perceived as ethnic or religious grievances. The records of increased state interference in cultural and religious spheres of its citizens have been plainly counterproductive if not explosive. In doing so, the government also subjects itself to political pressure from specific groups in its resolution of issues arising from such interference. Perception of the neutrality of the state and the judiciary system has suffered grave blows from one incident to another. The current way of dealing with interreligious litigations needs urgent reform to provide avenues for legal remedy for non-Muslims. Equitable solutions reached through sincere and open-minded dialogues and negotiations need to be found. Ultimately, a just resolution of these concrete though thorny issues without pandering to communalist sentiments is the only way forward to build a nation with a shared sense of belonging and destiny; its multiplicity of races, cultures and religions notwithstanding.

Notes

1. By the beginning of 1970s, as many as 20 million people was estimated to have died in ethnic conflicts, and that nearly half of the world's states have experienced varying degrees of "ethnically inspired dissonance" (quoted by McKay 1982, p. 395). Situation did not improve by 1990s. The United Nations Development Program noted in its Human Development Report of 1994 that between 1989 and 1992, only three out of the 82 armed conflicts were between states. Though many of the rest had a political or economic character, they were often cast in ethnic divisions (p. 47).
2. Regional disparity and conflict is another important issue central to nation-building agenda but it is out of scope of this chapter.
3. In a separate attempt to examine different "paradigms" used in Malaysian Studies, Shamsul (1998) proposed that ethnicity, class, culture and identity are the four existing paradigms applied in Malaysian studies. His ethnicity paradigm would correspond with the plural society approach discussed by Loh and Kahn (1992), whereas his class paradigm would match the political economy approach of the latter. What Shamsul referred to as "culture" and "identity" may arguably be regrouped as a deconstructionist approach.
4. As no scholarly analysis can be all embracing, each approach, applied judiciously, arguably contributes to a better understanding of a particular dimension of the reality. While deconstruction may contribute to a more critical perspective on an ethnic phenomenon, inappropriate or weak application may provide as partial or inadequate a perspective as an uncritical "plural society" or "ethnic" theorist.
5. Making a distinction between conflict and violence, Varshney (2005) notes that conflicts over resources, identity, patronage and policies are commonplace, hence "conflict per se is not a cause of concern", but "violent conflict is" (p. 13).
6. Ruling it out as "a random phenomenon", Horrowitz (2001) wrote that "… ethnic riots are not always quite as spontaneous as they may appear" (p. 8), "more like purposive, concerted activity than it is like sleepwalking" (p. 13) and that "… few riots occur with no organization whatever, and some are rather well organized … but apparently less instrumental and calculative than internal war" (p. 18).
7. Horowitz (2001) noted that: "In riot after riot, … regardless of context or the nature of the earlier provocations, rumors of aggression inflicted by the target group have been involved in setting a crowd on a course of mass violence against the target group. The rumors are false or exaggerated. They may report violence already accomplished or merely impending. The recurrent role of such rumors in precipitating attacks indicates that belief in the hostile intentions of the target group is an important facilitator of riot activity, as it can be in international warfare" (p. 79).

8. This distinction was made by Despres (1975) in relations to Guyana, whereby he observed that at the level of individual encounters, interethnic interaction appeared to be widespread at the superficial level (p. 105).
9. The importance of print capitalism in the spread of national perspective as an imagined community as raised by Benedict Anderson has been amply cited.
10. This does not discount people from responding occasionally to specific event or crisis of national significance.
11. Popularization of online electronic media has fostered a growing pool of internet savvy, socially well-connected users. Free access to information and alternative news sources has resulted in a declining effectiveness of government control over public opinion through mainstream print media.
12. In the case of political consciousness, it is noteworthy that more than 4 million or some 28 per cent of Malaysians above the age of 21 were not registered as voters as of January 2010.
13. "Although social and/or cultural unity is neither a necessary nor sufficient condition for political unity, government intervention in a community's cultural affairs may well lead to political turmoil" (Rabushka 1973, p. 101).
14. National Culture Policy prioritizes indigenous cultures and Islam as the central defining features of the national culture, with other cultures being adopted "when appropriate".
15. 1990s saw the abandonment of restrictive regulation of public performance of Chinese cultural practices such as the lion dance. Scholars have noted the relative absence of public contestations over cultural issues (Loh 2002). This illustrates how it was the inappropriate "nation-building" state policies (during the previous decades) which were the cause of conflicts and not cultural diversity *per se*.
16. Several studies found that a great majority of Chinese who converted to Islam during the 1970s were male of lower socio-economic background (Hew 2005, pp. 50–51).
17. Thirty years after, an analysis of an online debate on the same issue did not find many non-Malays who support the Malay special rights, even though the opinions expressed were not regarded as representative. While most of the Malay contributors expressed their support, a handful of them did not (Ong 2007).
18. A scholar analysing the problems of ethnic relations and national integration in Sabah, states that, "The issue of equality among all the Bumiputera groups in Malaysia, or more specifically the interests of the Malays of the Peninsula [sic] versus the interests of the natives of Sabah and Sarawak, will probably be among the most challenging issues of unity and national integration in Malaysia in the future. It has to be dealt with by the principle of equality and due recognition and respect for Sabah and Sarawak as important and equal partners in the Federation of Malaysia" (Mariappan 2010, p. 55).

19. For instance, political scientist, Farish Noor, has reportedly warned in February 2011 that "race relations in Malaysia is dangerously close to absolutely breaking down if racial politics is not kept in check" ("Ethnic strain: M'sia on brink of breakdown, says don", *Malaysiakini*, 17 February 2011).

References

Azizah Kassim. "Conversion into Islam and Inter-faith Marriages in Malaysia: An Exploratory Study". In *Proceedings of the Symposium "Islam in Southeast Asia: Transnational Networks and Local Context"*, edited by Ikuya Tokoro. Tokyo: ILCAA, Tokyo University of Foreign Studies, 2009.

Barth, Fredrik. "Introduction". In *Ethnic Groups and Boundaries: The Social Organisation of Culture Difference*, edited by Fredrik Barth, Bergen (Oslo). London: Univresitetsforlaget/George Allen and Unwin, 1969.

Bock, John Charles. "Education and Nation-Building in Malaysia: A Study of Institutional Effect in Thirty-Four Secondary Schools". Ph.D. dissertation submitted to the School of Education and the Committee on Graduate Studies of Stanford University, 1970.

Brubaker, Rogers. "Ethnicity Without Groups". *Archives europeenes de sociologie* XLIII, no. 2 (2002): 163–89.

Calhoun, Craig. *Nationalism*. Minneapolis: University of Minnesota Press, 1997.

Chatterjee, Partha. *The Nation and Its Fragments: Colonial and Postcolonial Histories*. Princeton, New Jersey: Princeton University Press, 1993.

Cheah Boon Kheng. *Malaysia: The Making of a Nation*. Singapore: Institute of Southeast Asian Studies, 2002.

Cohen, Abner. *Two-Dimensional Man: An Essay on the Anthropology of Power and Symbolism in Complex Society*. Berkeley: University of California, 1976.

Crouch, Harold. *Government and Society in Malaysia*. New York: Cornell University, 1996.

Daniels, Timothy P. *Building Cultural Nationalism in Malaysia: Identity, Representation, and Citizenship*. New York and London: Routledge, 2005.

———. "Urban Space, Belonging, and Inequality in Multi-ethnic Housing Estates of Melaka, Malaysia". *Identities* 17 (2010): 176–203.

Despres, Leo A. "Ethnicity and Resource Competition in Guyanese Society". In *Ethnicity and Resource Competition in Plural Societies*, edited by Leo A. Despres. The Hague/Paris: Mouton Publishers, 1975.

DongZong Chuban Zu 董总出版组 (comp.). *Dongzong sanshinian* 董总三十年 [Thirty Years of UCSCA] vols. 1–3. Kuala Lumpur: United Chinese School Committees' Association (UCSCA), 1987.

Duara, Prasenjit. *Rescuing History from the Nation: Questioning Narratives of Modern China*. Chicago and London: The University of Chicago Press, 1995.

———. "Historicizing National Identity, or Who Imagines What and When". In *Becoming National: A Reader*, edited by Geoff Eley and Ronald Grigor Suny. Oxford and New York: Oxford University Press, 1996.

Eriksen, Thomas Hylland. *Ethnicity and Nationalism: Anthropological Perspectives*. London/Boulder: Pluto Press, 1993.

———. *Common Denominators: Ethnicity, Nation-Building and Compromise in Mauritius*. Oxford and New York: Berg, 1998.

Fernando, Joseph M. *The Making of the Malayan Constitution*. Kuala Lumpur: Malaysian Branch of the Royal Asiatic Society, 2002.

Funston, John. *Malay Politics in Malaysia: A Study of UMNO and PAS*. Petaling Jaya: Heinemann Educational Books, 1980.

Geertz, Clifford. "The Integrative Revolution: Primordial Sentiments and Civil Politics in the New States". In *The Interpretation of Cultures*, edited by Clifford Geertz. New York: Basic Books, 1973.

Glazer, Nathan and Moynihan Daniel P., eds. *Ethnicity: Theory and Experience*. Cambridge (Massachusetts)/London: Harvard University Press, 1976.

Hew Wai Weng. *Identiti Cina Muslim dalam Kancah Budaya dan Sejarah Malaysia: Persempadanan, Perundingan dan Kacukan* [*Muslim Chinese Identity in the Cauldron of Malaysian Culture and History: Boundary Making, Negotiation and Hybridity*]. Master of Philosophy thesis submitted to Post-graduate Management Centre (PPS), Universiti Kebangsaan Malaysia, 2005.

Horowitz, Donald L. "Cause and Consequence in Public Policy Theory: Ethnic Policy and System Transformation in Malaysia". *Policy Sciences* 22 (1989): 249–87.

Horowitz, Donald. *The Deadly Ethnic Riot*. Berkeley: University of California Press, 2001.

———. "Approaches to Inter-ethnic Accommodation: A Comparative Perspective". In *Rethinking Ethnicity and Nation-Building: Malaysia, Sri Lanka and Fiji in Comparative Perspective*, edited by Abdul Rahman Embong. Kajang: Malaysian Social Science Association, 2007.

Joseph, Cynthia. "It is So Unfair Here ... It is So Biased: Negotiating the Politics of Ethnic Identification in Ways of Being Malaysian Schoolgirls". *Asian Ethnicity* 7, no. 1 (2006): 53–73.

Kaufmann, Eric. "Themed Section on Dominant Groups". *Nations and Nationalism* 14, no. 4 (2008*a*): 739–42.

———. "Dominant Ethnicity: From Minority to Majority". *Nations and Nationalism* 14, no. 4 (2008*b*): 743–67.

Kua Kia Soong, ed. *Malaysian Cultural Policy and Democracy*. Kuala Lumpur: The Resource and Research Centre, Selangor Chinese Assembly Hall, 1990.

Lim Khay Thiong 林开忠. *Jian gou zhong de "huaren wenhua": zu qun shu xing, guojia yu hua jiao yungdong* 建构中的"华人文化": 族群属性、国家与华教运动. [Development of "Chinese Culture": Ethnic Belonging, National and

Chinese Education Movement]. Kuala Lumpur: Huazi Resource and Research Centre 华社资料研究中心, 1999.

Loh, Francis and Joel Kahn. "Introduction: Fragmented Vision". In *Fragmented Vision: Culture and Politics in Contemporary Malaysia*, edited by Kahn Joel S. and Loh Kok-wah Francis. Sydney: Asian Studies Association of Australia in association with Allen and Unwin, 1992.

Loh, Francis Kok Wah. "Developmentalism and the Limits of Democratic Discourse". In *Democracy in Malaysia: Discourses and Practices*, edited by Loh Francis Kok Wah and Khoo Boo Teik. Surrey: Curzon Press, 2002.

Malaysian Court of Appeal. *Lina Joy v Majlis Agama Islam Wilayah Persekutuan and 2 Ors 2005* [*CA*]. Downloaded in 2006 from <http://www.malaysianbar.org.my/selected_judgements/lina_joy_v_majlis_agama_islam_wilayah_persekutuan_2_ors_2005_ca.html>.

Malaysian Federal Court. *Lina Joy v Majlis Agama Islam Wilayah Persekutuan and 2 Ors 2007* [*CA*], 21 June 2011. Available at <http://www.malaysianbar.org.my/>.

Mariappan, Kntayya. "Unity and Integration: Ethnic Relations and National Integration". In *Sabah Priority Issues: Setting the Course for Change*, edited by Ramzah Dambul et al. Kota Kinabalu: Penerbit UMS, 2010.

McKay James. "An Exploratory Synthesis of Primordial and Mobilizationist Approaches to Ethnic Phenomena". *Ethnic and Racial Studies* 5, no. 4 (October 1982): 395–420.

Merdeka Center. "Public Opinion Poll on Ethnic Relations". Consulted on 15 June 2011. Available at <http://www.merdeka.org/pages/02_research.html>, 2006, p. 25.

Milne R.S. and Mauzy Diane K. *Politics and Government in Malaysia*. Vancouver: University of British Columbia Press, 1978.

Nagata, Judith. *The Reflowering of Malaysian Islam*. Vancouver: University of British Columbia Press, 1984.

Ng Moon Hing. "Allah-Word and the Alkitab: Fact Sheet", 28 June 2011. Available at <http://stevblogs.wordpress.com/2010/07/04/allah-word-the-alkitab-fact-sheet/>, 2010.

Ong Puay Liu. "Ethnic Quotas in Malaysia: Affirmative Action or Indigenous Rights?". *Asian Profile* 18, no. 4 (1990): 323–34.

———. "Identity Matters: Ethnic Salience and Perceptions in Malaysia". In *Rethinking Ethnicity and Nation-Building: Malaysia, Sri Lanka and Fiji in Comparative Perspective*, edited by Abdul Rahman Embong. Kajang: Malaysian Social Science Association, 2007.

Ooi Kee Beng. *The Relunctant Politician: Tun Dr Ismail and His Time*. Singapore: Institute of Southeast Asian Studies, 2007.

Rabushka, Alvin. *Race and Politics in Urban Malaya*. Stanford, California: Hoover Institution Press, University Stanford, 1973.

Sanusi Osman. "Perkauman dan Perpaduan". *Akademika* 14 (1979): 53–68.

Shamsul A.B. "Ethnicity, Class, Culture or Identity? Competing Paradigms in Malaysian Studies". *Akademika* 53 (July 1998): 33–59.

———. "Making Sense of National Unity in Malaysia: 'Break-down' Versus 'Break-out' Perspectives". In *Readings on Ethnic Relations in a Multicultural Society,* edited by Muhammad Kamarul Kabilan and Zaharah Hassan. Serdang: Fakulti Pengajian Pendidikan UPM, 2005.

Shils, Edward. "Primordial, Personal, Sacred and Civil Ties". *The British Journal of Sociology* 8, no. 2 (1957): 130–45.

Singh, Ranjit. "Ethnicity, Development and Federal-State Relations in Sabah and Sarawak, 1963–1990". In *The State, Economic Development and Ethnic Co-Existence in Malaysia and New Zealand,* edited by Edmund Terence Gomez and Robert Stephens. Kuala Lumpur: CEDER, University of Malaya, 2003.

Tan Sooi Beng. "Counterpoints in the Performing Arts of Malaysia". In *Fragmented Vision: Culture and Politics in Contemporary Malaysia,* edited by Kahn Joel S. and Loh Kok-wah Francis. Sydney: Asian Studies Association of Australia in association with Allen and Unwin, 1992.

———. *Bangsawan: A Social and Stylistic History of Popular Malay Opera.* Oxford University Press, 1993.

———. "The Chinese Performing Arts and Cultural Activities in Malaysia". In *The Chinese in Malaysia,* edited by Lee Kam Hing and Tan Chee-Beng. Oxford: Oxford University Press, 2000.

Tey, Nai-Peng, Halimah Awang and Kuppusamy Singaravelloo. "Ethnic Interactions among Students at the University of Malaya". *Malaysian Journal of Economic Studies* 46, no. 1 (2009): 53–74.

Thio Li-ann. "Apostasy and Religious Freedom: Constitutional Issues Arising from the Lina Joy Litigation". *The Malaysian Law Journal,* vol. 2 (2006): 17.

Ting, Helen. "From Ketuanan Melayu to Bangsa Malaysia? A Study of National Integration and Identity in West Malaysia". Ph.D. thesis submitted to the Institute of Political Studies of Paris [Science Po] and defended in November 2007.

———. "The Politics of National Identity in West Malaysia: Continued Mutation or Critical Transition?". *Southeast Asian Studies* (Kyoto University) 47, no. 1 (June 2009*a*): 29–49.

———. "Malaysian History Textbooks and the Discourse of *Ketuanan Melayu*". In *Race and Multiculturalism in Malaysia and Singapore,* edited by Daniel Goh, Philip Holden, Matilda Gabrielpillai and Khoo Gaik Cheng. London and New York: Routledge, 2009*b*.

———. "Interethnic Relations in Malaysian Campuses: A Historical Review". *Malaysian Journal of Chinese Studies,* vol. 1 (2012): 60–84.

Varshney, Ashutosh. "Social Policy, Conflict and Horizontal Integration". Paper presented at Arusha Conference "New Frontiers of Social Policy", 12–15 December 2005. Downloaded on 15 June 2011 from <http://siteresources.

worldbank.org/INTRANETSOCIALDEVELOPMENT/Resources/Varshney %5B1%5D%5B1%5D.rev.1.pdf>, 2005.

Vasil, R.K. *Ethnic Politics in Malaysia*. New Delhi: Radiant Publishers, 1980.

Verdery, Katherine. "Whither 'Nation' and 'Nationalism'?". *Daedalus* 122, no. 3 (Summer 1993): 37–46.

———. "Ethnicity, Nationalism and State-Making: *Ethnic Groups and Boundaries*: Past and Future". In *The Anthropology of Ethnicity: Beyond "Ethnic Groups and Boundaries"*. Amsterdam: HET SPINHUIS Publishers, 1996.

Williams, Brackette F. "A Class Act: Anthropology and the Race to Nation Across Ethnic Terrain". *Annual Review of Anthropology* 18 (1989): 401–44.

5

RACE-BASED PARADIGM IN POVERTY ERADICATION AND INCOME DISTRIBUTION ANALYSIS AND POLICY

Ragayah Haji Mat Zin

INTRODUCTION

When analysing the issue of poverty and income distribution in the development literature, it is common for analysts to be guided by several paradigms as a framework for their analysis. These paradigms include the overall or total poverty incidence and income distribution in a country, followed by the strata (urban and rural) and the income class paradigms. In countries where there are state or provincial as well as regional differences, then it is also common for the problem of poverty and income distribution to employ the state/provincial and regional paradigms. However, the latter paradigms are not relevant for city-states like Hong Kong and Singapore, which are totally urban. The race[1] paradigm, which is widely used in Malaysia, is not such a common framework of analysis. A few examples of countries in Asia that employ the race paradigm and publish some statistics based on ethnic groups are Sri Lanka and Vietnam. Most of the past studies have employed the vertical inequality (inequality between individuals or households) approach to analyse inequality. In recent times, where there are group differences between race, class, religion, etc., then the horizontal inequality (inequality between groups) concept, made known by Frances Stewart (2001, 2004) and Stewart et al. (2005), has also been employed, especially in utilizing it as a framework for affirmative action. This paradigm has also been introduced to Malaysia in the last decade.

Most of the current generation of Malaysians associate the idea of poverty eradication and income distribution analysis with the introduction of the New Economic Policy (NEP) in 1971. However, available evidence shows that this approach had been employed since the beginning of the colonial period. It was the British policy of "divide-and-rule" as well as the failure of integration of a large immigrant population with the local population that led to the continuation of the race paradigm. Other countries in Southeast Asia such as Indonesia, Philippines and Thailand that also received immigrants from China and to a lesser extent from India, do not incorporate ethnic aspects into their poverty eradication and income distribution strategies as their immigrants are well integrated with the local population. In these countries, integration was facilitated by speaking the same language, using local names, as well as practising similar religion as the locals by many immigrants, and through widespread intermarriage. The situation is completely different in Malaysia (Malaya then). The race paradigm pervades through all the analysis of poverty and distribution especially since 1970. Taking note of this fact, the objectives of this chapter are to address the following questions:

- What are the economic and social rationales for the use of a race paradigm in poverty and income distribution policy and analysis;
- How is the race paradigm articulated in academic discourses and policy formulation?
- To what extent is the race paradigm embedded in poverty and income distribution academic and policy analysis?

This chapter will focus on the discourses on these three issues, that is, how the race paradigm evolved historically, how it is articulated in policies and the change in the emphasis from a race-based to a needs-based approach in poverty eradication. For this purpose, the next section traces the economic and social rationales for a race paradigm in poverty and income distribution analysis while Section 3 examines the articulation of the race paradigm in policies. Section 4 assesses the extent to which a race paradigm is embedded in poverty and income distribution academic and policy analysis. Section 5 concludes the chapter by summarizing the main arguments.

ECONOMIC AND SOCIAL RATIONALES FOR A RACE PARADIGM

In Poverty and Income Distribution Analysis

This section will trace the economic and social rationales for a race paradigm from the colonial period to the birth of the New Economic Policy 1971–90 (NEP).

Colonial Period

Malacca's strategic geographical importance attracted many traders from India, China, Middle East, Java, Sumatra, and elsewhere during the pre-colonial period. Some of them stayed and settled down, making Malaya their new home, where they freely assimilated into the dominant Malay society by speaking the same language, adopting similar customs, and many also became Muslims (Alatas 1977, p. 187). For example, large-scale immigration of Chinese to Malaya that started around the mid-nineteenth century to work in the lucrative tin mines led to approximately four-fifths of these immigrants in the Federated Malay States working in mining by the late 1870s (Arudsothy 1968, p. 17 as quoted in Jomo 1988, p. 157). This was followed by an influx of Indian migrants from the British Indian colony to open up new lands for rubber plantation and to work there. The major flow of Indian migration began in 1880s (Sandhu 1969, p. 60) and intensified with the "rubber rush" in the early years of the twentieth century (Sandhu 1969, p. 50) that continued until 1938 when all assisted immigration to Malaya was prohibited (Jomo 1988, p. 188). These two waves of immigration changed the racial composition of the country, as shown in Table 5.1. In the Straits Settlements, the Chinese population exceeded that of the Malays by 1891 and the latter fell to just one quarter of the total population by 1931. In the Federated Malay States, the Malay population's share fell from 55.7 per cent to 34.7 per cent over the same period. Malays remained a majority only in the Unfederated Malay States, but even then their share fell from 84.2 per cent to 69.2 per cent. Consequently, the Malay share in the total population of Peninsular Malaysia at the time of Independence was only slightly less than half of the total population.

The British did not make any serious effort to assimilate these immigrants into the Malayan social system, and these immigrants were left to settle in separate communities and retained their respective cultures.

Table 5.1
Peninsular Malaysia: Population by Ethnic Groups
('000)

Area and Year	Malays	%	Chinese	%	Indians	%	Others	%	Total	%
Straits Settlement										
1891	211	42.5	227	44.6	54	10.6	17	3.3	509	100.0
1901	214	37.6	282	49.6	55	9.7	18	3.2	569	100.0
1911	232	32.8	370	52.3	81	11.4	23	3.2	708	100.0
1921	249	28.3	501	57.0	102	11.6	28	3.2	879	100.0
1931	274	25.0	659	60.0	129	11.7	36	3.3	1,098	100.0
Federated Malay States										
1891	235	55.7	165	39.1	20	4.7	2	0.5	422	100.0
1901	315	46.3	302	44.4	58	8.5	5	0.7	680	100.0
1911	427	40.7	436	41.6	174	16.6	11	1.1	1,048	100.0
1921	516	38.6	498	37.2	309	23.1	14	1.1	1,337	100.0
1931	601	34.7	719	41.5	385	22.2	28	1.6	1,733	100.0
Unfederated Malay States										
1911	758	84.2	112	12.5	13	1.4	17	1.9	900	100.0
1921	862	76.6	181	16.1	62	5.5	21	1.9	1,125	100.0
1931	1,056	69.2	331	21.7	111	7.3	29	1.9	1,527	100.0

Table 5.1 *(Cont'd)*

Area and Year	Malays	%	Chinese	%	Indians	%	Others	%	Total	%
Peninsular Malaysia										
1911	1,373	58.6	695	29.7	240	10.2	35	1.5	2,342	100.0
1921	1,569 (1.4)	53.4	857 (2.3)	29.1	440 (8.3)	15.0	43 (2.3)	1.5	2,910 (2.4)	100.0
1931	1,863 (1.9)	49.1	1,285 (5.0)	33.9	573 (3.0)	15.1	67 (5.6)	1.8	3,789 (3.0)	100.0
1947	2,427 (1.9)	49.3	1,885 (2.9)	38.3	535 (–0.4)	10.9	76 (0.8)	1.5	4,923 (1.9)	100.0
1957	3,126 (2.9)	49.8	2,334 (2.4)	37.2	696 (3.0)	11.1	123 (6.2)	1.9	6,279 (2.8)	100.0
1970	4,672 (3.8)	53.0	3,131 (2.6)	35.6	936 (2.7)	10.6	70 (–3.3)	0.8	8,810 (3.1)	100.0
1980	6,316 (3.5)	55.3	3,865 (2.3)	33.8	1,171 (2.5)	10.2	75 (0.7)	0.7	11,427 (3.0)	100.0

Source: Population census (various years), taken from Jomo (1988, p. 324). Percentages and annual growth rates were calculated by present author.

Notes: "Malays" include immigrants of Malay stock and all the indigenous peoples of the Malay Peninsula and Archipelago.
Figures in parentheses are average annual growth rates.

They were allowed to maintain their loyalty to their homeland, thus constituting a barrier to shifting their allegiance to Malaya. The immigrants also had a different set of rules governing them. As in the case of the Chinese, they were placed under the Chinese Protectorate, unlike the rest of the residents. These immigrants were also not considered subjects of the Sultan, like the Malays, but were subjects of the British. The different political framework discouraged assimilation, and reinforced the presence of the dualistic socio-economic-political system. This separation was enhanced by the fact that the British allowed the development of a four-stream educational system in Malaya, divided along linguistic and ethnic lines, financed and managed differently, with different orientation and different syllabuses (Lim 1967, p. 297), thus eliminating an important avenue for social integration. Under the British, labour also had separate functions, where most of the Malays lived in rural areas, working as paddy farmers, fishermen and rubber small-holders, while the Chinese were involved in trade and commerce or worked in the tin mines that were concentrated urban areas. The Indians were mostly confined to the rubber estates.

The race paradigm in Malaya was initially conceptualized in the early nineteenth century by Thomas Stamford Raffles (Milner 2011, p. 12) and the colonial administration. Shamsul (1998, p. 42) argued that the establishment and consolidation of a plural society in some of the former British colonies including Malaysia, was the British labour immigration policy which facilitated the export of cheaply paid workers from one colony to another in the British Empire. The race paradigm was then operationalized through the construction of race in the census that enabled the "divide-and-rule" principle to be implemented in Malaya. For instance, the British administration had on official application forms for land acquisition a blank space labelled race that needed to be filled, while laws or Acts, such as the Malay Reservation Act or establishment of a corporation, the Rural and Industrial Development Authority (RIDA) were established for the Malays. The introduction of an identity card during the Emergency period of 1948–60 with some personal information, including one's race, enhanced the use of racial divisions within the society. The British also collected data such as on population, employment and ownership based on race categories. The same framework of data collection in race terms continued after independence till today.

The Malay Reservations Enactment 1913 for the Federated Malay States enabled the British Resident to declare certain areas suitable for rice cultivation to be given exclusively for Malay ownership. It also restricted the Malay credit market to Malay lenders, resulting in falling land prices by as much as 50 per cent. Jomo (1988, p. 60) also argued that since the reservation land could no longer serve as collateral for loans from non-Malays, this encouraged the participation of wealthier Malays in usurious activities as they are the only ones allowed to accept this land as collateral. With this monopoly, Malay creditors could charge higher interest rates and impose more stringent conditions on loans, making it difficult for borrowers to repay their loans, resulting in wealthier Malays being able to purchase the devalued land and increasing wealth inequality among the Malays. RIDA was supposed to promote economic development programmes for the Malays, but by the end of the 1950s, "RIDA's record — with some exceptions like training schemes — remained unimpressive, especially in the promotion of Malay industry that was mainly undertaken through credit provision and technical assistance" (Jomo 1988, p. 248).

British policy was never intended for poverty eradication among the Malays. Their main objective was to maximize what they could extract from their colonies. This can be seen in their policies for the Malays in rice and rubber production. With respect to the former, up to the 1960s shifting cultivation of dry padi was more common than wet padi cultivation in the Peninsula. However, colonial restrictions on shifting cultivation were imposed on the Malay peasants. This dealt a blow on their livelihood as these policies were not accompanied by the necessary infrastructural and financial support to make sedentary agricultural alternatives more attractive when the environment was not conducive to wet padi cultivation (Jomo 1988, p. 55). The rapid increase in immigrant population led to a shortage that necessitated imports. In order to minimize the foreign exchange loss to pay for the rice imports and to curb the Malay peasants from moving into cash-crop cultivation that would compete with British enterprises, Malays were encouraged to stick to padi production (Jomo 1988, p. 56), a move that trapped most of them in poverty until recently. Moreover, superior land were not alienated to the peasants but reserved for colonial interests. To restrict the Malays from shifting to rubber, the colonial government strictly enforced cultivation conditions on land use, normally disallowing rubber as well as imposing low production quotas under the 1922 Stevenson Restriction Scheme and only small acreages were alienated for smallholdings compared to the estates (Jomo 1988, pp. 66, 68–69).

Similarly, living conditions were also deplorable for many of the migrant workers and many were living in dire poverty. The heavy work of clearing virgin jungle and malarial swampland for new mines and plantations, new roads and railways plus minimal pay and inadequate diet resulted in a heavy death toll. Moreover, the growth of new towns without sound sanitation system, or clean water supply caused frequent outbreaks of Malaria, dysentery, smallpox, cholera, typhoid and other diseases (Ting 1999, p. 92). Many were opium addicts that spent on average about two-thirds of their annual income on the drug (Li 1982, p. 150). Consequently, the death rates were inordinately high, where the death rate for the Chinese indentured labour[2] was more than 200 per thousand, while that of the un-indentured ones was 100 per thousand, compared to the death rate of the local European population of 7–9 per thousand. The situation was just as bad for the Indian indentured labourers working in the rubber plantations where, in some estates, "as many as 60 rising to 90 per cent of the labourers die within a year of arrival" (Sandhu 1969, p. 171). However, it must be pointed out that the Chinese businessmen were the recruiting agents of the Chinese indentured labour and the *kanganys*, or Tamil foremen, were responsible for recruiting Indian indentured labour.

Post Independence: Market-led Development, 1957–70

This socio-economic separation was continued after independence in 1957, as there was hardly any effort to integrate the diverse communities or re-balance their employment pattern or productivity with the employment pattern showing specialization between different ethnic groups. The Malays were mainly employed in the agriculture sector where per capita productivity was the lowest while the Chinese were concentrated in mining, manufacturing, and construction where per capita product was more than 150 per cent that of the agriculture sector and about 60 per cent higher than the economy's average (Ragayah 1988, p. 31).

In 1970, 49.3 per cent of all households in Peninsula Malaysia received income less than the poverty line in 1970 (Malaysia, 1976, p. 160) and inequality was high, the Gini ratio being 0.513. The potential social instability associated with the inequality problem is mainly due to its close correspondence with the various ethnic groups in the country and not due its degree or its rate of increase as Malaysia's Gini was comparable to other countries at the same stage of development. The situation is worsened by the fact that some states were also predominantly inhabited by one ethnic group, leading to regional imbalance. Hence, a potentially unstable situation emerged because inequality had important racial parallels with the country's racial composition that was in turn also accompanied by racial specialization in economic activities and the distribution of wealth ownership. The industrial policies pursued, especially the promotion of pioneer-status industries and the centralization of manufacturing in the industrial estates, further exacerbated the problem. Though wages for all industries increased by 12 per cent between 1962 and 1972, this ranged between –27 per cent and 89 per cent for individual industries (Edwards 1975).

Government policy for reducing inequality and overcoming poverty during this period focused at accelerating the increase in income of the Malays who were mainly in the rural areas by modernizing the agriculture sector, instead of hastening the development of the industrial sector. Unfortunately, the imbalance between the ethnic groups could not be remedied in this way. In May 1969, Malaysia experienced a racial riot that was believed to originate from the inadequate efforts to redress the socio-economic disparities within the Malaysian society. In the aftermath, there was a fundamental shift in public policies by the enunciation of the NEP in 1971. National unity to maintain political stability was stated as the overriding objective of the Government. Consequently, it was deemed that the country needed more than high economic growth rates. Instead, the government must also simultaneously ensure that there is social justice, equitable sharing of income growth, and opportunities for employment. Thus, national unity is to be attained via the two-pronged NEP which sought to "eradicate poverty among all Malaysians and to restructure Malaysian society so that the identification of race with economic functions and geographical location is reduced and eventually eliminated, both objectives being realized through the rapid expansion of the economy over time" (Malaysia 1976, p. 7). The 1970 level of poverty is targeted to be reduced by about two-thirds, that is, from 49 per cent to 17 per cent in 1990. By the same date, the employment pattern is supposed to reflect the racial composition of the population and the shares of the Malays and other indigenous people, collectively known as the Bumiputera, in the ownership of the corporate sector is to be increased from 2.4 per cent in 1970 to at least 30 per cent in 1990. It is important to bear in mind that these "policies and programmes will be implemented in such a manner that no one will be deprived of his rights, privileges, income, job or opportunity" (Malaysia 1971, p. 6). In other words, redistribution has to emanate from a larger economic pie.

THE ARTICULATION OF THE RACE PARADIGM IN POVERTY AND INCOME DISTRIBUTION ACADEMIC DISCOURSES AND POLICY FORMULATION

Malaysia had employed overall poverty incidence, strata, regional as well as race paradigms for the analysis of the poverty and the income distribution. The analysis of these two issues cannot really be separated as in most cases, statements regarding poverty are accompanied with the articulation concerning inequality and distribution, often in terms of income, but sometimes also in terms of wealth. This is not surprising as analysing income distribution is actually looking at relative poverty, which has been a policy focus since the National Development Policy 1991–2000 (NDP) and currently re-emphasized under the New Economic Model.

British Period and Prelude to the NEP

The problem of Malay backwardness and poverty had been discussed by a number of Malay intellectuals. It began with Abdullah Munshi (1796–1854) who discussed the problem of poverty among the Malays since the mid-nineteenth century when he observed that it was widespread in Pahang, Terengganu and Kelantan at that time (Shaharuddin Maaruf 1988, p. 35). For Abdullah, the way out of poverty was to overcome the exploitation by feudal lords, embrace the "modern" and "rational" values of the British society and practise the "genuine teachings of Islam".

More than half a century later, the discourse on Malay poverty was continued by several other Malay intellectuals such as Syed Sheikh Alhady, Za'ba or Zainal Abidin bin Ahmad and Abdul Rahim Kajai. Like Abdullah Munshi, they lamented about the future of the Malays. However, according to Abdul Rahman Embong (1999, pp. 11–14), each author attributed the causes of Malay poverty to different factors. Syed Sheikh Alhady attributed Malay backwardness to laziness, an indifferent attitude, in-fighting and inability to work together for the common good because they did not practise the genuine teachings of Islam (Rolf 1994, p. 57 as quoted by Abdul Rahman Embong 1999, pp. 11–12). He recommended the reformation of religious study to enable people to use independent reasoning rather than blind faith.

Za'ba had written an article on "Malay Poverty" and "The Way to Malay Salvation" (Jalan Keselamatan bagi Orang Melayu) in December 1927. He described poverty among the Malays as two types: "poverty of the mind" (lack of education) and poverty in behaviour (lack of ability to be independent and pride in their own effort, lack of concentration, easily bored, wasting time and lack of ambition and purpose in life (Abdul Rahman Embong 1999, ibid.). On the other hand, Abdul Rahim Kajai attributed Malay poverty to the British colonialists who neglected the welfare of the Malays and who pushed, threatened, cheated, tortured and abused Malays as well as other migrants. He agreed with Syed Sheikh Alhady in the way to overcome poverty.

The idea of poverty among the Malays has been explored and refined by Ungku Abdul Aziz (1964, 1987) who discussed poverty in the context of rural development. He argued that poverty arose from the unequal distribution of income and wealth, as well as through the neglect by the colonial administrators, middlemen exploitation and the absence of a credit institution to help the Malays. He introduced the first poverty index, known as the "sarong" index per capita to measure poverty among the Malays in the villages. Extreme rural poverty was represented by an index of less than two sarongs per capita.

The discourse on poverty and inequality was not limited only to public intellectuals. Politicians also entered the fray. Tun Abdul Razak Hussein, in the Preface of the Second Malaysia Plan 1971–75, stated that the objectives, priorities and strategies of the Plan have been shaped by the over-riding need to promote national unity. The Plan is the blueprint for the NEP that incorporated the two-pronged objectives of eradicating poverty, irrespective of race, and restructuring society to reduce and eventually eliminate the identification of race with economic function (Malaysia 1971, p. v). While economic growth is important, there is a concurrent need to ensure that social justice; equitable income distribution and increasing employment opportunities. It is also the first time when the race paradigm was raised in a development plan when the Preface stated that it "aims at the creation of a viable and dynamic commercial and industrial community of Malays and other indigenous people, and the emergence of a new breed of Malaysians living and working in unity to serve the nation with unswerving loyalty". And it is also the first time that statistics on employment imbalances between races and ownership of share capital of limited companies by racial groups were provided in a development plan. With his demise, it was Tun Hussein Onn, Malaysia's third prime minister, who put the NEP into action, with explicit targets for the eradication of poverty and the restructuring of society given for the first time (Malaysia 1976, p. v).

Tun Hussein's successor, Tun Mahathir Mohamad, was more concerned with income and wealth distribution than poverty eradication. He is known to have defined equity as each of the major racial group having equal number of millionaires. ... "In trying to redress the imbalance, it will be necessary to concentrate your efforts on the Malays, to bring out more Malay entrepreneurs and to make Malay millionaires, if you like, so that the number of Malays who are rich equals the number of Chinese who are rich, the number of Malays who are poor, equals the number of Chinese who are poor and the number of unemployed Malays equals the number of unemployed Chinese, then you can say that parity has been achieved", Low (1971) as quoted by Ishak and Ragayah (1983). Mahathir had made a similar statement when he officiated the *Konvensyen Ekonomi Bumiputera* held on the 19–22 March 1978 at Universiti Kebangsaan Malaysia. In his book *The Malay Dilemma* (1970), Mahathir also criticized the weaknesses of the Malays from the aspect of culture and value such as leaving things to fate, having no motivation, not working hard enough, not valuing time and having no plans for the future, which became a stumbling block to their progress. To progress, they needed a renewal that should begin with the leaders because when the leaders change, the followers will also change.

At the same time, politicians also gave their views and ideas arguing the need for a "Mental Revolution" among the Malays, expressed in the book *Revolusi Mental,* edited by Senu Abdul Rahman (1971). Abdul Rahman Embong (1999, p. 13) summarized that the root cause of Malay poverty was not "monetary" poverty but "poverty of the soul", was their main stand. The book listed what the contributors consider seventeen negative characteristics of most Malays, such as lack of initiative, unwillingness to learn, weak in rational thinking, lack of originality, lack of imagination, believe in fate and others. In order to change and progress, the Malays were encouraged to revolutionize their mentality and be like the the successful capitalists from the United States and Europe.

In his review of both Mahathir's and Senu's books, Syed Hussein Alatas in *Siapa Yang Salah: Sekitar Revolusi Mental dan Perbadi Melayu* (1973), criticized the two writings as confusing the readers with regards to the Malay character and demeaning the Malay personality and culture. He argued that both authors discussed the Malay culture in an unacademic manner and their approaches were erroneous when they generalized the characteristics of certain Malay individuals to the whole Malay culture and race. For instance, if there are one or two lazy Malays or a few with mental instability leading them to run *amok*, this does not mean that "laziness" and *amok* are the main chacteristics of the Malays.

However, published official poverty statistics were only available from 1970 onwards as the NEP targets required some quantitative assessments. As Jomo (1988, p. 256) put it, "poverty is rather arbitrarily defined by the government in terms of an undisclosed poverty line". Burton et al. (1992, p. 196) also stated that "Data on poverty, as distinct from inequality, always have a considerable component of arbitrariness about them" and pointed out to the fact that Snodgrass (1980, p. 80), in calculating the poverty incidence among households based on the Household Budget Survey 1957–58, had assumed a poverty line income (PLI) of RM120 per month.

The New Economic Policy, 1971–90

As mentioned above, the NEP was enunciated in the aftermath of the 13 May 1969 racial riots. With the implementation of this policy, poverty eradication and income distribution policies are inevitably based on ethnicity. As the mean Malay household income in 1970 was only just over 44 per cent of Chinese average household income and 57 per cent of Indian average household income, and Malay poverty incidence was 65 per cent compared to 26 per cent Chinese poverty incidence,[3] with the Malays accounting for 74 per cent of those under poverty (Malaysia 2001, p. 32), the poverty prong was accepted as an appropriate policy by most at that time.

Hence it is not surprising that the various Malaysia Plans have emphasized on rural development to raise the income of the rural poor and alleviate poverty. Among others, rural development involves a multi-sectoral approach that includes agricultural development, rural industrialization, infrastructural development and welfare programmes. However, since majority of the rural population are engaged in agriculture-related employment and activities, agriculture (in the form of Integrated Agricultural Development Programmes) and land developments (FELDA and FELCRA) normally formed the core of rural development programmes. This came in the form of agricultural-income-productivity-related programmes, which attempted to transform traditional to modern agriculture with the infusion of modern technology together with the provision of assistance, subsidies and basic amenities, to yield greater impact. All these are targeted at increasing productivity and income in order to reduce poverty among rural households. Since agricultural development alone is inadequate to significantly reduce rural poverty, it was supplemented by rural industrialization, sponsored rural outmigration, creation of non-farm employment, population control programme, community development and rural urbanization. These rural development programmes together with the provision of infrastructure, basic needs and welfare programmes serve to better the quality of life and well-being of the rural population as well as bring about greater integration between the rural sector and the national economy.

Under the Fifth Malaysia Plan, 1986–90 (Malaysia 1986), the focus was on rural urbanization and land development. Some new programmes to eradicate poverty were also put into practice, including the introduction of group farming systems. This strategy facilitated smallholders to benefit from estate type technology and management systems. Hard-core poverty was getting increasing attention to ensure that the poorest had direct access to the benefits of the various development programmes. Some special programmes tailored to the needs of the poorest were implemented during 1989–90. At the same time, a non-governmental project run by Amanah Ikhtiar Malaysia (AIM), patterned after the Grameen Bank concept, provided interest-free loans to poor households to undertake income-generating activities. This project is said to be effective in eradicating poverty, when it is closely supervised (Gibbons and Sukor Kasim 1990).

Education has been recognized as the best tool for poverty eradication and increasing social mobility. Thus, the NEP focused on education as a means to attain its two-pronged objectives. The provision of universal primary education had resulted in widespread higher wages due to increased productivity of Bumiputera. Educational programmes, which include university enrolment quotas (until 2002), scholarships, public boarding secondary schools and other educational subsidies, aided the Bumiputera to improve their wage earning capacities. However, as of 2007, the share of Chinese in accountancy, architecture and engineering far exceeded their population share while the share of the Indians as veterinarians, doctors, lawyers and dentists also well exceeded their population share.

The promotion of export-oriented labour-intensive manufacturing sector (mainly through FDI) as well as the public sector,[4] provided employment for many Bumiputera. This absorption of increasingly educated rural labour into the higher income occupations in urban industrial and service sectors was the most important avenue to reduce rural poverty. The Free Trade Zone Act of 1971 had encouraged large inflows of FDI but this was affected by the Investment Coordination Act of 1975 (ICA), which aimed at controlling the industrial development in order to ensure the attainment of the NEP objectives. However, after an amendment was made in 1977, FDI surged again towards the end of the 1970s and early 1980s. A very significant role in industrial development was assigned to state enterprises based on the premise that private enterprise development would result in inequity. Thus, existing agencies were strengthened, public enterprises, trust agencies and regional authorities were established with disastrous results (Ismail and Ragayah 1988).

The second prong of the NEP also sought to redress the imbalances in the ownership of assets and wealth in the society. The NEP envisaged the creation of a Bumiputera Commercial and Industrial Community (BCIC), whereby within one generation, Bumiputera would own and manage at least 30 per cent of the total commercial and industrial activities and become full partners in the economic life of the nation. Still, not all policies and programmes implemented to reduce poverty and improve income distribution during this period were ethnic-based as there were also those that have been characterized as supply and demand side policies (Bhalla and Kharas 1992). On the supply side, this policy includes the strategy of maintaining an open economy with export promotion and imposing low tariff rates as well as providing infrastructure, education and health facilities. On the demand side, appropriate policies, such as controlling the rate of inflation and fostering foreign direct investment, were also able to decrease poverty and narrow income inequality.

The National Development Policy (NDP), 1991–2000

The NDP aimed to attain *balanced development* in order to create a more united and just society (Malaysia 1991, p. 4). Based on the NEP objectives of eradicating poverty and restructuring society, it still emphasized the strategy of *growth with equity*. It encompasses, among others, the need to strike an optimum balance between growth and equity, ensure a balanced development of major sectors to optimize growth as well as reduce inequalities between regions and among Malaysians. However, it relies more on the private sector to be responsive and proactive in attaining these objectives. Hence, the private sector was the engine of growth in the 1990s, with the public sector playing a supportive and complementary role. Nevertheless affirmative actions was continued. It should be noted that the reduction in relative poverty, focusing on the bottom 40 per cent of households, was already stated in the Sixth Malaysia Plan 1991–95 (Malaysia 1991, p. 33).

The National Vision Policy (NVP), 2001–10

The NDP was succeeded by the National Vision Policy (NVP) contained in the Third Outline Perspective Plan 2001–10 (Malaysia 2001). In essence, the NVP represents a consolidation of all past development efforts (NEP and NDP) to attain a united, progressive and prosperous Malaysian society. The quest of the nation is to become a developed nation in its own mould, and in meeting the challenges towards this end the same strategies expounded in the NEP and NDP of building a resilient, competitive nation and an equitable society to ensure national cohesion and social stability is also emphasized in the NVP. It continued the attempts to promote an equitable society by eradicating poverty and reducing imbalances among and within ethnic groups as well as regions. It was during this phase that the government revised the methodology and definition of the hardcore poor.

New Economic Model (NEM)

The New Economic Model aims at moving towards inclusive socio-economic development — focusing support on those most in need and reforming affirmative action policies. Affirmative action policies and programmes will focus on the bottom 40 per cent of households through programmes designed to raise earning potential. The NEP will be reformed, with a market friendly, merit based, transparent and needs-based approach. Under the Tenth Malaysia Plan 2011–15, Bumiputera in Sabah and Sarawak and *Orang Asli* of Peninsular Malaysia, the Chinese in new villages and the estate workers (who are the Indians) are specifically mentioned with particular programmes been tailored to their needs.

POVERTY AND INCOME DISTRIBUTION ANALYSIS: TO WHAT EXTENT IS THE RACE PARADIGM EMBEDDED?[5]

Not all the analysis of poverty and income distribution was based on race. The race issue was introduced to the analysis only whenever it is relevant or when there is available data. In general, except for case studies where researchers normally collected their own data, macro level analysis tend to be dependent on the data provided by the government (or the Economic Planning Unit as it is the custodian of the relevant data). Hence, there is not as much study done from the ethnic perspective as official data were hard to come by. Ragayah and Chamhuri (2007) concluded that relatively few studies have taken the ethnic paradigm as almost all of the poverty studies they examined look at the issue from the overall as well as the urban and rural perspectives.

Poverty and Inequality

Some authors examined the issue of poverty and income distribution concurrently. This is exemplified by Bhalla and Kharas (1992), Zainal Aznam (2001), Ragayah (1994, 1999*a*, 1999*b*, 2000, 2004, 2009*a*, 2009*b*), Kumpulan Penelitian Sosial UKM (1990), Shireen (1998) and Leete (2007), who examined the impacts of public policies on growth, poverty and equity during the NEP and later periods. Ishak (1995) examined the phases of industrialization in relation to the progress made in eradicating poverty and reducing income inequalities during the 1971–90 period. He concluded that while industrialization played a significant role in reducing poverty and income inequality, there were other factors that helped to mitigate these problems. Only Bhalla and Kharas, Kumpulan Penelitian Sosial UKM, Shireen, and Ragayah (1994, 2000, 2009*a*, 2009*b*) and Leete have incorporated the ethnic dimension in their analysis.

Poverty

In one of the earliest estimates for poverty incidence, Snodgrass (1980, p. 80) assumed RM120 per month as the household PLI and using the Household Budget Survey 1957–58, he found that there were 55.7 per cent earning less than RM120 per month, with Malays 55.7 per cent, 13.1 per cent Chinese, 19.8 per cent Indian households in poverty, which seemed to be a fair representation of the situation at that time. During the early years of the NEP, the main concern was more to understand the concepts and measurements (Cheong and Fredericks 1977, Chamhuri and Mohd. Haflah 1988*a*). One of the earliest collections of essays on poverty after the launch of the NEP was Mohkzani and Khoo (1977). The book is structured into five parts, covering definitions and measurement of poverty, poverty in selected sectors, poor groups, socio-psychological implications of poverty and strategies for eradicating poverty. Jamilah

(1994) introduced the volume with a review on concepts, trends and research patterns on poverty in Malaysia.

As the policies of the NEP were being implemented, the discourse became more focused on trying to elaborate on the policies and strategies for poverty eradication as well as to describe the poverty characteristics such as the various dimensions of poverty and problems faced by the poor [Chamhuri and Mohd. Haflah 1988*b* (policies and strategies for poverty alleviation); Osman Rani 1995 (dimensions and characteristics of ten poorest districts in Peninsular Malaysia); Chamhuri 1994 (an overall summary of Osman Rani 1995), Chamhuri and Nor Aini 1996 (poverty perspective and rural-urban poverty), Ataul Huq Pramanik 1998 (multi-dimentional perspectives of poverty based on a micro level study of seven Malaysian villages), Ragayah (1999*a*, 1999*b*) (assessing policies and strategies for poverty alleviation and relationship of growth with equity)]. Jamilah (1994) added a gender dimension in poverty studies, while Ishak and Osman-Rani (1996) studied the extent and causes of poverty in Sarawak and reaffirmed that, like elsewhere, poverty there was caused by multiple factors, including low productivity, low income occupations, falling prices of agricultural products, low education and skill, rural-urban migration of youths, lack of productive assets and credit facilities, inaccessibility in rural areas, and lack of dynamic grass-root leaderships. Sulochana (2005) examined the incidence of poverty by looking at the overall situation and in the urban and rural areas, but added a racial dimension by stressing that poverty among the Indians in the urban areas needed serious attention. Similarly, Ragayah (2011*b*) also included the trends of poverty incidence among the ethnic groups when assessing the impact of the strategies for poverty eradication.

The discourse on poverty from various dimensions also has a more rural focus as rural poverty is more predominant. Other than Ungku Aziz (1964), Fisk (1964) attributed rural poverty to uneconomic farm size and the small portion of the return from the land as tenants and share-croppers received by farmers. To Kamal Salih (in Mohkzani and Khoo 1977), the causes of rural poverty were low income and a lack of access to services and resources while others attributed it to inefficiencies in rural and agricultural development policies and strategies (Peacock 1979, Galenson 1980, Ishak 1992, Corner 1993, Ishak 1994, Jomo and Abdul Aziz 1996, and Ragayah and Muhammad 1996). Mehmet (1988) also analysed the structure of persistent poverty in rural Malaysia and highlighted the salient features of the problem by exploring the estate and rubber smallholding sectors as well as the padi farmers, noting that the highest poverty incidence were among the Malays.

Several of the chapters in Mohkzani and Khoo (1977) also dealt with urban poverty problems as did a chapter in Jamilah (1994), particularly on the squatter issue. Similarly, the volume by Chamhuri and Nor Aini (1996) also had chapters dealing with poverty issues such as women in the informal sector and housing and urbanization problems. Chamhuri and Mohd. Yusof (1997), Chamhuri Siwar (1999), Mohd. Zin (2001), Chamhuri and Nor Aini (2003) and Ragayah (2005*b*) discussed the urbanization process and the patterns and trends in the incidence of urban poverty in Malaysia. Characteristics and causes of poverty as well as strategies to eradicate urban poverty were also described.

As Malaysia is an open economy, economic downturns would impact negatively on the vulnerable as they tend to create the new poor. The effects of crisis on poverty have been noted by many authors (Faridah et al. 2001; Ishak and Abdul Rahman Embong 1998; Ishak 2001; Jomo and Lee 2000; Ragayah 1999*a*, 2001*a*, 2002; Zulridah et al. 2001, Sulochana 2002). Crises have been shown to be the rule rather than the exception, with an attending need to provide poor and the vulnerable with social safety nets. Otherwise, new poor would emerge as in the 1997–98 Asian financial crisis. Some of these papers also raised the issue of the need for more formal type of social safety nets, while Ragayah (2008) argued that globalization does not negatively impact Malaysia's policy space in poverty reduction issues.

Prior to 2004, the government had utilized the 1977 Methodology of measuring the poverty line income (PLI). However, this methodology had a number of weaknesses and several studies highlighted the weaknesses of calculating the PLI such as Ishak (1995), Shireen (1998), Ragayah (2001, 2007), Sulochana (2005). In 2004, the Malaysian Government revised the methodology for determining the poverty line after taking into account weaknesses in the 1977 methodology as well as other realities (see Malaysia 2006, p. 347, Ragayah 2007*b*).

Dissatisfaction with the poverty eradication achievement continues to be debated. ASLI (2005) Centre for Public Policy Studies tried to analyse the lack of effectiveness of government measures among the Indian poor. The paper claimed that rural development programmes during the NEP period never reached them because the plantations were classified as private property and little was done to improve their lot. When these plantations were acquired for property and township development, little was done to assist the Indians. It further asserted that though the Government has acknowledged the seriousness of the socio-economic problems faced by these two groups, there has been a noticeable absence of programmes and budgetary resources provided to assist the community. However, most of the claims were not rigorously substantiated and a more serious, balanced study should be conducted. A similar claim was also made by HINDRAF.[6] These problems could have arisen because, while EPU is racially and politically neutral in its poverty eradication policies, the implementing arm of the government could have acted with some racial biasness.

Income Distribution

Empirical analyses on income distribution by racial groups have been carried out even before Independence, as exemplified by Putthucheary (1960, reprinted in 2004). The study took a class approach but it was also sensitive to ethnic inequalities and focused on wealth rather than income distribution unlike later writings. Puthucheary's main thesis was that the corporate economy of Malaya and Singapore was owned and managed by the foreigners, primarily the British by examining the distribution of ownership and control in the economy in four primary sectors in 1953: agriculture, manufacturing, trade, and mining. He concluded that foreign control inhibited economic development and progress towards equality, as the profits were not reinvested but were being repatriated to the home country of the capitalists, that is, Europe, China and India.

As data from the government on income distribution were more accessible up to the 1970s, there were several writings that examined the patterns and trends of income distribution (overall, by strata and by ethnic groups) as for example in Lim (1974*a*, 1974*b*) and Snodgrass (1975, 1980). Analysts had faced tremendous difficulty in accessing the Household Income Surveys data throughout the Mahathir era as these data were deemed racially sensitive, although there were occasional partial information published. Consequently, the analysts of Malaysian income distribution data relied totally on published government statistics and never had access to the raw data for deeper analysis. Again the focus of the discourse was to explain the patterns and trends of income distribution, the changes over time as well as the factors explaining the changes since some of these researchers updated their writings according to available data.

Anand (1983) conducted one of the most thorough studies using the 1970 PES data, using decomposition with the Theil Index. He found that the overall income inequality was rather high, especially when he compared with the results of the 1957/58 HBS with the caveat that the findings were not conclusive since the two surveys were not methodologically comparable. The decomposition showed that only 13 per cent of the overall inequalities arose from income disparities between ethnic groups, implying that income disparity problem in Malaysia was more a class than an ethnic problem. Studies that also decomposed income inequality in Malaysia by Shireen (1998), UNDP (2008), Ragayah (1978, 2011*a*) and Ragayah and Ishak (1978) also came to the same conclusion. The decomposition analysis is a suitable tool in discussing horizontal inequalities, a concept that was employed by Brown (2005), Ragayah (2009*b*, 2011*a*).

Like Anand, Ragayah (1978), Ragayah and Ishak (1978) and Ishak and Ragayah (1983) based their analysis on the Post Enumeration Survey 1970 (PES), with some efforts made to compare with the Household Budget Survey 1957/58. The main objective of these studies was to decompose inequality within the sub-groups and between group factors, or by stratum (rural and urban) and by race, and to explain the results. The decompositions of these inequality measures into the "within" and "between" components indicated that the latter contributed only a small proportion of the total inequality of incomes in the country and most of the inequality is apparently due to inequalities within each group, thereby confirming Anand's (1983) earlier findings.

Tan (1982) investigated the major factors that determined income and wealth among different ethnic and occupational groups in this country. He emphasized that ownership and control of the various major industries and the structure of marketing would determine the past, present and future distribution of income. One of his important findings is that higher income groups comprising both Malays and non-Malays were the major beneficiaries in terms of income since independence (1982, p. 332). After the implementation of the NEP, Malay middle and upper income groups experienced an extremely fast and unusually high rate of post-independence benefits and their expectations were similarly inflated. The non-Malay middle and upper income groups also had high hopes for themselves and their families (p. 335). Hence, conflicts inevitably occurred and were magnified to the extent that the crux of the issues — the welfare of the poor of any race — was subordinated in attention.

Faaland et al. (2003) argued that, contrary to the perception that the NEP discriminates against the non-Bumiputera, in reality it is quite the opposite as the non-indigenous population advanced economically at a much faster rate than the Bumiputera. While on the one hand, the non-indigenous population obtained citizenship "by a stroke of a pen" as the other side of the bargain, the development of an ethnically balanced economy, required a gradual change over a long period of time.

Due to the inaccessibility to raw data, studies like Ishak and Ragayah (1990, 1997), Jomo and Ishak (1981, 1986), Ragayah (1994, 2000) employed inequality indicators provided by the government in its official documents such as the five-year Malaysia Plan and its mid-term review and the outline perspective plans. As the government has been tracking the ethnic income distribution, they published some aggregate inequality indices that have been included in all these studies. However, with the changing of the guards, these data became more accessible and thus Ragayah (2007*a*, 2008*b*, 2011*c*) was able to incorporate more recent developments with respect to the overall, rural-urban, state and ethnic income distribution.

The intensification of the globalization process leading to changes in the industrial structure of the economy would also have impact on wages (and thus income) of workers in the various types of industry. As official data were not accessible then, Ishak et al. (2000*a*, 2000*b*) and Ragayah (2001*a*) undertook their own respective surveys of the workers and their results (with some caveats) showed that the gaps in wages between the unskilled and the skilled workers were widening. Ragayah (2006) also examined the rise of China and India on income inequality in Malaysia, with some ethnic dimensions in the discussion.

CONCLUSION

The race paradigm has existed since the colonial times because it was British policy to separate the various races into their own enclaves. Their data collection was also patterned along ethnic lines and this was continued after independence. This resulted in the identification of race with economic function and the lack of national unity that the NEP wants to address. Unfortunately for some, the government had chosen the recommendations of the DNU (Department of National Unity) School that emphasized redistribution rather than that by the EPU (Economic Planning Unit) School that emphasized growth although both parties were agreeable on poverty eradication.

Malay intellectuals had articulated the race paradigm since the colonial times and the discourse was continued up to the introduction of the NEP. From then on, the race paradigm pervades in government policies on poverty eradication and distribution as the government tried to attain the stated objectives of the NEP. However, it was not the only paradigm used as analysis was also based on the overall, strata, income class, state and regional paradigms. In analysing the race paradigm, the concept of horizontal inequality has also been introduced as a framework for affirmative action.

In terms of the embeddedness of the race paradigm in the poverty and income distribution discourse, this may be divided into three phases: the first phase is from the colonial time up to the 1970s, the second is during Mahathir's tenure as Prime Minister, and the third is post-Mahathir. During the first phase, researchers did manage to get the raw data and constructed their own tables for income distribution. Hence, they had a free hand whether to include the ethnic dimension or not. However, as the 1977 PLI methodology was only very newly created and not well disseminated, the poverty data was relatively scarce at this time. During the second phase, these types of data really became inaccessible, except for snippets provided in the government publications. Nevertheless, things became relatively transparent during the Abdullah Badawi's tenure and EPU responded likewise. While one still cannot get hold of the various HIS raw data, one can request for certain parts of the survey to be made available to researchers. Moreover, EPU itself has even published some of the frequently requested statistics on its website. It can be seen that the ethnic paradigm has been revived in the more recent discourse on poverty and income distribution. Thus, it can be concluded that the embeddedness of the race paradigm in the poverty and income distribution discourse has really been determined by EPU's willingness to share the data.

The NEP has often been acclaimed as a successful model of redistribution without sacrificing growth, but the record in income distribution has been mixed, achieving growth with equity in the 1980s but inequality fluctuating since the end of the NEP and remaining high[7] throughout the period, which poses a serious challenge to inclusive growth. Thus, in order to overcome this obstacle and achieve Vision 2020 of being a developed nation, the government has introduced the New Economic Model (NEM) to be achieved through an Economic Transformation Program (ETP) that will drive Malaysia to achieve a high income status with inclusiveness and sustainability. Thus the NEM seeks to improve the economic standing of everyone, irrespective of income level or ethnicity, particularly for the bottom 40 per cent of households, implying that the government, at least officially, wants to shift to a class-based approach. However, objections from some and the rise of PERKASA do not bode well for its effective implementation in both poverty eradication and redistribution. It also means that the race paradigm will still be dominant in the twenty-first century unless there is a change in the political landscape of the country.

Notes

1. In this chapter, the word "race" is used interchangeably with "ethnic".
2. The infamous indenture system binds the worker to a single employer for an agreed period of time, usually one and three years, with the former often subject to employer abuse (Ting 1999, p. 93).
3. Figures calculated from EPU (2011).
4. Through the implementation of "*Operasi Isi Penuh*" (Full Employment Operation) that raised the public sector workforce from 398,000 in 1970 to 804,000 in 1983, which generally bypassed non-Bumiputera.
5. Only selected works will be discussed here.
6. HINDRAF is a coalition of 30 Hindu non-governmental organizations committed to the preservation of Hindu community rights and heritage in a multiracial Malaysia. It also appears to be fighting for a bigger slice of the economic pie for the Indian community.
7. Defined by UNRISD (2010, p. 65) when the Gini coefficient is more than 0.40.

References

Abdul Rahman Embong. "Melayu Baru" dan Wacana Tentang Pemodenan Masyarakat Melayu. Working Paper Series No. 2. Jabatan Antropologi and Sosiologi, Universiti Kebangsaan Malaysia, 1999.

Alatas, Syed Hussien. *Siapa Yang Salah: Sekitar Revolusi Mental dan Peribadi Melayu* [*Who is at fault: Mental Revolution and Malay psyche*]. Singapore: Pustaka Nasional Singapura, 1972.

———. *The Myth of the Lazy Native.* London: Frank Cass, 1977.

Anand, S. *Inequality and Poverty in Malaysia: Measurement and Decomposition.* New York: Oxford University Press for the World Bank, 1983.

ASLI. "Ensuring Effective Targeting of Ethnic Minorities: The Case of Low Income Malaysian Indians". Centre for Public Policy Studies, 2005.

Ataul Huq Pramanik. *Poverty from Multi-dimentional Perspectives: A Micro Level Study of Seven Malaysian Kampungs (Villages).* Kuala Lumpur: Cahaya Pantai (M) Sdn. Bhd., 1998.

Bhalla, S. and Homi Kharas. "Growth and Equity in Malaysia: Policies and Consequences". In *Malaysia's Economic Vision: Issues and Challenges*, edited by Teh Hoe Yoke and Goh Kim Leng. Kuala Lumpur: Pelanduk Publications, 1992.

Brown, Graham K. "The Political Economy of Regional Inequalities: Malaysia in an International Perspective". Mimeograph. Centre for Research on Inequality, Human Security and Ethnicity (CRISE), University of Oxford, 2005.

Bruton, Henry J. In collaboration with Gamini Sanderatne and Zainal Aznam Yusuf. *Sri Lanka and Malaysia: The Political Economy of Poverty, Equity, and Growth*. New York: Oxford University Press, 1992.

Chamhuri Siwar. "Poverty Profile in Malaysia: Findings from 10 Districts in Peninsular Malaysia", in *Poverty Amidst Plenty*, edited by Jamilah Ariffin. Kuala Lumpur: Pelanduk Publications, 1994.

Chamhuri Siwar and Mohd Haflah Piei, eds. *Isu, Konsep dan Dimensi Kemiskinan*. Kuala Lumpur: Dewan Bahasa dan Pustaka, 1988*a*.

———. *Dasar dan Strategi Pembasmian Kemiskinan*. Kuala Lumpur: Dewan Bahasa dan Pustaka, 1988*b*.

Chamhuri Siwar and Mohd Yusof Kasim. "Urban Development and Urban Poverty in Malaysia". *International Journal of Social Economics*, vol. 24, no. 12 (1997): 1178-89.

Chamhuri Siwar and Nor Aini Idris, eds. *Kemiskinan dalam arus Pembangunan Ekonomi Malaysia*. Bangi: Penerbit Universiti Kebangsaan Malaysia, 1996.

Cheong Kee Cheok and L.J. Fredericks. "Theory and Measurement of Poverty: Tentative Views on An Amorphous Topic". In *Some Case Studies on Poverty in Malaysia: Essays Presented to Professor Ungku A. Aziz*, edited by Mokhzani Abdul Rahim and Khoo Siew Mun. Kuala Lumpur: University of Malaya Press, 1977.

Corner, L. "The Persistence of Poverty: Rural Development Policy in Malaysia". *Kajian Malaysia* 1, vol. 1. Penang: Universiti Sains Malaysia, 1993.

Edwards, C.B. "Protection, Profits and Policy: An Analysis of Industrialization in Malaysia". Ph.D. thesis. University of East Anglia, 1975.

Faaland, Just, Jack Parkinson and Rais Saniman. *Growth and Ethnic Inequality: Malaysia's New Economic Policy*. Kuala Lumpur: Utusan Publications and Distributors Sdn. Bhd., 2003.

Faridah Shahadan, Madeline Berma, Zulridah Mohd. Nor and Mohd. Azlan Shah Zaidi. "Implikasi Krisis Ekonomi Terhadap Taraf Sosio-ekonomi Golongan Berpendapatan Rendah di Bandar Utama di Malaysia". In *Pascasidang Bengkel Hasil Penyelidikan Kumpulan Wang Pengajian Pembangunan [Bank of Tokyo]*, edited by Rahmah H. Ismail, Zulridah Mohd. Noor and Nor Aini Hj. Idris. Fakulti Ekonomi, Universiti Kebangsaan Malaysia, 2000.

Fisk, E.K. *Studies in the Rural Economy of Southeast Asia*. Singapore: Eastern Universities Press for University of London Press, 1964.

Galenson, Alice. "Agriculture and Rural Poverty". In *Malaysia: Growth and Equity in a Multiracial Society*, edited by K. Young, Willem Bussink and Parvez Hasan. Baltimore: John Hopkins University Press, 1980.

Gibbons, D.S. and Sukor Kasim. *Banking on the Poor*. Penang: Amanah Ikhtiar Malaysia, 1990.

Ishak Shari. "Rural Development and Rural Poverty in Malaysia: The Experience during the New Economic Policy (1971–1990) Period". In *Poverty Amidst Plenty: Research Findings and the Gender Dimension in Malaysia*, edited by Dlm. Jamilah Ariffin (pynt.). Petaling Jaya: Pelanduk Publications, 1994.

———. "Industrialization and Poverty: The Malaysian Experience". In *Jurnal Antropologi dan Sosiologi* 22 (1995): 11–29.

———. "Kemiskinan Bandar di Malaysia: Satu Tinjauan Semula". Paper presented at the Seminar Kemiskinan Bandar Peringkat Kebangsaan, organized by the Ministry of Rural Development, Kuala Lumpur, 12–13 July 1996.

———. "Economic Growth and Income Inequality in Malaysia, 1971–1995". *Journal of the Asia Pacific Economy*, vol. 5, nos. 1 and 2 (2000*a*): 112–24.

———. "Globalization and Economic Disparities in East and Southeast Asia: New Dilemmas". *Third World Quarterly* 21, no. 6 (2000*b*): 963–75.

———. "Financial Crisis and Its Social Impact in Malaysia". In *The Social Impact of the Asian Financial Crisis*, edited by Yun-Peng Chu and Hal Hill. Cheltenham: Edward Elgar, 2001.

Ishak Shari and H. Osman-Rani. "Poverty Eradication in Sarawak: Problems and Remedies". *Jurnal Ekonomi Malaysia* 30 (1996): 3-30.

Ishak Shari and Ragayah Hj. Mat Zin. "Agihan Pendapatan Di Kalangan Orang Melayu Di Semenanjung Malaysia" [Income Distribution Among Malays in Peninsular Malaysia]. In *Masalah dan Prospek Ekonomi Bumiputera*, edited by Jaafar Muhammad dan A. Shukur Ariffin. Universiti Kebangsaan Malaysia Press, 1983.

———. "The Patterns and Trends of Income Distribution in Malaysia, 1970–1987". *The Singapore Economic Review*, vol. XXXV, no. I (April 1990): 102–23.

———. "Economic Growth and Equity in Malaysia: Performance and Prospects". In *Southeast Asia on the Growth Path: Book of Readings*, edited by Ahmad Mahdzan. Kuala Lumpur: Universiti Putra Malaysia Press, 1997.

Ishak Shari and Abdul Rahman Embong. "Rapid Participatory Assessment of the Social Impact of the Financial and Economic Crisis in Malaysia". Draft Final Report prepared for The United Nations Development Program Regional Bureau for Asia and the Pacific (UNDP/RBAP), 14 December 1998.

Ishak Shari, Ragayah Haji Mat Zin, Rahmah Ismail and Nik Hairi Omar. "Liberalisasi Perdagangan, Perubahan Teknologi dan Agihan Pendapatan di Malaysia". Paper presented at the *Seminar Pemantauan IRPA RMK-7 "Ke Arah Penyelidikan Bertaraf Dunia"*, Melaka, 20–22 October 2000*a*.

Ishak Shari, Ragayah Haji Mat Zin, Rahmah Ismail, Nik Hairi Omar and Shukri Haji Noor. "The Effects of Industrialization on Income Distribution". Final report of the research project financed by the Bank of Tokyo Fund, UKM, 2000*b*.

Ismail, M.S. "Rural Development and Improving Inequality". In *Globalisation, Culture and Inequalities*, edited by Abdul Rahman E. Bangi: Universiti Kebangsaan Press, 2004.

Ismail Muhd. Salleh and Ragayah Haji Mat Zin. "Fiscal Policy and Structural Adjustment: The Malaysian Case". In *Analisis*, Jun and Dis. vol. 3, nos. 1 and 2 (1988): 1–21.

Jamilah Ariffin. "Women, Development and Poverty: Globalised Issues and Empirical Findings Elevant to Studying Poor Women in Malaysia". In *Poverty Amidst Plenty: Research Findings and the Gender Dimension in Malaysia*, edited by Jamilah Ariffin. Petaling Jaya: Pelanduk Publications, 1994.

Jomo, K.S. *A Question of Class: Capital, the State, and Uneven Development in Malaya*. New York: Monthly Review Press jointly with Manila: Journal of Contemporary Asia Publishers, 1988.

Jomo K. S. and Ishak Shari. "Income Distribution and Role of the State in Peninsular Malaysia". In *Jurnal Ekonomi Malaysia*, nos. 3/4 (1981): 212–54.

———. *Development Policies and Income Inequality in Peninsular Malaysia*. Monograph Series: SM No. 1. Malaysia: Institute of Advance Studies, University Malaya, 1986.

Jomo K.S. and Abdul Aziz Abdul Rahman. "The Effects of Price Liberalization and Market Reforms on Poverty Situation of Rural Communities and Farm Families". In *Economic Liberalization and Rural Poverty*. United Nations, ESCAP, 1996.

Jomo K.S. and Lee Hwok Aun. "Some Social Consequences of the 1997–98 Economic Crisis in Malaysia". In *Social Impacts of the Asian Economic Crisis in Thailand, Indonesia, Malaysia and the Philippines*. Bangkok: Thailand Research Development Institute, 2000.

Kamal Salih. "Unbalanced Growth and Persistent Poverty: The Consequences of Unequal Access in Urban and Rural Development". In *Some Case Studies on Poverty in Malaysia: Essays presented to Professor Ungku A. Aziz*, by Mokhzani Abdul Rahim and Khoo Siew Mun (pynt.). Kuala Lumpur: University of Malaya Press, 1977.

Kumpulan Penelitian Sosial UKM. *Setelah 1990: Ekonomi dan Pembentukan Bangsa*, Debat Ekonomi Dewan Masyarakat. Kuala Lumpur: Dewan Bahasa dan Pustaka, 1990.

Leete, Richard. *Malaysia: From Kampung to Twin Towers — 50 years of Economic and Social Development*. Kuala Lumpur: Oxford Fajar Sdn. Bhd., 2007.

Li Dun Jen. *British Malaya: An Economic Analysis*. Kuala Lumpur: Institute for Social Analysis, 1982.

Lim Chong Yah. *Economic Development of Modern Malaya*. Kuala Lumpur: Oxford University Press, 1967.

Lim Lin Lean. "The Pattern of Income Distribution in West Malaysia 1957–1970". World Employment Programme Research (Working Papers). Geneva: International Labour Office, 1974*a*.

———. "Income Distribution in West Malaysia 1967–68". Paper presented at the seminar sponsored by the Japan Economic Research Centre and the Council for Asian Manpower Studies on "Income Distribution, Employment and Economic Development in Southeast and East Asia", 1974*b*.

Low, Patrick. "Trends in Malaysia 1". Singapore: Institute of Southeast Asian Studies, 1971.

Malaysia. *Second Malaysia Plan, 1971–1975*. Kuala Lumpur: Government Press, 1971.

———. *Third Malaysia Plan, 1976–1980*. Kuala Lumpur: Government Press, 1976.

———. *Fifth Malaysia Plan, 1986–1990*. Kuala Lumpur: National Printing Department, 1986.

———. *Sixth Malaysia Plan 1991–1995*. Kuala Lumpur: Percetakan Nasional Malaysia Berhad, 1991.

———. *The Third Outline Perspective Plan 2001–2010*. Kuala Lumpur: Percetakan Nasional Malaysia Berhad, 2001.

———. *Tenth Malaysia Plan 2011–2015*. Economic Planning Unit, Prime Minister's Department. Kuala Lumpur: Percetakan Nasional Malaysia Berhad, 2010.

Mahathir bin Mohamad. *The Malay Dilemma*. Singapore: Asia Pacific Press, 1970.

Mehmet, Ozay. *Development in Malaysia: Poverty, Wealth and Trusteeship*. Beckenham: Croom Helm Ltd., 1986.

Milner, Anthony. *Malaysia's Dominent Societal Paradigm: Invented, Embedded, Contested*. Bangi: Universiti Kebangsaan Malaysia Press, 2011.

Mohd. Zin bin Mohamed. "The Role of Local Government in Urban Poverty Alleviation: A Case Study of the Kuala Lumpur City Hall, Malaysia". In *Environmental Management, Poverty Reduction, and Sustainable Regional Development*, edited by James E. Nickum and Kenji Oya. Westport, Connecticut and London: Greenwood Press, 2001.

Mokhzani Abdul Rahim and Khoo Siew Mun, eds. *Some Case Studies on Poverty in Malaysia: Essays Presented to Professor Ungku A. Aziz*. Kuala Lumpur: University of Malaya Press, 1977.

National Economic Advisory Council (NEAC). *New Economic Model for Malaysia: Part 1: Strategic policy Directions*. Putrajaya: Malaysia National Printers Limited, 2010.

Nor Aini Haji Idris and Chamhuri Siwar, eds. *Kemiskinan Bandar dan Sektor Tidak Formal di Malaysia*. Bangi: Penerbit Universiti Kebangsaan Malaysia, 2003.

Osman Rani Hassan, ed. *Daerah-daerah Kemiskinan*. Kuala Lumpur: Dewan Bahasa dan Pustaka. 1993.

Peacock, F. "The Failure of Rural Development in Peninsular Malaysia". In *Issues in Malaysian Development*, edited by J.C. Jackson and M. Rudner. Canberra: Australian National University, 1979.

Puthucheary, J. J. *Ownership and Control in the Malayan Economy*. Singapore: Eastern Universities Press, 1960 (reprinted in 2004).

Ragayah Haji Mat Zin. "Some Aspects of Income Inequality in Peninsular Malaysia, 1957–1970". Council of Asian Manpower Studies (CAMS) Discussion Paper Series No. 78–01. Manila, 1978.

———. "A General Equilibrium Approach to Fiscal Incidence and Redistribution Policies in West Malaysia". Ph.D. dissertation. Vanderbilt University, U.S., 1988.

———. "The Effect of the New Economic Policy on Poverty and Income Distribution in Peninsular Malaysia and Challenges in the 1990s (in Malay)". In *Rancangan Malaysia Keenam: Prioriti Pengukuhan Negara*, edited by Supian A. and Zainudin S. Bangi: National University of Malaysia Press, 1994.

———. "Growth with Equity: Policy Lessons from the Experience of Malaysia". In *ESCAP Growth with Equity: Policy Lessons from the Experiences of Selected Asian Countries*. (ST/ESCAP/2007). New York: United Nations, 1999*a*.

———. "Policies and Strategies of Poverty Alleviation in Malaysia". In *Poverty Reduction in Developing Countries: Experiences from Asia and Africa*, edited by V.S. Vyas and Pradeep Bhargava. Jaipur dan New Delhi: Rawat Publications, 1999*b*.

———. "The Challenges to Poverty Eradication and Redistributing Income (in Malay)". In *Facing and Managing the Challenges in the 21st Century*, edited by Md. Zhahir Kechot dan Mansor Jusoh. Bangi: Universiti Kebangsaan Malaysia Press, 2000.

———. "The Impact of Globalization on Income Distribution in Malaysia". Paper presented at the APEC Study Centre Consortium Conference, Tianjin, China, 18–20 May 2001*a*.

———. "Meningkatkan Keutuhan Daya Tahan Kualiti Hidup: Beberapa Dilema". Paper presented at the Workshop Meningkatkan Keutuhan Daya Tahan dan Daya Saing Ekonomi Malaysia, Port Dickson, Malaysia, 29–30 December 2001*b*.

———. "The Impact of the Financial Crisis on Poverty and Inequality in Malaysia". In *Impact of the East Asian Financial Crisis Revisited*, edited by Shahid Khandker. Manila: The World Bank Institute and the Philippine Institute for Development Studies, 2002.

———. "Income Distribution and Poverty Eradication in Malaysia: Where Do We Go from Here". In *Globalisation, Culture and Inequalities*, edited by Abdul Rahman Embong. Bangi: Penerbit Universiti Kebangsaan Malaysia, 2004.

———. "Concepts and Measurement of Poverty". Paper presented at National Seminar on Poverty Eradication Through Empowerment. Kuala Lumpur, Malaysian Institute of Economic Research (MIER), 23 August 2005*a*.

———. "Revisiting Urban Poverty and the Issue of Social Protection in Malaysia". In *Emerging Urban Poverty and Social Safety Net in East Asia*, edited by Zhang Yunling. Beijing: World Affairs Press, 2005*b*.

———. "China and India: Challenges and Opportunities for Poverty Eradication and Moderating Inequality in Malaysia". *The Philippine Review of Economics*, vol. XLIII, no. I (June 2006): 109–30.

———. "Income Distribution in Malaysia". Paper presented at the 5th Asian Economic Policy Review Conference on "Growing Inequalities?". Tokyo, 29 September 2007*a*.

———. "Understanding the Formulation of the Revised Poverty Line". *Akademika* 70 (January 2007*b*): 21–39.

———. "Poverty Eradication, Development and Policy Space in Malaysia". In *Globalization and Autonomy: The Experience of Malaysia*, edited by Joan Nelson, Jacob Meermen and Abdul Rahman Embong. Singapore: Institute of Southeast Asian Studies and IKMAS, 2008*a*.

———. "Explaining the Trends in Malaysian Income Distribution". In *Income Distribution and Sustainable Economic Development in East Asia: A Comparative Analysis*, edited by Ragayah H.M.Z. and Medhi K. Bangi: Universiti Kebangsaan Press, 2008*b*.

———. "Growth and Equity: Reality and Aspiration: Professorial Inaugural Lecture (in Malay)". Bangi: Universiti Kebangsaan Press, 2009*a*.

———. "Poverty Reduction, Social Integration and Development: The Formula for Peace?". Public Lecture and Keynote Speech Publication Series. Bangi: Universiti Kebangsaan Press, 2009*b*.

———. "Strategies for Poverty Eradication". In *Malaysia: Policies and Issues in Economic Development.* Kuala Lumpur: Institute of Strategic and International Studies (ISIS), 2011*a*.

———. "Sharing the Pie: Towards a More Equitable Malaysian Society". In *Malaysia at a Crossroads: Can We Make the Transition?*, edited by Abdul Rahman Embong and Tham Siew Yean. Bangi: Penerbit Universiti Kebangsaan Malaysia, 2011*b*.

———. "The New Economic Policy: Growth with Equity". In *Malaysia: Policies and Issues in Economic Development.* Kuala Lumpur: Institute of Strategic and International Studies (ISIS), 2011*c*.

Ragayah Haji Mat Zin and Chamhuri Siwar. "Review of Poverty Studies in Malaysia". Paper presented at the "Bengkel Kebangsaan Mengenai Kemiskinan". University of Malaya, Kuala Lumpur, 12–13 March 2007.

Ragayah Haji Mat Zin and Ishak Shari. "Some Aspects of Income Inequality in Peninsular Malaysia, 1957–70" (abridged). In *Income Distribution by Sectors and Over Time in East and Southeast Asian Countries*, edited by H.T. Oshima and

T. Mizoguchi (pynt.). Selected papers presented for the CAMS-Hitotsubashi Seminar, CAMS, Quezon City, Philippines and IADRPHU, Institute of Economic Research, Hitotsubashi University, Tokyo, January 1978.

Ragayah Haji Mat Zin and Muhammad Haji Alias. "The Effects of Price Liberalization and Market Reforms on the Poverty Situation of Farm Communities and Rural Familie". In *Economic Liberalization and Rural Poverty: A Study on the Effects of Price Liberalization and Market Reforms in Asian Developing Countries* (25)(ST/ESCAP/1686). New York: United Nations, 1996.

Rolf, Williatti R. *The Origins of Malay Nationalism*. 2nd ed. Kuala Lumpur: Oxford University Press, 1994.

Sandhu, Kernail Singh. "Indians in Malaya: Some Aspects of their Migration and Settlement (1786–1957)". Cambridge: Cambridge University Press, 1969.

Senu Abdul Rahman, ed. "Revolusi Mental". Kuala Lumpur: Utusan Melayu (M) Berhad, 1971.

Shaharuddin Maaruf. "Malay Ideas on Development: From Feudal Lord to Capitalist". Singapore: Times Books International, 1988.

Shamsul A.B. "Ethnicity, Class, Culture or Identity: Competing Paradigms in Malaysian Studies". *Akademika* 53 (July 1998): 33–59.

Shireen Mardziah Hashim. *Income Inequality and Poverty in Malaysia*. Lanham, Maryland USA: Rowman and Littlefield Publishers, Inc., 1998.

Snodgrass, Donald R. "Trends and Patterns in Malaysian Income Distribution, 1957–1970". In *Readings on Malaysian Economic Development*, edited by David Lim. Kuala Lumpur: Oxford University Press, 1975.

———. *Inequality and Economic Development in Malaysia*. Kuala Lumpur: Oxford University Press, 1980.

Stewart, Frances. "Horizontal Inequalities: A Neglected Dimension of Development". Working Paper 1. Centre for Research on Inequality, Human Security and Ethnicity, CRISE, Queen Elizabeth House, University of Oxford, United Kingdom, 2001. Available at <http://www.crise.ox.ac.uk>.

———. "Development and Security". Working Paper 3. Centre for Research on Inequality, Human Security and Ethnicity, CRISE, Queen Elizabeth House, University of Oxford, United Kingdom, 2004. Available at <http://www.crise.ox.ac.uk>.

Stewart, Frances, Graham Brown and Luca Mancini. "Why Horizontal Inequalities Matter: Some Implications for Measurement". Working Paper 19. Centre for Research on Inequality, Human Security and Ethnicity, CRISE, Queen Elizabeth House, University of Oxford, United Kingdom, 2005. Available at <http://www.crise.ox.ac.uk>.

Sulochana Nair. "Globalisation: Help or Hindrance to Poverty Alleviatio". Paper presented at the Conference on Poverty Alleviation and Social Stability, Kuala Lumpur, 22-23 October, 2002.

———. "Causes and Consequences of Poverty". Paper presented at National Seminar on Poverty Eradication through Empowerment. Malaysian Institute of Economic Research (MIER), Kuala Lumpur, 23 August 2005.

Tan Tat Wai. *Income Distribution and Determination in West Malaysia.* Kuala Lumpur: Oxford University Press, 1982.

Ting, Mu-hung Helen. "A Historico-Systematic Analysis of the Development Process in Malaya between 1400–1940". M.A. thesis. Universite Catholique de Louvain, 1999.

UNDP. "Malaysia: Measuring and Monitoring Poverty and Inequality". Kuala Lumpur: United Nations Development Programme (UNDP) Malaysia (second print), 2008.

Ungku Abdul Aziz. "Poverty and Rural Development in Malaysia". *Kajian Ekonomi Malaysia,* vol. 1, no. 1 (June 1964): 70–97.

———. *Jejak-jejak di Pantai Zaman.* Kuala Lumpur: Jabatan Penerbitan Universiti Malaya, 1987.

United Nations Research Institute for Social Development (UNRISD). *Combating Poverty and Inequality.* Geneva: UNRISD, 2010.

Zainal Aznam, Yusof. "Growth and Equity in Malaysia". In *Malaysian Development Experience: Changes and Challenges.* Kuala Lumpur: National Institute of Public Administration, 1994.

Zulridah Mohd. Nor, Faridah Shahadan, Madeline Berma and Mohd. Azlan Shah Zaidi. "Krisis Ekonomi: Tindakbalas Golongan Berpendapaatn Rendah di Malaysia". In *Pascasidang Bengkel Hasil Penyelidikan Kumpulan Wang Pengajian Pembangunan* [Bank of Tokyo], edited by Rahmah Ismail, Zulridah Mohd. Noor and Nor Aini Hj. Idris. Fakulti Ekonomi, Universiti Kebangsaan Malaysia, 2000.

6

FOREIGN WORKERS IN MALAYSIA IN THE POST-INDEPENDENCE ERA
Race Paradigm in State Policy, Academic Writings and Public Discourse

Azizah Kassim

INTRODUCTION

Large scale labour migration into the constituent regions of Malaysia i.e., Malaya, Sabah and Sarawak began in late nineteenth century when these regions were under British rule. For Malaya, the first of the three regions to attain independence the large inflow was induced by the introduction of capitalistic economic enterprises at a time when the region was sparsely populated. Millions of workers were brought in from India, China and Indonesia to work in the expanding production of tin and agricultural products for exports and the accompanying infrastructural development (see among others, Kaur 2006 and Khoo 2008, pp. 11–31). Many of the early labour migrants stayed on such that on independence in 1957, there were millions of foreigners comprising mainly those from China, India and Indonesia in Malaya. On independence, the immigrants were accorded citizenship by naturalization made possible by Article 16 of the

Federal Constitution. The newly independent Federation of Malaya adopted a democratic government, based on a power sharing formula between the three major ethnically based political parties — the United Malay National Organization (UMNO), Malayan Chinese Association (MCA) and the Malayan Indian Congress (MIC) who formed the Alliance party. The Alliance party which gained power in 1957 election was later enlarged to form the Barisan Nasional (BN or National Front) with the incorporation of more political parties in the early 1970s. With the establishment of Malaysia in 1963 which saw the incorporation of Singapore,[1] Sabah and Sarawak into the federation, this political power sharing formula was continued with more ethnically based or ethnically dominated political parties joining the BN. Since then the BN which now comprises thirteen political parties from the Peninsula, Sabah and Sarawak remains the party in power. Given this demographic and political background, managing race/ethnic relations is highly problematic and ethnic conflicts and violence occur once in a while, the worst being the May 13 incident in 1967. The balance of power between the ethnic political parties is keenly guarded by the respective ethnic party leaders. This race paradigm is not confined to the political arena only; it also pervades into almost every aspect of Malaysian life.

In the years after independence, transnational inflow returned on a massive scale in 1970s and Malaysia is increasingly inundated by millions of foreigners many of whom are low skill workers from at least fourteen designated countries. Their presence further accentuates the ethnic diversity of the Malaysian population and makes the management of ethnic relations even more difficult. This chapter attempts to unravel how the race paradigm affects and shapes the foreign worker policy and its strategies. To ascertain the relevance (or otherwise) of the race paradigm in the policy, this chapter will also examine other paradigms that are often used to analyse the presence of foreign workers in Malaysia namely security, economics and human rights. Legally recruited migrant workers in Malaysia consist of two major categories — the legally recruited low skilled workers and the expatriates. In addition there are a large number of irregular migrants officially referred to as illegal immigrants. Legally recruited workers are estimated at around 1.9 million in 2010; and irregular migrants at least 1.3 million,[2] some of whom are also in the workforce. This chapter confines itself only to the low-skill foreign workers, both legal and otherwise, as their presence in large numbers is acutely challenging to the state, the general public and to the migrants themselves.

TRANSNATIONAL INFLOWS IN THE POST-INDEPENDENCE ERA

In the years after independence, transnational inflows were restricted with the formulation and enforcement of the Immigration Act 1959/63 and the Passport Act 1966. However, cross-national inflows and outflows continued, albeit at a subdued rate especially in border areas viz. between the Peninsular and Thailand, Sarawak and East Kalimantan and between Sabah and the southern Philippines and west Kalimantan, where existing communities were broken apart by foreign powers and the establishment of nation states. Members of families, kin and ethnic groups who found themselves divided into different nationalities continued to visit one another, across their national boundary, as in the case of traditional cross-border traders and workers. Much of the cross-border flows were irregular, using traditional routes outside the authorized port of entry. With the expansion of employment opportunities in Malaysia due to increased economic activities since the early 1970s, nationals from neighbouring countries began to enter in large numbers. In Sabah, the shortage of workers in the agricultural sector necessitated the recruitment of workers from the Philippines, Indonesia and the Peninsula as early as 1968 under the Malaysian Migration Fund Board. Inflows of Filipinos into the state increased in the early 1970s with political instability in the Mindanao region in southern Philippines. Over 100,000 refugees were reported to have entered Sabah where the refugees were "welcomed" by the state administration and employers partly because of labour shortage, especially in the logging industry (Bahrain and Rachagan 1984). Hence some of the refugees became foreign workers, a situation that continues to the present day.

In the Peninsula, the early 1970s saw a large inflow of refugees from Vietnam and a small number from Cambodia along with economic migrants from Indonesia and Thailand. Sarawak was spared the entry of refugees, but not foreign workers who began to make their presence felt in the late 1970s in the agricultural and plantation sectors. In the Peninsula, they were initially engaged mainly in the agricultural and rural sector, opening up new land for development; but by the mid-1970s, many began to move into the construction sector especially in the Klang Valley. As there were no legal mechanisms to recruit and employ low-skilled foreign workers then, they arrived and worked illegally. Thus by the early 1980s official sources estimated that there were around 500,000 illegal immigrants in Malaysia. Their presence was accompanied by various socio-cultural, economic and security problems which forced the government to take steps towards formulating a policy on foreign workers.

The inflow continues until today due to Malaysia's relatively better economic performance, smaller population and fussy workers compared to other countries in ASEAN, thereby making it a favourite destination for economic migrants from these countries. In addition, political instability in Acheh, Indonesia until 2006; the Mindanao region in southern Philippines; and in Myanmar which continues to the present pushed out more asylum seekers to Malaysia. New developments in the fields of education and tourism in the last two decades provide further reasons for other categories of migrants to come viz. foreign students and participants in the Malaysia My Second Home project (MM2H). The result is a continuous increase in the number of foreign nationals in the last four decades (see Figure 6.1). The Malaysian Population Census

Figure 6.1
Increase in Foreign Population in Peninsula Malaysia, Sabah and Sarawak
(1970–2010)

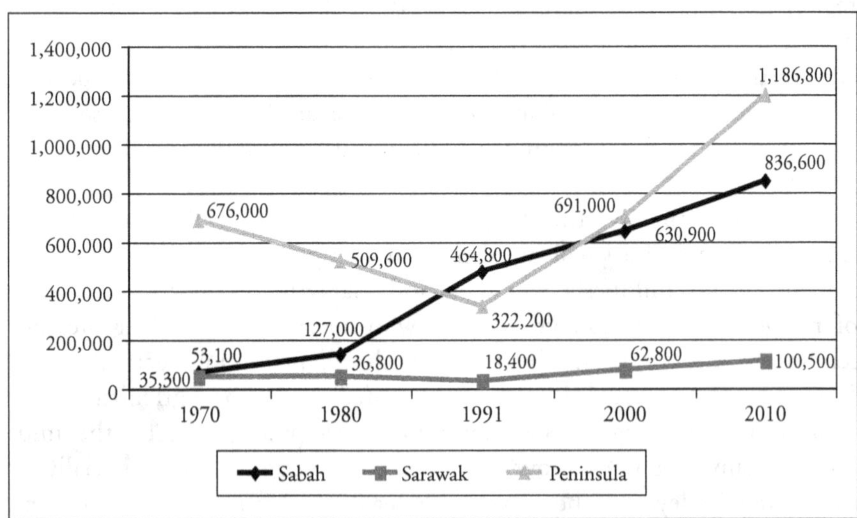

Source: Government of Malaysia — Housing and Population Census, 1970, 1980, 1991, 2000 and 2010. Department of Statistics, Malaysia.

in 1970 shows there were over 670,000 foreign nationals in the country then forming about 7 per cent of the population. Of these, the majority (88.4 per cent) were in the Peninsula. By 2010, their number rose to over 2.3 million or 8.2 per cent of the total Malaysian population of over 28 million.

As shown in Figure 6.1, expansion rate of the foreign population in the three regions differs greatly. Sabah and Sarawak has about the same number of foreign nationals in 1970, but in the following decades, those in Sabah increased at an unprecedented rate compared to Sarawak. In the Peninsula, the number of foreigners declined sharply in the 1991 census, and rose again steadily in the following decade. The decline in 1991 could be due to a number of factors. Firstly, regularization exercises carried out on illegal immigrants from the second half of 1980s may have affected illegal inflow or induced many to return home. Secondly, it may have caused some illegal immigrants not to participate in the census. Thirdly, some may have been granted citizenship.[3]

The majority of foreign nationals in Malaysia are economic migrants. Over 95 per cent are low skilled workers or *pekerja asing* as they are officially referred to, while the rest are expatriates comprising the highly skilled professional, managerial and technical group known officially as *pegawai dagang*. The actual number of *pekerja asing* is difficult to determine in view of the large number of irregular workers. However, the number of registered legal workers provides a good indication. There were only 3,484 foreign workers in the first registration exercise in 1985; by 1990 the number rose to 24,152. In 2001, their number increased exponentially to over 769,566 but their annual increase between 2001 and 2010 fluctuated in tandem with Malaysian's economic performance, reaching a peak of over 2 million in 2007. The number declined in the following years to over 1.9 million in 2009 (see Figure 6.2). Initially designated source countries were mainly Malaysia's immediate neighbours — Indonesia, Thailand and the Philippines. This was induced by economic and socio-cultural reasons. The close proximity of these countries such as Indonesia in the case of the Peninsula and the Philippines in the case of Sabah was expected to reduce the cost of recruitment; and the close cultural similarities between the dominant population in Malaysia with the majority of the migrant workers was expected to facilitate their adaptations. Following a change in policy strategies in 2002 (see section 3) the number of source countries was increased to fourteen of which major ones are indicated in Table 6.1.

Figure 6.2
Number of Foreign Workers in Malaysia
(1993–2009)

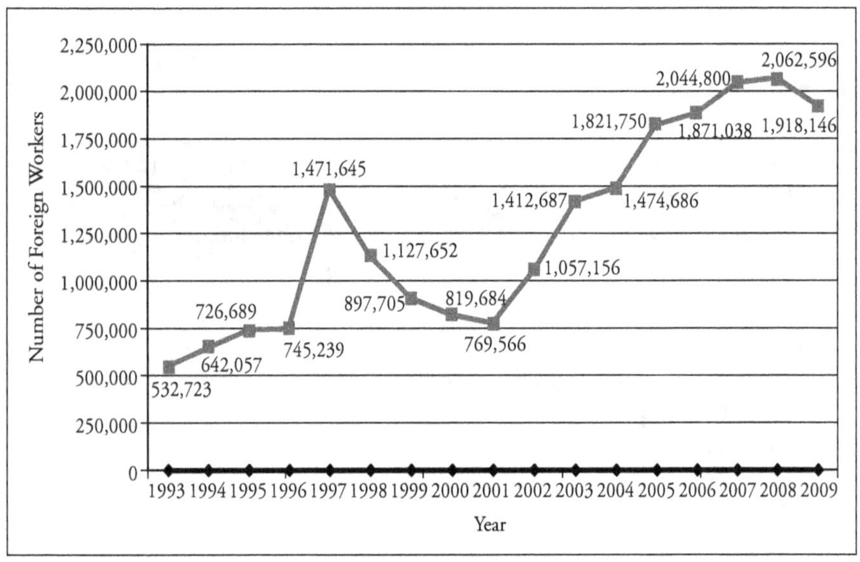

FORMULATION AND IMPLEMENTATION OF STATE POLICY ON FOREIGN WORKERS

As stated earlier, migrant workers who arrived in the 1970s were irregular and undocumented as they entered Malaysia clandestinely outside the authorized port of entry. Border infiltration by a large number of foreigners soon was seen as a threat to border security. Other negative consequences of their presence came under official scrutiny. They were also seen as a serious health risk with the recurrence of diseases such as tuberculosis and malaria which were already under control in Malaysia. Economically, they were accused of posing unfair competition to Malaysian workers because of their readiness to accept low pay, long working hours and poor working conditions, which in turn, frustrated trade unions' attempts to fight for better remunerations for workers. In the urban areas, their presence led to stiff competition for low cost accommodation especially in squatter areas and in Malay reserve "villages" thus causing a great stress on social

Table 6.1
Five Major Source Countries
(2001–10)

Countries	2001	2002	2003	2005	2006	2007	2008	2009	2010*
Indonesia	566,983	754,845	886,308	1,209,127	1173863	1,148,050	1,085,658	991,940	792,809
Nepal	—	78,314	85,563	192,332	213090	189,389	201,997	186,668	251,416
Myanmar	—	26,678	32,985	88,574	108414	104,305	144,612	139,731	160,504
India	—	37,362	51,150	137,946	138321	142,031	130,265	122,382	95,112
Vietnam	—	31,380	51,723	81,194	106545	113,903	87,806	72,682	51,956

Notes: * Until June only.
Source: Abdul Wahap (2011).

amenities and public utilities; and for petty trading opportunities at the expense of local traders, especially the newly emerging Bumiputra traders. Consequently, their presence in the urban areas were strongly opposed especially by the local poor such as the squatters and petty traders as evidenced by a protest march by local traders against their presence in the late 1980s. Eventually, illegal foreign workers were also seen as a threat to internal security.

The policy on foreign workers was formulated to address the various problems associated with the large pool of irregular migrants. It has two inter-related objectives; firstly, to encourage legal recruitment of foreign workers; and secondly, to stem the expansion of irregular migrants or "illegal immigrants" (*pendatang asing tanpa izin or* PATI for short) as they are officially referred to. The policy which is a short term measure to overcome labour shortages in some sectors of the economy is exclusionary in nature designed to employ workers on a rotation basis that will deter permanent stay. Policy and strategy formulations are the responsibilities of the Cabinet Committee on Foreign Workers whose name was changed in 2008 to Committee on Foreign Workers and Illegal Immigrants (CFWII) to reflect its true functions. The Committee decides on major issues such as the sectors and jobs where foreign workers can be employed, their number, the source country, the rights and responsibilities of the workers and employers; and the procedures for recruitment.

Major institutions for policy implementation are the Ministry of Home Affairs (MOHA), especially the Department of Immigration (DOI), the Division for Foreign Workers,[4] the Military, Royal Malaysian Police (RMP), Marine Operation Force (MOF), Malaysian Maritime Enforcement Agency (MMEA); and the Department of Labour (DOL) in the Ministry of Human Resources. Policy instruments devised by the CFWII and its amendments are relayed to the respective implementing agencies internally via directives. It was only in 2006 that the procedure for foreign worker recruitment was published by the DOL (Jabatan Tenaga Kerja 2006). However, no comprehensive guidelines for stemming out irregular migrants were published and enforcement officers are guided by the Immigration Act 1959/63, Passport Act 1966, Anti-Trafficking in Persons and Smuggling of Migrants Act 2007 (ATIPSOM), and other directives periodically issued by their respective Departments/Ministries.

While the policy on foreign workers remains the same, some of its strategies and policy instruments are scrapped, replaced or amended from time to time in response to border or internal security, economic and political challenges. Table 6.2 indicates that the country's economic

Table 6.2
Foreign Workers (FW), Economic Growth and Policy Measures
(1970–2010)

Year	Number of Legal FW	Economic Growth (%)	Impact on Policy Measures
1970–75	NA	8.0*	No mechanisms for legal recruitment. Illegal entry and employment of FW.
1976–80	NA	8.6*	-do-
1981–84	NA	5.2*	May 1984, Medan Agreement — to legalize irregular Indonesian workers in the plantations.
1985–90	Between 3,484–24,152	6.9*	Regularization of plantation workers
1991		9.6	Regularization of domestic maids
1992		8.9	Regularization of FW in const. services & manufacturing Policy implementation — legal recruitment began
1993	532,723	9.9	Offshore legal recruitment
1994	642,057	9.2	-do-
1995	726,689	9.3	-do-
1996	745,239	10.0	Amnesty in the Peninsula — voluntary repatriation
1997	1.471,645	7.3	
1998	1,127,652	–7.3	Ban on recruitment of FW, voluntary repatriation, compulsory contribution to EPF by FW & employers.
1999	897,705	6.1	None
2000	819,684	8.9	Ban on FW recruitment lifted

Table 6.2 *(Cont'd)*

Year	Number of Legal FW	Economic Growth (%)	Impact on Policy Measures
2001	769,566	0.5	None
2002	1,057,156	5.4	Number of source countries increased to 14.
2003	1,412,697	5.8	None
2004	1,474,686	6.8	Nationwide amnesty of IM-voluntary repatriation.
2005	1,821,750	5.3	Nationwide amnesty of IM extended until February.
2006	1,871,038	5.8	Cap imposed on FW recruitment at 1.5 million.
2007	2,044,800	6.5	None
2008	2,062,596	4.7	Ban on recruitment of FW in manufacturing. Proposal by government to increase levy in some sectors but the proposal was shelved due to strong opposition from employers.
2009	1,918,146	–1.7	Ban lifted due to demand for rubber gloves. Regularization of IM exercise in Sabah (Phase 1).
2010	N.A	7.0	Policy review to phase out low skill FW. Regularization of IM exercise in Sabah (Phase 2).

Notes: *Average, N.A: Not available, FW: Foreign workers, IM: Irregular migrants & Const.: Construction.
Source: Dept. of Immigration, Putrajaya as shown in Azizah Kassim (1991 and 2008) and Tham S.Y. (2011).

performance played an important role on the strategies taken. Table 6.3 outlines the changes and amendments made to policy measures from 1992 to 2010 and the rationales for doing so. Apart from economic factors, a concern for internal security also accounts for some major changes in policy measures. For example, before 2002, Malaysia sanctioned the import of workers from Indonesia, Philippines, and Thailand based on former Prime Minister Mahathir's "prosper thy neighbour" policies. Bangladeshi workers, who are Muslims, were also accepted on the assumption that their religious similarity with the majority Muslim population in Malaysia will ease the adaptation for these workers and facilitate accommodation by the locals. However, this was changed in mid-1990s following gang fights between Bangladeshi workers and local men in Johor Bharu in 1995 and the spread of such incidents in Penang and Kuala Lumpur the same year. The presence of a large concentration of Bangladeshi workers was soon seen as a threat to public order and a ban was imposed on their recruitment. In early 2002, a riot by Indonesian workers at a garment factory in Nilai forced the government to revise its decision on the quantum for Indonesian workers. The riot erupted due to a misunderstanding over drug abuse tests run by the police on some Indonesian workers at the factory which angered many of their countrymen. Consequently, hundreds of Indonesian workers clashed with the police causing much injury and destruction to public properties.

The Nilai incidence drove home the danger to internal security on the dependence on foreign workers from a single source country. A temporary ban on the recruitment of Indonesian workers followed (which was reversed within a few weeks) and the quota for Indonesian workers was subsequently reduced. Malaysia soon increased the number of source countries to include other countries in ASEAN (such as Cambodia, Myanmar and Vietnam), the Indian subcontinent (India, Pakistan, Nepal, and Sri Lanka) and four countries from western Asia (Kazakhstan, Uzbekistan, etc.). However, recruitment from West Asian countries remains inactive due to the high cost of recruitment and language problem which renders them less attractive to Malaysia's employers. However, there is also recruitment made from countries not listed as designated source countries such as the People Republic of China (PRC). The government gives exceptions to such recruitment in cases where certain services required by Malaysia are not available from the designated source countries. Workers from non-designated countries, whose number is negligible, are put under the "others" category. In the case of PRC, for example, there are a number of Chinese workers in the reflexology businesses in urban areas. Malaysia's reluctance to include PRC

Table 6.3
Rationales for Changes in Policy Measures and Instruments
(1992–2011)

No	Year	Changes In Policy Strategies and Instruments	Facilitating Circumstances/Purpose	Rationales
1.	1992	Launch of FW policy	The presence of a large pool of IM and their various negative impacts.	Economic and Security
2.	1994	Decision to allow FW in manufacturing sector	Growth in the manufacturing sector	Economic
3.	1996	Ban on recruitment of Bangladeshi workers	Gang fight over women between Bangladeshi workers and Malay men in JB which spread to other states.	Security
4.	1997	i. Voluntary repatriation for FW ii. Ban on FW recruitment iii. Immigration Act amended heavier penalties for breach of immigration rules	i. Asian Financial Crisis — Recession ii. Existing penalty too lenient to act as effective deterrent to IM	Economic and Security
5.	1998	i. Compulsory contribution to EPF by FW and increase in levy ii. Compulsory medical examination for all FW	i. To reduce outflow of FW remittances ii. To check the spread of infectious diseases by FW	Economic Security
6.	2001	i. Ban on FW recruitment lifted	i. Economic recovery	Economic
7.	2002	i. Temporary ban on Indon. workers ii. Reduction of quotas on Indonesian workers and number of source countries raised to 14 iii. Immigration Act amended	i. Riot by Indon. factory workers in Nilai ii. Reduce dependence on Indon. workers iii. To impose sanctions against employers and harbourers of IM; human traffickers	Security

8.	2005	i. Restructuring of recruitment procedures, formation of outsourcing agencies, OSC and JCS. ii. Increase in levy for FW. iii. Introduction of a Special Court for IM.	i. Inadequacy in present system — contributes to expansion of IM and marginalization of Malaysian workers. ii. Discourage employers from engaging FW. iii. Overcome backlog in Malaysian courts which delayed deportation of IM.	Security and Economic
9.	2006	Ceiling imposed of FW recruitment at 1.5 million.	To reduce dependency on FW, phase out labour intensive enterprises and encourage capital intensive and high technology.	Economic
10.	2007	Ban on recruitment of Bangladeshi workers lifted.		Economic
11.	2008	2nd ban on recruitment of Bangladeshi workers reinstated.	Economic slowdown Fraudulent exercise by recruiting agencies led to a glut of unemployed Bangladeshi workers and expansion of IM.	Economic and Security
12.	2009	Ban on recruitment of FW in manufacturing (rubber gloves) lifted in March.	High demand for rubber gloves due to widespread incidence of H1N1 epidemic.	Economic
13.	2010	Compulsory payment of levy by employers imposed.	To discourage employers from engaging FW and encourage expansion of capital intensive, high technology industries.	Economic
13.	On-going	Signing of MOUs with source countries.	To provide guidelines for FW recruitment from specific countries esp. recruitment cost and work contract.	Political/ Diplomatic Security

Notes: IM: Irregular migrants; FW: Foreign workers; OSC: One Stop Centre, Indon.: Indonesia and JCS: Job Clearing System.
Source: Compiled by the author.

in the list of officially recognized source countries could be due to the latter' adherence to communism as a state ideology to which Malaysia was strongly opposed to previously.

The ban on Bangladeshi workers was lifted in 2007, but it was re-instated in 2008 due to fraudulent recruitment practices by Bangladeshi recruiting agencies in cahoots with Malaysians. These agencies brought in thousands of Bangladeshi workers, more than required by local employers, creating a glut of unemployed Bangladeshis, many of whom were abandoned by their agents at the Kuala Lumpur International Airport and other areas in the Klang Valley. This caused an outcry from the Malaysian public and damaged Malaysia-Bangladesh relations. It was unclear how the problem was resolved, but many of the stranded workers soon found themselves joining the ranks of irregular migrants in Malaysia.

Political and diplomatic considerations also account for recent changes in policy measures (see Table 6.4). The decline in Malaysia's ranking from Tier 2 to Tier 3 in 2009 in the United States Trafficking in Persons Report is a case in point. The report lumped Malaysia in the same category as countries with serious human rights abuses such as Myanmar. A year earlier, another report by United States Committee on Refugees and Immigrants (USCRI) declared Malaysia as one of the worst places for immigrants and refugees. To salvage its reputation Malaysia was compelled to widen the scope of its Anti-trafficking in Persons Act to include victims of forced labour in 2009.

Under the second policy objective designed to stem the inflow of irregular migrants, five policy measures were adopted — regularization, amnesty, border control (Ops Nyah 1), weeding out irregular migrants already in the country (Ops Nyah 2) and deportation. Migrant workers who breached Malaysian immigration law and/or the guidelines for foreign labour employment (Jabatan Tenaga Kerja 2006) such as changing their approved work sector or running away from a designated employer are to be compounded, fined, caned and/or imprisoned depending on the types of violation committed. On paying the compound or fines, or on completion of their sentence, irregular migrants are to be deported. However, these measures failed to reduce the number of illegal immigrants in the country. To overcome this setback, in early 2010, the Ministry of Home Affairs set up a laboratory for foreign workers and illegal immigrants where a group of stakeholders in the government and others sat down for a month to study the associated problems and to seek ways to overcome them. The outcome is a comprehensive programme called the "6P" which includes

Table 6.4
Recent Changes in Policy Measures

No.	Year	Policy Formulation & Changes in Policy Instruments	Facilitating Circumstances/Reasons	Rationale
1.	2009	Application of Anti-Trafficking in Persons Act on victims of forced labour.	i. Negative TIP Report 2008 by USA where Malaysia's ranking declined from Tier 2 to Tier 3.	
	2010	Introduction of Anti-Trafficking in Persons and Anti-Smuggling of Migrants Act, 2007 (Amended).	ii. Pressure from human rights groups at the international and national levels. iii. To curtail activities of transnational syndicates involved in human trafficking & smuggling which contribute to the expansion of IM.	Diplomatic/ Political & Security
2.	2011	Introduction of new initiatives called the 6P Programme which includes: i. Registration (*Pendaftaran*) ii. Regularization (*Pemutihan*) iii. Amnesty (*Pengampunan*) iv. Monitoring (*Pemantauan*) v. Enforcement (*Penguatkuasaan*) vi. Deportation (*Pengusiran*) (To run for 6 months starting 11 July 2011).	i. Outcomes of consultations at the Laboratory on Immigrants in Malaysia held by MOHA in Feb 2010. ii. To overcome the inadequacies of the present policy measures.	Security

Notes: IM = Irregular migrants; FW = Foreign workers; TIP Report = Trafficking in Persons Report, MOHA = Ministry of Home Affairs.
Source: Mohd. Zamberi Abdul Aziz (2011) and National Council for Anti-Trafficking in Person and Anti-Smuggling of Migrants, MOHA.

Pendaftaran (registration), *Pemutihan* (legalization), *Pengampunan* (amnesty), *Pemantauan* (monitoring), *Penguatkuasaan* (enforcement) and *Pengusiran* (deportation) to be implemented in succession over a period of six months beginning 1 July 2011.

There are also a substantial number of refugees who are in the workforce. As Malaysia is not a signatory to the Geneva Convention 1951 and the New York Protocol 1967 Relating to Status of Refugees, there are no clear guidelines on how they should be treated. Refugees are allowed to stay temporarily on humanitarian grounds but their position is unclear as there are no legal or administrative procedures to deal with them. Until 2010, asylum seekers and refugees in the country were given similar treatments as illegal immigrants. Although there is now an implicit understanding between the enforcement authorities and United Nation High Commissioner for Refugees (UNHCR) that refugees registered with the international agency were not to be arrested, many asylum seekers and refugees are detained by enforcement personnel either because they are not registered with UNHCR or because the enforcement officers refused to acknowledge the UNHCR registration card.

DOMINANT PARADIGMS IN ACADEMIC AND PUBLIC DISCOURSES ON MIGRANT WORKERS

There are at least four dominant paradigms in discourses on migrant workers in Malaysia — security, economics, human rights and racial. The main elements in each of the paradigms are discussed in the following sections.

Security Elements

The formulation of the foreign worker policy was based on perceived threats to both border and internal political stability. Views of state officials on immigrants as security threat can be gauged from a paper by Che Moin Umar (2003),[5] an unpublished report by the Department of Immigration, Putrajaya (2005) and a seminar paper by Mohd Zamberi (2010) an official of the Immigration Department in Putrajaya.

Confining himself to illegal immigrants in Sabah, Che Moin not only viewed them as a serious challenge to border security but also associated them with separatist activities such as *Gerakan Aceh Merdeka* (GAM) and the Moro Islamic Liberation Front (MILF) and the Moro National Liberation Front (MNLF) which, according to him, have been intercepted by the authorities for arms smuggling and soliciting financial support from their countrymen working in Malaysia. He also linked them with violent crimes and gang fights; social ills and involvement in forgery of official documents, all of which if left unchecked can undermine the rule of law, hence a threat to internal security. Similar views on illegal immigrants are reflected in an unpublished report by the Department of Immigration (2005) which referred to illegal immigrants as "Public Enemy Number Two", a security threat that is next in term of seriousness to that of drug menace which is "Public Enemy Number One". Such a depiction of illegal immigrants persisted among official circles as mentioned in a seminar paper by Mohd Zamberi on illegal immigrants in 2010. In a nutshell, in the view of the Malaysian state, migrant labour is not a just labour issue, but a security issue.

There are also statements by some Ministers in the Malaysian cabinet that indicate migrant workers as a grave security concern. For example, in the aftermath of the riot by Indonesian workers in the Nilai incidence in early 2002, the previous Law Minister, Rais Yatim was quoted as saying,

> Besides defying the authority, they had the cheek to wave the Indonesian flag. They are not in Jakarta. They are in Malaysia. Indonesia's Ambassador here need not say sorry anymore. We are going to take stern action. Malaysians in general cannot tolerate the violent behaviour of the Indonesians who are being extreme and ungrateful (*The Star*, 22 January 2002).

Security issues are also prevalent in academic writings on migrant workers especially those specializing in strategic studies, international relations or on policy. Many of these works are done by university students as part of their final year degree programme or for their Diploma courses. Most of them remain unpublished. Among published works are those of Azizah (1991, 1994, 1997 and 2005) and Ramli, Wan Shawalludin, Peters and Marja Azlima (2003) and Liow (2004). In explaining the rationales for the formulation of the Malaysian foreign worker policy and the challenges in its implementation, Azizah (1991 and 1994) highlighted the impact of a large pool of illegal immigrants on the security of Malaysia in the 1980s, which include border infiltration and a threat to internal political stability (or non-traditional security). In a subsequent paper on illegal immigrants, Azizah (1997) further elaborated on the security implications of their presence. She explained how foreign criminals and subversive political activists entered Malaysia disguised as economic migrants; and by using statistics from the Royal Malaysian Police, she pointed out that there was an increase in the percentage of crimes committed by foreign nationals to total crime, increasing from 1.5 per cent in 1985 to 3 per cent in 1991. She emphasized that crimes committed by illegal immigrants are serious ones such as murder (between 14.7 per cent and 18.2 per cent) and gang robbery (between 32.7 per cent and 48.2 per cent). Rampant illegal occupation of land for housing in the Klang Valley also occurred, which led to much resentment and antagonisms on the part of the local poor who had to compete with the immigrants for affordable housing. Azizah also noted that while Malays and non-Malays in the Peninsula opposed the presence of illegal foreign workers, their reasons are dissimilar. Many non-Malays, as represented by their political leaders, did so for political reasons; many Malays, especially the poor, resented their presence as they competed with the locals for scarce resources.

In a later paper (Azizah 2005), she also referred to the growing number of undocumented children of illegal migrants with no access to education, training and decent jobs who may also be a possible threat to future internal security. There were also elaborations on violations of Islamic law by migrant workers, particularly the case of bigamy committed by Indonesian women workers who contracted another marriage in Malaysia while they are still legally married in Indonesia. These marriages, which are contrary to Islamic teachings, were conducted without authorization of the state Islamic Department, which is an offence under the Malaysian Islamic law. In his paper on securitization of illegal immigrants in Malaysia, Liow (2004) not only concurred with Azizah on the list of issues that caused Malaysia to view labour inflow as a security issue, but also added more cases to the list such as the spread of deviationist Islamic teachings by Indonesian migrants, the revelations that some Indonesians were behind terrorist networks operating in Indonesia and Singapore; and proselytizing activities by Christian Indonesian migrants among the Malay Community (Liow 2004, pp. 15 and 17).

Studies on the security dimension of foreign workers by Ramli, Wan Shawalludin, Peters and Marja Azlima (2003) and Wan Shawaluddin and Ramli (2003) focused on Sabah where about 25 per cent of the population comprised foreign nationals in 2000. They wrote on the security impact of Filipino migrants, both refugees and economic migrants in the state. Their main concerns were border and internal security. The former relates to their illegal entry which is often accompanied by trafficking of drugs and other commodities, involvement in sea piracy or *Mundu*, while the latter discussed their illegal occupation of land for housing in the urban areas, their infiltration into petty trading especially in contraband goods, which negatively affects local traders. The writers also mentioned the involvement of foreigners in crimes and the conspicuous presence of undocumented children with no access to education, training and limited job opportunity, which is then expected to push them into criminal activities in the future.

Many NGOs also share the state's concern on security in Malaysia's heavy dependence on foreign workers. A group called *Persatuan Pemikir Profesional Melayu* is a good example. Its President, Kamaruddin Kacar is reported to have said that he fears an increase in the number of migrant workers will be difficult to control and it may lead to conflicts between the local and immigrants due to cultural clashes when he commented on a recent government plan to employ 45,000 more workers from India, (*Utusan Malaysia*, 3 March 2011). His fears are not unfounded for such conflicts have happened before. SUHAKAM, a government linked human rights organization, also views the inflow of foreign workers as a security risk. This is demonstrated in an opening speech delivered by its then Vice-President, Simon Sepaun at its Round Table Conference in 2007. Sepaun referred to the increasing number, "... of refugees, illegal immigrants, stateless and undocumented people in Sabah as one of the biggest problem in the state ... which appears to be out of control" (SUHAKAM 2007, p. 33). He blames the Federal authorities for taking a light view of the problem and the Federal Special Task Force[6] for failing to perform its task.

The views of the laymen as expressed in the national dailies also reflect security and safety considerations. The large concentration of foreigners such as Africans in some housing areas creates fear among the locals who see these big and strong young men with their unfamiliar culture as a moral threat to their young girls and women. In Selayang, nine local associations got together to appeal to the government to take immediate action against foreigners in their neighbourhood (*Utusan Malaysia*, 1 March 2011). Such fears are further aggravated by the many and frequent reports on foreigners' involvement in crimes such as house break-ins, armed gang robbery, murder, rape, drug trafficking, etc. With the latest report that a large number of public low cost flats in Kuala Lumpur are now being rented out by unscrupulous owners to foreigners, many local poor are incensed as they feel they have been robbed of their rights to these accommodations (*New Straits Times*, 9 November 2011). Such anger can easily be translated into a backlash on the unsuspecting foreign tenants.

Elements of a Race Paradigm

While it appears that the race paradigm hardly played any role in the FW policies, a closer examination at the rationales for changes in policy strategies, however, reveals the dominant presence of a race paradigm, subsumed under security considerations. Malaysia adopts the notion of comprehensive security which "... goes beyond the traditional military or the internal violence and disorder that arise from ethnic conflicts It includes all other issues ... which are threats to stability ..." (Zarina Othman 2009, p. 1041). Any perceived threats to internal political stability are a security issue and the biggest challenge to internal security is inter-ethnic conflict as in the 13 May 1969 incident. Thus in deliberating who can be allowed to work in Malaysia, for how long and in which sector, attempts are made by the policy-makers to ensure that the recruitment of foreign workers will not negatively affect racial (and political power) balance between the various ethnic groups in Malaysia. This obsession with racial demographic numbers is attributable to the nature of political parties in Malaysia which are primarily based on ethnic groupings or, if they are formed as multi-ethnic parties; by the dominance of one ethnic group in the party. The urgent need to maintain the balance of political power between the various political parties has given way to allegations and counter allegations by leaders of different ethnic groups that labour inflow has been used by some to enhance their political power base, at the expense of others. In Sarawak where the immigrant population is small, their presence has not turned into security and political issue.

It should be noted that the migrant worker employment contract is made deliberately short, a minimum of three and maximum five years (3+1+1), after which he must go home for six months before he can resume work in Malaysia. This is less than the required period a foreign resident should stay before he can apply for the permanent resident status (PR). This arrangement disqualifies him from applying for the PR status, if he has any intention of doing so. A PR status would automatically confer their children citizenship. Hence, the exclusionary nature of the policy is deliberate, designed to stop migrant workers from access to citizenship.[7]

Nevertheless, the issue of race in discourses on migrant workers are clearly manifested among politicians, both from the ruling coalition Barisan Nasional (BN) and the opposition. Consistent with the nature of political parties which are predominantly ethnic-based, each political leader wants the ethnic balance of power to be maintained and is continuously suspicious that other leaders may use the inflow of migrant workers as a means to increase their political support. Hence there are common allegations by many non-Malay (non-Muslim) leaders that the UMNO (Malay/Muslim) led BN is using (or misusing) labour inflows to augment the number of party members and political power as mentioned earlier. In the Peninsula, such allegations began more than three decades ago as mentioned by Dorall (1989). According to him, many opposition non-Malay leaders alleged that the lack of sanctions against illegal immigrants, most of whom were Indonesians, for over a decade in the 1970s by the UMNO led BN government was deliberate. It was a means to increase the number of Malays and eventually Malay voting strength as Indonesians were assumed to eventually assimilate with the Malays. Thus, the UMNO led BN under the Mahathir administration was accused of granting citizenship to asylum seekers, refugees and illegal immigrants by fraudulent means so as to augment UMNO's political strength in the state. In the Peninsula such allegations have subsided but usually re-emerge before a general election.

In Sabah, when the state was infiltrated by thousands of Filipino asylum seekers trying to escape civil war in the Mindanao region in southern Philippines in the early 1970s, the accommodating attitude shown by the then Chief Minister Tun Mustapha was interpreted by Bahrin and Rachagan (1984) as an act of charity by him to the refugees who had close ethnic links and religious similarity with the Chief Minister. It was also according to the authors, induced by economic and political reasons. The Chief Minister, they believed, was hoping to use the new arrivals to boost the number of supporters for his political party, the United Sabah National Organization (USNO)[8] and with it his political power. Similar allegations persisted until today.

In the 1998 Sabah state election for the Likas constituency, for instance, Chong, the candidate who lost the election challenged the outcome of the election in court on grounds that many of the voters were not Sabahans, but illegal immigrants who have received their citizenship through the backdoor from the ruling BN. Chong, who won the court case, wrote a small book to provide proof of his allegation to the public (Chong 2009). Using official statistics as evidence, Chong claimed there was a large increase in the number of Malays in Sabah between 1970 and 2000. According to him, while the Sabah interior is inhabited largely by Sabah Bumiputra group the Kadazan/Dusun and Muruts (KDM), the increase in their population is only 162 per cent within this period (from 215,811 to 564,600). However, Chong claims that the number of Malays increased by 1,552 per cent from 18,362 to 303,500 during the same period. Such an increase in the Malay population, he argued, could not have been the result of natural increase. As further proof to support his claim that many foreigners have been granted citizenship status, he also scrutinized a list of identity card numbers issued during this period. He notes that most of the numbers begin with "H" which implies that the card owners are Bumiputra of Sabah, most of whom have attained their identity card via statutory declaration. He concluded that the granting of blue identity card (as evidence of citizenship) to foreigners were based on fraudulent claims by the aliens through statutory declaration that they were undocumented Bumiputra of Sabah.[9] This has negatively affected the status and political power of non-Muslim Bumiputra political parties in Sabah.

Among the locals in Sabah one person who deserves mention here for his consistent opposition to the immigrants in the state is Mutalib, a vocal journalist who are among those who accuse the Federal government of granting citizenship to illegal immigrants under the Mahathir administration. Since the 1990s he has written a series of titles on the subject such as *Pengundi: Voters for Hire* (1999*a*) and *IC Palsu Merampas Hak Anak Sabah* (1999*b*). Mutalib main contention was that immigrants have robbed (*merampas*) Sabah Bumiputra of their rights. The illegal immigrants who had obtain their blue IC (citizenship) by fraudulent means are now enjoying the rights of the local Bumiputra — access to native land, jobs, state schools, public housing, and the right to vote. He claims that a few of the "new Sabahans" are also now holding positions in UMNO (Mutalib 1999*a*, p. 109).[10] His brave disclosure, which won him much support from local politicians and others in Sabah, is clearly predicated on a race paradigm.

Chong's and Mutalib's conviction is shared by Bernard Dompok a veteran politician in Sabah and the head of a Sabah political party, the United Pasuk Momogun Kadazandusun Murut Organization (UPKO), one of the constituent parties in Barisan Nasional. This is manifested in his continuous resistance to the issuance of permanent residence (PR) status to the Muslim Filipino refugees who have been in Sabah since the early 1970s. As a veteran political leader one would have expected him to welcome the announcement made by the Federal government to grant PR status to the Filipino refugees in 2006, as it would help overcome many of the problems associated with the community. However, Dompok and his party members opposed its implementation and instead called for the refugees' repatriation (*New Straits Times*, 2 July 2007 and *Daily Express*, 1 July 2007). One can only infer that the basis of his objection is political, as a leader of a Christian dominated political party, he may have envisaged that the granting of PR to the Filipinos will benefit UMNO, the

Muslim Malay based political party in Sabah at the expense of his own. Due to strong opposition to the PR project by politicians like Dompok, the granting of PR to the Filipinos have been aborted as the Sabah state has the right to disregard directives from the Federal government in matters related to immigration.

In the Peninsula, a vocal critic of foreign worker policy is the independent member of Parliament, Ibrahim Ali, who expressed his concerns over the government's announcement to take in more foreign workers from India in a two part article published in a national daily (*Utusan Malaysia*, 14 and 15 March 2011). He questioned the need to import more Indian workers as Malaysia already has too many foreign workers, both legal and irregular. He bemoaned the fact that facilities to encourage tourism such as the VOA (Visa on Arrival) procedure have been abused mainly by Indian tourists, with a few others from outside Nusantara such as from China, Sri Lanka and Pakistan. As approximately 40,000 Indian tourist have "disappeared" in Malaysia, he fears that these tourists and other workers from India will claim to be Malaysians without birth certificates and identity cards[11] and then seek the help of Indian politicians and syndicates (probably local Indians ones) to get Malaysian identity cards. This in turn, according to Ibrahim, will contribute to problems between ethnic groups in Malaysia which will eventually affect national security. In the second part of his article, he elaborated further on the negative consequences in allowing a large number of foreign workers especially those from outside the *Nusantara* area to enter Malaysia and appealed to the government to reconsider its sanctions on importation of workers from non-Muslim source countries especially from India and China. According to him such action is necessary as many among the new migrants had acquired and will soon acquire PR status or become citizens with the collusion of crooked enforcement officers and syndicates dealing in organized cross-border crimes. He further added that many of the "new Malaysians" are now trying their best to subvert the status quo of the Malays, Muslims and Bumiputra. It is clear that Ibrahim in the Peninsula as well as Dompok, Chong and Mutalib in Sabah conceive and responded to the policy on foreign workers in terms of a race paradigm. Their views reflect their need to defend the interests of their own ethnic group i.e., their power base; the Malays, in the case of Ibrahim and the non-Muslim Bumiputra in the case of Dompok and Chong in Sabah. Mutalib is driven by the desire to protect his rights and that of other Sabah Bumiputra from being taken away by the "new Sabah citizens".

Economic Issues

There are a number of published works that analyse migrant workers in Malaysia from the economic perspective, see among others, Rima Devi (1996), Anja Rudnik (1996), Halim and Abdul Rashid (1997), Tham and Liew (2004) and Ragayah (2010). Apart from these there are scores of small scale works by students at the undergraduate level and a few at the postgraduate, which remain unpublished. Such works revolve around several themes — the push and pull factors that accounts for foreign workers entry into Malaysia, the cost of their recruitment, utilization of their labour between and within designated sectors, the nature of their employment, wages and other benefits, their productivity, impact of their employment on local workers, their contributions to economic growth and their remittances to the home country.

Writing on contract labour in Peninsular Malaysia, Rima Devi (1996) devoted a chapter on immigrant contract labour. She elucidated the nature of their inflow, highlighted the distinction between "legal contract immigration" and "legal immigration" and how migrant labour were being utilized in the construction and plantation industries and in government FELDA land schemes in particular KEJORA. She revealed that many employers prefer to engage foreign workers because local labour is expensive to hire. The writer mentioned complaints made by local workers in the national press in the mid-1980s that employers, "... had been blatantly denying local workers jobs ... preferring instead to employ immigrants ... Locals found themselves discriminated against vis-a vis immigrant workers" (1996, p. 89). In the plantations and constructions, wages for foreign workers were lower than locals' as illegal foreign workers also did not receive social security provisions and protection and are outside the labour legislation. Migrant workers, legal or otherwise, worked long hours (between twelve to fourteen hours a day); usually out of choice so as to augment their income especially because they had nothing else to do in their spare time. Housing in the private estates were provided for, however, in the land development schemes basic housing provision was lacking and living conditions according to the writer was "sub-human" (1996, p. 92). The study by Halim and Abdul Rashid (1997) on illegal construction workers in the Peninsula supports Rima Devi's findings in many respects — on why employers preferred foreign workers especially illegal ones, the low and discriminatory wages and poor living conditions. Both writers attributed the persistence of foreign, albeit illegal workers in the construction sector to the nature of work allocation in this sector where the main contractor usually allocate jobs to sub-contractors, and the latter to sub-sub contractors. Such a system puts foreign labour at some distance from the "principal employer" and this creates ample room for exploitation.

In a study on manufacturing workers, Rudnik (1996) focused her attention on Bangladeshi workers in five textile factories in Penang. In general, her findings with regards to pay and working conditions bear some similarities with that of Rima Devi's. The workers she studied were directly employed, they were legally recruited workers and covered by the Malaysian labour law, but they were deprived of their right to equal treatment and wages. They were paid half of what they were promised by the recruiting agencies back home and it took many of them two years before they are able to cover the agency fees (between RM5,000–RM7,000). Many ran away as a result and became illegal immigrants. Rudnik believed that "... the problem of illegal immigrant workers cannot be solved without tackling the unfair treatment of legal migrant workers" (1996, p. 76).

Tham and Liew (2004) also studied the manufacturing sector but their objective was to examine the impact of foreign workers on the productivity in this sector. The authors noted that within the manufacturing sector, the manufacture of wood products has the highest percentage of foreign to total workers, a pattern that has existed since 1991. This is followed by rubber products; and textile and garments. This, they believe may be due to the labour intensive nature of production in these industries which are rejected by local workers. Based on data from the Malaysian Department of Statistics, they found that "the increasing presence of foreign labour was found to worsen the productivity of labour in the manufacturing sector" (2004, p. 271). The writers lent support to the government's plan to reduce the dependence on foreign workers and called for firms "... to restructure their operation towards high technology, capital and high skill activities" (p. 272) and for the government to come up with a consistent policy that is not influenced by fluctuations in Malaysia's economic performance.

As alluded to by Tham and Liew, Malaysia has taken several measures to reduce the dependency on foreign workers each time there is an economic crisis or downturn. However, when the economy recovered, the government would again face strong pressures from industries to reverse its decision and it would very often, cave in to these pressures. A good example is the 2007/08 economic downturn due to the global financial crisis, precipitated by the sub-prime problems in the United States. The announcement to reduce the intake of foreign workers in the manufacturing sector in 2008 was reversed in early 2009 due to strong pressures from rubber glove manufacturers that were facing a surge in demand because of the H1N1 epidemic.

On the part of the public, economic consideration is also a major factor influencing their perception of foreign workers. Those who benefit from the presence of foreign workers such as employers, house owners, traders, etc. generally do not oppose their presence. It is those whose lives are negatively affected who want the number of foreign workers to be reduced. Such people who often articulate their displeasure with foreign workers in the national dailies include those who must compete with them for jobs, affordable housing, and trading opportunities and for public amenities and social services (*New Straits Times*, 26 November 2011).

Human Rights

Malaysia's policy on foreign workers have been criticized for its lack of human rights by many local and international human rights groups. Among the academia, the issue of human rights of migrant workers is a much neglected subject. The writer found only two such studies, the first by Hilsden (2006) which focused on Muslim Filipinos in Sabah and the second by Azizah (2007). Hilsden, who did her fieldwork in Kota Kinabalu, carried out an anthropological study of sixteen Filipino Muslim refugees, soliciting information through in-depth interviews. She found that many of them were exposed to violence and oppression at many fronts: by the state, and at the micro level, in the family and at the workplace. Such violence and oppression, differentiates these Muslim Filipinas from local women and women in the Philippines. While the article addresses the issue of violence and women's resilience, it also invokes the question as to who ought to defend and protect the basic rights of these migrant women. In the second paper, Azizah confined herself to legally recruited foreign workers. She began by examining the terms and conditions of the foreign worker employment as shown in the guideline by the Department of Labour (2006) and the foreign worker's employment contract. According to the writer there are terms and conditions that violate the fundamental rights of the workers such as the prohibition to marry while in service and to take along family members. As such clauses are in contradiction to a person's basic needs, they are frequently violated. Many migrant workers sent for their family members once they are settled in Malaysia, arranging for them to enter legally on tourist visas, and then to overstay. Single workers too often get married secretly and such marriages are not registered. Consequently, children born to them are also not registered with the authorities, be it the Malaysian National Registration Department or the workers' embassy in Malaysia, thereby contributing to the expansion of the illegal immigrant population.

Much of the advocacy work on the rights of migrant workers are done by SUHAKAM which is critical of state handling of the policy on foreign workers for its lack of emphasis on human rights. This is best reflected in a report of a Round Table Discussion (RTD) on "Human Rights and Citizenship in Sabah" held in February 2007. Some of the participants were leaders and representatives of non-government organizations (NGO). In his opening speech the then Vice Chairman of SUHAKAM, Simon Sipaun, a Sabahan, acknowledged the contributions made by the illegal immigrants to development in Malaysia. He said,

> Sabah without them would be at a standstill. Illegal they may be, they are no less human beings like the rest of us ... they have rights which ought to be respected. At the same time illegal immigrants are essentially law breakers and the process of law should therefore take its course. The exercise of human rights must be in line with the laws of the country (SUHAKAM 2007, p. 35).

Sipaun also referred to allegations made by some Sabahans that many illegal immigrants in the state were granted citizenship by fraudulently declaring themselves as natives of Sabah and of his believe and fear that "... a process of reverse takeover has slowly but surely long started economically, socially, culturally and politically speaking" (p. 36).

Although Sipaun emphasized the need to observe the fundamental rights of the "illegal immigrants", the theme of the discussion that followed took a different course. The focus was the erosion of the rights of Sabahan due to the alleged granting of citizenship to thousands of illegal immigrants by the Federal government under the administration of Prime Minister, Mahathir. Some participants reiterated the allegation about the dubious issuance of identity cards to foreigners as mentioned earlier and a participant openly announced that this was to "... give illegal immigrants who are Muslims citizenship ... voting rights in the state election" (SUHAKAM 2007, p. 12). The participants lament the fact that the new citizens also have access to social services (education and health) and public amenities (water and electricity) thus reducing the Bumiputra access to these facilities. The migrants are also whittling the rights of the bona fide Bumiputra to land and housing; contributing to rising crimes; the emergence of undocumented children and street kids; and that they are a threat to national security and sovereignty. The RTD ended with SUHAKAM appealing to the Federal government to immediately investigate the influx of foreigners and the alleged fraudulent claims to citizenship in the state, to strengthen the mechanisms for issuance of citizenship; to review judiciously the state electoral roll to ensure only bona fide voters can vote; and to enforce border control to curb influx of more illegal immigrants.

It is obvious that the core issues in the discourse on the illegal immigrants and "new citizens" at the RTD was the ethnic paradigm manifested in the need to safeguard the interest of the participants' respective ethnic groups against the challenges imposed by the foreigners. However, many NGOs are in agreement with SUHAKAM that foreign workers, be they legal or otherwise, ought to be given some space to exercise their fundamental rights as residents and workers in Malaysia. Among the NGOs with such objectives are SUARAM, TENAGANITA, Caram Asia, Aliran, and the Bar Council in addition to MTUC (Malaysian Trade Union Congress). Apart from the MTUC, perhaps, among the most vocal are SUARAM and TENAGANITA. The former devotes a chapter in all its yearly report to the ill treatment of illegal immigrants and refugees by state authorities. The 2007 report also alleges the rise in the incidence of human rights abuse in 2006 by Malaysia's voluntary force RELA in its handling of undocumented migrants.

Like SUARAM, many other NGOs are also critical of Malaysia's policy on migrant workers because of its disregard for their basic rights. Their stand is clearly reflected in the papers presented at a seminar held by the Malaysian Bar Council and ILO in early 2008. All papers by NGOs — TENAGANITA, MTUC, Bar Council, Caram Asia and Aliran unanimously took the Malaysian authorities to task for their lack of action against human rights abuses on migrant workers; with each paper highlighting one aspect of the abuse. Gabriel of Caram Asia elaborated on the vulnerability of foreign workers to all kinds of ailments and their lack of access to state health facilities and Yap of Aliran on the need to give them social and cultural rights. Suppiah from the Malaysian Bar, on the other hand, zooms in on their lack access to seek redress, while MTUC's Balasubramaniam describes the foreign workers lack of rights to organize themselves. Netto of Aliran criticized the discriminatory practices against migrant workers by the state while conferring privileges to the expatriate; and Fernandez of TENAGANITA, denounced the rules pertaining to recruitment and placement of foreign workers as "... unclear, deregulated and without a human rights approach". In conclusion, Ramachelvam presented a paper on a rights based policy framework consistent with the fundamental principal in the Universal Declaration of Human Rights where every worker will be given equal treatment irrespective of his nationality. He calls for a comprehensive policy on migrant workers with the issue of "work" as its core and not "security". The proposed policy framework fits the objective of the International Labour Organization (ILO), which provided support for the seminar. However, given the fractious nature of ethnic relations in Malaysia and the prime role of security in all public endeavours, the proposed policy appears idealistic and impractical.

CONCLUDING REMARKS

The maintenance of peace and security takes top priority in the functioning of the state. Malaysia is no different. The policy on foreign workers in Malaysia is predicated on security considerations because of the large number of foreign workers in the country, particularly irregular migrants; and the high potential for legal migrant workers to change their status to that of an illegal. With over three million foreign workers in a population of over 28 million, the migrant workers has proven to be a serious challenge to border and internal security especially with the many attendant negative consequences of their presence as explained above. The policy which was formulated with the twin overt objectives to combat the expansion of illegal immigrants; and to encourage, regulate and monitor legal recruitment is exclusionary in nature as it has the covert intention of restricting migrant workers access to citizenship.

The Malaysian notion of security covers both traditional and non-traditional security and race paradigm is embedded in the latter. For as long as the Malaysian political parties are based on ethnic affiliations, racial issues will continue to shape and influence state policies, including the employment of foreign workers. It must be emphasized that although the migrant worker policy strategies are amended or changed more by economic factors, security concerns which encapsulate the race paradigm remains the foundation of the policy. In spite of the economic transformation programme in place and that many Malaysians now embrace and commit themselves to 1Malaysia, it is unlikely that this will change.

Notes

1. Singapore left the Malaysian federation in 1965.
2. The number of illegal immigrants who have registered with the Immigration Department until November 2011 in the current legalization exercise under the 6P programme.
3. In a survey on foreign workers in the Klang Valley in 2008–09, I met a number of Indonesian workers who arrived in the 1970s and 1980s who said they obtained red identity card (permanent resident status) within a few years. Children born to them are now citizens. Many of them, who are now in their late eighties, are found in Indonesian settlements in Gombak, Serdang and Sungai Buloh area.
4. Since 2005 only.
5. Che Moin Umar was then attached to the National Security Council, in the Prime Minister's Department. Putrajaya.
6. Specially formed in 1992 to manage and reduce the number illegal immigrants in Sabah and Labuan.
7. Under Article 19 of the Federal Constitution, anyone who has lived for twelve years in Malaysia can apply for citizenship by naturalization.
8. USNO was disbanded in the early 1990s and its members joined UMNO.
9. Such fraudulent claims can easily be made in Sabah as many Bumiputra in the state especially those living in the interior do not have official documents as their births were not registered with the National Registration Department. Attempts have been made to overcome this setback with the introduction of mobile registration units in 2000.
10. Based on information from the ex-deputy Head of an UMNO Branch in Anjung Teduh Felda Sahabat, in Lahad Datu, Mutalib reported the case of an illegal Filipino woman who became a member of Wanita UMNO and a party official at the branch level. He also mentioned the case of an illegal Indonesian man, holder of a fake identity card, who became a committee member of an UMNO branch and community leader (Penyelia Masyarakat) (Mutalib 1999*a*, p. 109).
11. Among reasons usually given by undocumented Malaysian residents are: they were living in some remote estates and were unable and too scared to go out, they lost touch with family members, etc.

References

Abdul Wahab bin Abdul Hamid. "Realty Check: Foreign Workers are Shunning Malaysia Since 2008". Paper presented at the *Bengkel Pekerja Asing dan Pendatang Asing Tanpa Izin di Malaysia: Dasar, Pelaksanaan Serta Respon Perekrut, Majikan dan Pekerja*. Puri Pujangga, UKM, 5 May 2011.

Azizah Kassim. "Recruitment and Employment of Indonesian Workers: Problems and Policy Issues". Paper presented at the ILO Inter-country Workshop on Migrant Workers in the Plantation Industry. Kuala Lumpur, 12–17 November 1991.

———. "Amnesty for Illegal Foreign Workers in Malaysia: Some Attendant Problems". *Manusia dan Masyarakat*, New Series, vol. 9. Department of Anthropology, Universiti Malaya, 1994.

———. "From Neglect to Legalization: The Changing State Response to the Inflow of Illegal Labour in Malaysia". Paper presented at the *Conference on Globalization: Local Challenges and Responses*, organized by Malaysian Social Science Association, Universiti Sains Malaysia, Penang, 19–21 January 1995.

———. "Illegal Alien Labour in Malaysia: Its Influx, Utilization and Ramifications". *Indonesia and the Malay World*, No. 71. School of Oriental and African Studies, Oxford University Press, 1997.

———. "Security and Social Implications of Cross National Migration in Malaysia". In *Pacifying the Pacific: Confronting the Challenges*, edited by Mohamad Jawhar Hassan. Malaysia, Kuala Lumpur: Institute of Strategic and International Studies, 2005.

———. "Development and International Migration in Malaysia: Patterns, Policy and Human Rights". In *Social Science and Malaysian National Development*, edited by Rahman Embong. Bangi, Selangor: Malaysian Social Science Association, 2007.

———. "Migrant Workers and Undocumented Persons in Malaysia". Report submitted to Suruhanjaya Hak Asasi Manusia (SUHAKAM) Kuala Lumpur (confidential), 2008.

Bahrin, T.S. and Rachagan, S. "The Status of Displaced Filipinos in Sabah: Some Policy Consideration and Their Long Term Implications". In *Arms Separatism in Southeast Asia*, edited by Lim J.J. and Vani S. Singapore Institute of Southeast Asian Studies, 1984.

Balasubramaniam, A. "Right to Organize: Developing a Comprehensive Policy Framework for Migrant Labour". *National Conference on Developing a Comprehensive Policy Framework for Migrant Labour*. Organized by the Malaysian Bar Council, Petaling Jaya, 18–19 February 2008.

Che Moin Omar. "Overview of National Security Challenges With Special Focus on Sabah". In *Reinventing Sabah: Global Challenges and Policy Responses*, edited by Mohd. Yaakub Hj. Johari and Chong S.Y. Kota Kinabalu, Sabah: Konrad Adenauer Foundation and Institute of Development Studies, 2003.

Chong, E.L. *Lest We Forget: Security and Sovereignty of Sabah*. Kota Kinabalu, 2009 (Publisher not indicated).

Dorall, R.F. "Foreign Workers in Malaysia: Issues and Implications of Recent Economic Migration from the Malay World". In *The Trade in Domestic Workers: Causes, Mechanisms and Consequences*, edited by Noleen Heyzer Geertje Lycklama A. Jijeholt, Nedra Weerakoon. Kuala Lumpur: Asia Pacific Migration Centre, 1989.

Fernandez, I. "Recruitment and Placement of Migrant Workers in Malaysia: Inconsistent, Unclear and Deregulated without a Human Rights Approach". *National Conference on Developing a Comprehensive Policy Framework for Migrant Labour*. Organized by the Malaysian Bar Council, Petaling Jaya, 18–19 February 2008.

Gabriel, C. "Access to Health Care and Living Conditions". *National Conference on Developing a Comprehensive Policy Framework for Migrant Labour*. Organized by the Malaysian Bar Council, Petaling Jaya, 18–19 February 2008.

Halim Salleh and Abdul Rashid Abdul Aziz. "Illegal Foreign Labor in Malaysia in the Construction Industry". Paper presented at the *1st International Malaysian Studies Conference*, University Malaya, Kuala Lumpur, 11–13 August 1997.

Hilsden, A.M. "Migration and Human Rights: The Case of Muslim Filipino Muslims in Sabah". *Women Studies International Forum* (2006): 405–16.

Kanapathy, Vijayakumari. "International Migration and Labour Market Adjustments in Malaysia: The Role of Foreign Labour Policies". In *Asia Pacific Migration Journal*, vol. 10, nos. 3–4. Manila, Philippines: Scallabrini Migration Centre, 2001.

———. *Controlling Irregular Migration: The Malaysia Experience*. ILO Regional Programme on Governance and Labour Migration, Working Paper No. 14. Regional Office for Asia and the Pacific, 2008.

Kaur, Amarjit. *International Migration in Malaysia and Singapore since 1880s: State Policies, Migration Trends and Governance of Migration*. The fourth James C. Jackson Memorial Lecture, University of New England Asia Centre (UNEAC), 2006.

Khoo K.K. "The Emergence of Plural Communities in the Malay Peninsula Before 1874". In *Multiethnic Malaysia: Past, Present and Future*, edited by Ghee L.T, Gomes, A. and Azly Rahman. Petaling Jaya, Strategic Information and Research Development Centre and MDAS@UCSI University, 2009.

Liow J.C. "Malaysia's Approach to Its Illegal Indonesian Migrant Labour Problem: Securitization, Politics or Catharsis?" Paper presented at the *IDSS-Ford Workshop on Non-Traditional Security in Asia*. Singapore, 3–4 September 2004.

Mohd Zamberi Abdul Aziz. "Pendatang Asing Tanpa Izin: Dasar dan Pelaksanaannya". Paper presented at the *Seminar Pekerja Asing dan Pendatang Asing Tanpa Izin di Malaysia*. Organized by IKMAS, UKM, 5 May 2011.

Mutalib M.D. *Pengundi: Voters for Hire*. Kota Kinabalu: Borneo Line Printing Sdn. Bhd. 1999*a*.

———. *IC Palsu Merampas Hak Anak Sabah*. Lahad Datu, Sabah, Kerja Percetakan Perak, 1999*b*.

Neeko, Ravi. "Arrest, Detention and Prosecution of Migrant Workers". *National Conference on Developing a Comprehensive Policy Framework for Migrant Labour*. Organized by the Malaysian Bar Council, Petaling Jaya, 18–19 February 2008.

Netto, A.N. "Violence and Xenophobia towards Migrant Workers". *Conference on Developing a Comprehensive Policy Framework for Migrant Labour.* Organized by the Malaysian Bar Council, Petaling Jaya, 18–19 February 2008.

Rachagan. S. "Refugees and Illegal Immigrants: The Malaysian Experience with Filipino and Vietnamese Refugees". In *Refugees: A Third World Dilemma*, edited by Rogge J.R. Rowan and Littlefield, University of Minitoba, 1991.

Ragayah Haji Mat Zin. "Economic Activities of Migrants in the Klang Valley". Paper presented at *the Malaysian Studies Conference 7*. Penang, 16–18 March 2010.

Ramachelvam, M. "A Rights Based Policy Framework and Plan for Action". *Conference on Developing a Comprehensive Policy Framework for Migrant Labour.* Organized by the Malaysian Bar Council, Petaling Jaya, 18–19 February 2008.

Ramli Dollah, Wan Shawalludin Wan Hassan, Diana Peters and Marja Azlima Omar. "Pendatang Asing Filipina di Sabah: Satu Pemerhatian Dari Sudut Keselamatan". *JATI*, Jabatan Asia Tenggara, Universiti Malaya, 2003.

Rima Devi. *Contract Labour in Peninsular Malaysia.* Kuala Lumpur: Institute Kajian Dasar, 1996.

Rudnik, A. *Foreign Labour in Malaysian Manufacturing*. Kuala Lumpur: Insan, 1996.

Sadiq, Kamal. "When States Prefer Non-Citizens over Citizens: Conflict over Illegal Immigration in Malaysia". *Harvard Asia Pacific Review* 5 no. 1 (2005): 14–18.

SUARAM. Malaysia Human Rights Report, various years.

SUHAKAM. *Human Rights and Citizenship in Sabah: Its Impact on Economic. Social and Cultural Rights.* Kuala Lumpur, 2007.

Suppiah, M. "Access to Justice and Employment". *Developing a Comprehensive Policy Framework for Migrant Labour.* Organized by the Malaysian Bar Council, Petaling Jaya, 18–19 February 2008.

Syed Shahir Syed Mohamud. "Protection of Migrants and Refugee Rights in Malaysia". *Proceeding of Conference on the Challenges of Global Migration and Forced Displacement.* Kuala Lumpur: UNHCR, 2006.

Tham, S.Y. "Revitalising Growth in Malaysia: Towards a High Income Economy". Paper presented at the *CAPAS-CSEAS Workshop for Young Scholars of Southeast Asian Area Studies "Exploring frontiers of Southeast Asian Area Studies: Asian Perspectives"*. Taipei, Taiwan, 9–11 August 2010.

Tham, S.Y and Liew C.S. "Foreign Labour in Malaysian Manufacturing: Enhancing Malaysian Competitiveness?". In *Globalisation, Culture and Inequalities*, edited by Abdul Rahman Embong. Bangi: Penerbit Universiti Kebangsaan Malaysia, 2004.

Wan Shawalludin Wan Hassan and Ramli Dollah. "Filipino Migrants in Sabah: An Early Survey from the Security Angle". Paper presented at the *Seventh Biennial Borneo Research Council International Conference.* Kota Kinabalu, July 2002.

Yap Swee Seng. "Social and Cultural Rights of Migrant Labour in Malaysia: An Overview from a Rights based Perspective". *Developing a Comprehensive Policy Framework for Migrant Labour*. Organized by the Malaysian Bar Council, Petaling Jaya, 18–19 February 2008.

Zarina Othman. "Human Security Concepts, Approach and Debates in Southeast Asia". In *Facing Global and Environmental Change: Environmental, Human, Energy, Food, Health and Water Security Concepts*, edited by Brouch H.G. et al. Springer, vol. 4. Hexagon Series on Human and Environmental Security and Peace, 2009.

Official Reports/Documents

Akta Imigresen 1959/63 (Akta 155) dan Peraturan-Peraturan Dan Akta Pasport 1966 (AKTA 150). International Law Books Series. Petaling Jaya, Selangor.

Federal Constitution (as at 25 July 1992). International Law Book Series. Petaling Jaya.

Government of Malaysia. *Anti-Trafficking in Persons Act 2007* (*Act 670*). Jabatan Tenaga Kerja Semenanjung Malaysia, 2006. Dasar, *Prosedur Dan Syarat-Syarat Penggajian Pekerja Asing Di Malaysia*, Putrajaya.

Government of Malaysia. *Housing and Population Census, 2010*. Department of Statistics, Putrajaya.

Jabatan Imigresen Malaysia. *Laporan Program Khas Pengampunan Tahun 2004–2005*. Putrajaya, 2005.

Jabatan Perdana Menteri Malaysia. *Rancangan Malaysia Kesembilan, 2006–2010*. Unit Perancangan Ekonomi, Putrajaya.

Trafficking in Persons Report, June 2007. Department of State, United States of America.

Newspaper Reports

Daily Express. "UPKO protests giving IMM13 holders PR", 1 July 2007.

New Straits Times. "Stopping PPR abuse", 26 November 2011.

———. "Reasons to be vigilant", 16 November 2011.

———. "Giving PR Status to Refugees not Solution to Problem", 2 July 2007.

———. "Syed Hamid: We Won't Recognize Refugees", 9 March 2007.

The Star. "Sorry is not enough", 22 January 2002.

Utusan Malaysia. "Impak kebanjiran warga asing ke atas keselamatan Negara", 14 March 2011.

———. "Bekukan seluruh pengambilan buruh asing ke Malaysia", 15 March 2011.

———. "Rimas gangguan warga Afrika", 1 March 2011.

———. "Lagi desakan batal keputusan bawa masuk pekerja India", 3 March 2011.

———. "Delima peniaga Melayu Jalan TAR", 9 November 2011.

7

TRADE POLICY FORMULATION IN MALAYSIA
Navigating between the Economic and Race Paradigms

Tham Siew Yean

INTRODUCTION

Trade policy can be used by governments as a means for intervening in an economy to promote certain sectors. But such interventions can be costly. Protection, for example, affects allocative efficiency due to the misallocation of resources between protected and non-protected sectors. It can also create rents and rent-seeking behaviour. At the same time, in developing countries, tariff revenues can contribute to the coffers of a country. The demand and supply for protection therefore exerts an influence in the formulation of the trade policies of a country (Rajapatirana 2000, p. 12). Two main factors shape the supply of protection, namely the preferences of trade policy-makers, which may be influenced by the prevailing ideology globally as well as locally, and the institutional structure of the government (democratic, authoritarian, multiparty or bi-party). Demand for protection is influenced by individuals, domestic groups and organizations.

The literature on trade policy formulation, especially in developed countries, tends to focus on bottom-up approaches whereby the economic interests of domestic groups as well as foreign lobbying can exert a major influence on the design of trade policies (Ladewig 2006; Gawande et al. 2004). However, the distribution of the costs and benefits of protection are asymmetrical; while the costs of protection in terms of its inefficiency in resource allocation is distributed over the whole society, the gains accrue to the beneficiaries of protection, namely the producer or producers of the protected industry. Hence the outcome of the bottom-up approach depends on the relative strengths of the different interest groups in the demand for protection. For example, producers' interests rule when they are more powerful than consumers' interests groups.

In the top-down approach that determines the supply of protection, economic ideology may affect the adoption of protectionist policies. For example, in the 1960s and 1970s, the prevailing economic ideology as well as protectionist lobbies contributed to the use of protection in most countries. However, subsequently, the role of infant industry protection in industrial development is hotly debated with two different schools of thought dominating the literature. In the first school, protection is abhorred based on the 1980s Washington Consensus framework while in the second school of thought, or the 1980s developmental school of thought, government support in the form of protection for infant industries, is deemed to be a key contributory factor to the successful industrialization process observed in South Korea and Taiwan (Woo 2011). Different governments have embraced the two different schools of thought on infant industry protection at different points in time.

In Malaysia, the birth of the New Economic Policy (NEP) in 1970 has national unity as the overriding objective (Malaysia 1971). There are two prongs in the NEP, namely poverty reduction and interethnic redistribution which is to be accomplished by means of "... rapid expansion of the economy over time" or economic growth. There are therefore two key paradigms driving economic policy formulations, including trade policy. The first is the race paradigm as encapsulated in the interethnic redistribution policies (see Chapter 5) while the second paradigm is economic growth as this is vital for enlarging the economic pie that is needed to finance the redistributive policies. As noted by McCrudden and Gross (2006, p. 166), the government sees the redistributive policy as a means for achieving racial stability, while economic growth provided the resources for redistribution so that the two went hand in hand. Consequently, the NEP itself encompasses both a race and an economic paradigm. More importantly, the racial and economic imperatives of the NEP are continued in subsequent policies such as the National Development Policy (NDP) and the National Vision Policy (NVP), after the NEP had officially ended in 1990. Thus, trade policy as in in the other policies in Malaysia has to continue to capture both the economic and race paradigms.

In view of the above, the objectives of this chapter are: first, to assess how trade policy formulation in the country navigates between the economic and race paradigms as articulated in the NEP and second, to examine the impact of trade policy on these two paradigms. The chapter is organized as follows: following the introduction in Section 1, Section 2 examines how the formulation of trade policy in the country navigates between the economic and race paradigms while Section 3 analyses the converse, namely how trade policy affects the economic and race paradigms. A case study of the national cars is used in Section 4 to illustrate the key issues brought up in Sections 2 and 3. The conclusion in Section 5 highlights the main findings of this chapter.

FORMULATING TRADE POLICY: NAVIGATING BETWEEN THE ECONOMIC AND RACE PARADIGMS

The objective of trade policy in the country as stated in documents provided by Malaysia to international organizations such as the Association of Southeast Asian Nations (ASEAN) Secretariat and the World Trade Organization (WTO) refers explicitly to the economic mandate, namely to increase trade and market access for Malaysia's exports as this is implicitly assumed to contribute towards the much needed economic growth of the country (ASEAN Secretariat undated; WTO 2001). This objective is reiterated in the Client's Charter of the key institution that is responsible for formulating trade policy in the country, namely the Ministry of International Trade and Industry (MITI). In the Charter, increasing the export performance of goods and services is stated as one of the objectives of MITI and this objective is to facilitate the country's aim to be among the most competitive trading nations in the world by 2020 (<www.miti.gov.my> accessed 7 June 2011). The Charter has five other goals, namely to increase domestic and foreign investments, high income and knowledge based employment, to inculcate innovation, productivity and application of latest technology in manufacturing and services for enhancing Malaysia's global competitiveness, nurture Small and Medium Enterprises (SMEs) and Bumiputera entrepreneurs who are dynamic and globally competitive, as well as to enhance the performance of MITI's delivery. Thus, the race paradigm in terms of developing Bumiputera entrepreneurs is explicitly stated in the Client Charter of MITI as this is part of the mandate in the industrial development arm of the ministry.

MITI is also the key agency for the implementation of the Industrial Coordination Act (ICA), a law that governs the procedures for the issuance of manufacturing licenses. The Act requires manufacturing activities above a certain size to be licensed subject to certain conditions, including compliance with NEP requirements in terms of 30 per cent Bumiputera equity and employment (Jesudason 1989). Non-manufacturing activities also have to comply with the NEP requirements and this is monitored by the respective Ministries that govern these activities and the Foreign Investment Committee (FIC) that was located in the Economic Planning Unit (EPU).[1]

Therefore, although the stated objective of trade policy is primarily oriented towards promoting growth, it is also used as part of the industrial policies that are employed for facilitating redistribution in the country. The academic literature on trade policy in Malaysia commonly identifies four main phases in the trade policy orientation that is used as part of Malaysia's industrial strategies (see for example Jomo 1993). These are: (i) first phase of import-substitution (1958–68), (ii) first phase of export-promotion (1968–80), (iii) second phase of import-substitution (1980–85) and, (iv) second phase of export-promotion (1985–2020) (see for example, Tham 2008; Lim 2011; Rasiah 2011). However, it should be emphasized that these four phases are not mutually exclusive as the strategy highlighted for each phase merely denotes the dominant trade strategy utilized during that phase and does not signify a complete shift from one strategy to another.

In the first phase of export-promotion, Free Trade Zones (FTZs) were used to encourage inward FDI by providing good infrastructure, cheap labour and duty-free imports. These zones also allowed a flexible implementation of the 30 per cent Bumiputera equity ownership requirements, as 100 per cent foreign owned companies were reportedly found there (Rasiah 1993). But the use of tariffs during this period was not related to the redistributive requirements of the NEP. Instead, it reflected the common ideology in trade policy of that period, namely the use of import substitution for industrial development and growth. Tariffs were implemented based on recommendations from the World Bank in 1963 for the development of import-substitution industries as a means for fostering industrial development. Industrialization, in turn, is meant to reduce the country's dependency on primary commodity production and exports as this dependency can lead to economic instability due to the volatility in commodity prices and deteriorating terms of trade for primary commodity producing countries.

However, the motivation to use protection for the second phase of import-substitution is completely different from the first phase. First, the call to re-invoke import substitution in 1980 went against the international trend to shift out of import-substitution policies due to the negative macroeconomic consequences of this policy. Second, the decision to increase protection is attributed to Dr Mahathir's launch of the heavy industrialization strategy in 1980 when he was Prime Minister. This, in turn, is tied to the desire to create Bumiputera entrepreneurship in the manufacturing sector. In 1980, the Heavy Industries Corporation of Malaysia (HICOM) was established by the government for this purpose as well as the development of linkages via the development of heavy industries. HICOM's establishment represented a significant departure from the earlier industrialization strategy that had relied on the private sector. Instead, HICOM is a state-owned enterprise that worked with Korean and Japanese multinationals and represents the government's foray into private enterprise.

The use of industrialization to meet the NEP objectives is stated in the Fourth Malaysia Plan (FMP: 1981–85 in Malaysia, 1981, p. 298). In addition, the academic literature on Malaysia's heavy industrialization strategy often emphasizes the twin objectives in the development of heavy industries which is namely, to build a strong capital goods sector with domestic linkages as well as to create Bumiputera enterprises that can participate fully in the manufacturing sector (see for example, Lim 2011, p. 20; Mahani 2011, p. 481; Machado 1994, p. 295).

Trade policy in the form of tariff protection was utilized to protect the development of these heavy industries, with the effective rate of protection increasing from 34 per cent at the end of the 1970s to over 70 per cent by the early 1980s (Lim 2011). Besides tariff protection, other forms of protection such as import restrictions, subsidized credit and preferential government procurement were also utilized. Malaysia's membership in the General Agreement on Tariffs and Trade (GATT), a multilateral agreement on tariffs and trade, did not affect the increase in tariffs for the new heavy industries as less developed member countries (LDCs) were exempted from the GATT rules prior to Uruguay Round (Tham 2008). In contrast, progressive trade liberalization under the GATT, has actually led to declining tariff barriers in the developed country members of the GATT.

The development of heavy industries received criticisms from the academia and the public.[2] Economic criticisms were raised as Malaysia had no comparative advantage in the production of such industries (Chee 1994) while racial issues were also raised because the use of HICOM to promote the development of linkages, especially among Bumiputera companies implied that the predominately Chinese controlled manufacturing sector at that time, would be by-passed (or ethnic by-pass) (Gomez and Jomo 1999). Public criticisms were raised both in and outside the country as mentioned by Mahathir in his message as Proton's Advisor in the car company's 25th anniversary publication (Kadir and Cheah 2010). Kadir Jasin, the editor-in-chief of that same publication, also noted that the launch of Proton was met with much skepticism (Kadir and Cheah 2010).

Economically, the country had grown at an average rate of 8 per cent per annum from 1971–75 and at 8.5 per cent per annum from 1976–80. Hence, the launch of the heavy industries was done after a period of fairly high growth. Nevertheless, it should be emphasized that while the venture into protection and heavy industries is meant to deepen industrial development as well as to support the redistributive imperatives of the NEP, the growth imperative was never neglected. Instead, the country continued to seek for FDI and to promote export-based manufacturing. Consequently, protection for selected heavy industries was utilized in conjunction with export promotion in the FTZs.

However, being a small open economy also meant that Malaysia is vulnerable to changes in the external environment. The emergence of the global recession in the early 1980s as well as the fall in the prices of tin and palm oil, which were among the main exports of the country during that time, affected the economy negatively. This negative impact was further aggravated by the emergence of internal problems such as the twin deficits or the fiscal and balance of payments deficits that was attributed to the development of the heavy industries.

The primary trade policy stance was reversed from inward to outward-orientation again, resulting in the launch of the second round of export promotion in 1986 in an attempt to stimulate the economy out of its first recession in 1985 since independence. Foreign equity constraints were liberalized together with tariff reforms for the light industries. The effective rate of protection fell to 28 per cent for the manufacturing sector as a whole (Alavi 1996). But significantly, the heavy industries continued to be protected. Therefore, the shift toward export-promotion did not negate the earlier venture into heavy industries. Again, the shift in the trade policy stance of the country was not done at the complete sacrifice of the race paradigm.

Consequently, from the time the NEP was launched until 1995, trade policy could and did accommodate to both the race and economic paradigms as protection was kept for the heavy industries while other sectors supported free enterprise, especially multinational production. The latter, in turn, increased manufactured exports that contributed towards the growth of the country. The NEP requirements were reportedly implemented flexibly and waivers were given, especially for export-oriented foreign companies (Rasiah 1993; Tham 1998). While external circumstances affected the growth strategy used in the country, global trade governance in the form of international trade agreements did not impinge on the policy space of the country in terms of Malaysia's choice of an appropriate trade policy for supporting its economic development.

IMPACT OF TRADE POLICY ON THE ECONOMIC AND RACE PARADIGMS

The establishment of WTO in 1995 has changed fundamentally the understanding of what constitutes trade policies as trade policies now extends to all possible policies that can affect trade, including intellectual property rights, labour, environment, etc. In other words, trade policies or global trade governance has extended its reach to anything that can affect international trade. This shift is part of the initiatives to lower non-tariff barriers (NTBs) in international trade since progressive liberalization had reduced the importance of tariff barriers. International trade law therefore sought to limit NTBs, including domestic regulations or other measures that may not be protectionist in their intentions but may have the same or equivalent impact as a tariff on the imports.

WTO also signalled another shift in global trade governance as members of the WTO are legally bound to their commitments and can be brought before the WTO Dispute Settlement Mechanism in the event of a trade dispute with another member of the WTO. In addition, countries have to undergo scheduled policy reviews that are used to monitor the implementation of a country's commitments in the WTO. The use of binding rules through irreversible commitments in the WTO therefore impinges on the policy space of a country. Global trade governance further emphasizes transparency, predictability and consistency in trade policies which obviously does not support the previous approaches used to negotiate between the race and economic imperatives of Malaysia in its trade policies. These are a dual track approach (namely export-oriented and protected sectors) as well as the use of flexibility in its implementation of the trade policies of the country as foreign equity constraints can be waived under stipulated conditions.

Nevertheless, there are several features in the existing WTO commitments that allow Malaysia to maintain her policy space to choose trade policies that meets the redistribution requirements of the NEP. First, the use of a positive list approach[3] under the WTO meant that Malaysia could choose the sectors for binding commitments. Consequently, Malaysia excluded 97 per cent of the tariff lines in the automotive sector and 92 per cent of the tariff lines in the iron and steel sectors from binding, which is important for the continued protection of these heavy industries (Tham 2008). Similarly, Malaysia could choose to open only selected sub-sectors of services that are deemed ready for liberalization. Even then, limitations on the extent of liberalization accorded could be used to restrict the commitments made. For example, a commonly used limitation is the percentage of foreign equity that is allowed for commercial presence in each of the sub-sectors, which is also important in terms of the redistributive policy of the NEP.

Second, the use of a plurilateral rather than multilateral approach on particularly sensitive issues such as government procurement also provided breathing space on a key policy instrument that is used for implementing the redistributive requirements of the NEP. Many governments, including Malaysia, use public procurement for their redistributive and developmental goals. There is a clearly stated preference programme in the Treasury (or the implementing agency) circulars to all government bodies to choose Bumiputera suppliers, producers, works and other providers as well members of the Malay Chamber of Commerce for government contracts (McCrudden and Gross 2006). It should however be noted that there is also a preference programme for domestic providers, without any ethnic conditions attached. It is therefore not surprising that Malaysia is not a member of the Plurilateral Agreement on Government Procurement. Malaysia has also used her negotiating capacity to form a coalition with other developing countries such as India, Pakistan and China to resist the inclusion of a multilateral agreement on government procurement in the protracted negotiations under the Doha Round. This coalition appears to have succeeded in suspending indefinitely all work on negotiating for such an agreement (McCrudden and Gross 2006, p. 184).

There is very little research written on the issue of government procurement in the country due to the lack of data on this matter. McCrudden and Gross (2006) documents some of the public debate on government procurement from the international as well as local media. Four main problems are highlighted in the public debate, namely rent seeking; the lack of competitiveness of Bumiputera entrepreneurs who have become too dependent on government contracts in contrast to the increasing need for competitiveness due to the implementation of the ASEAN Free Trade Area (AFTA); and the tendency for Bumiputera contractors to subcontract the jobs offered to them or to sell their contracts for quick profits. McCrudden and Gross (2006) further noted that the Treasury Division of the Finance Ministry has almost complete discretion to make rules which govern government procurement at all levels of the government. In view of the general opaqueness in the government procurement process, Ariff and Nambiar (2011) argue for greater transparency even though they agree that an accession to a government procurement agreement may be more suitable in the distant future in order to accommodate national interests and socio-economic development goals.

Nevertheless, some constraints on the use of trade policy for redistributive purposes have also emerged with the establishment of the WTO. The Agreement on Trade-Related Investment Measures (TRIMs) prohibits the use of investment performance measures that violate the principles of national treatment established under GATT (Tham 2008). However, the agreement is rather vague in its scope as it only provides an illustrative list of inconsistent measures, including local content requirements for goods. Such requirements are used in developing countries to develop local capacity in manufacturing production. In the case of Malaysia, it is also used to promote Bumiputera entrepreneurship, especially in the national car project that will be explained later in the case study of this chapter. TRIMs, for example, disallowed the use of local content policies for whatever purposes and illustrate how international trade agreements can lead to Malaysia having to choose between the economic and race paradigms instead of accommodating both in its trade policy.

More importantly, the policy space for determining a trade policy that can accommodate both the economic and racial imperatives appears to be narrowing, with the likely failure of the Doha Round to conclude despite eleven prolonged years of negotiations. Bilateral trade agreements have instead proliferated in place of multilateral liberalization. These agreements are likely to further impinge on the policy space of Malaysia for two main reasons: first, bilateral trade agreements aim to push trade liberalization beyond what has been achieved at the WTO. In other words, they aim to be WTO-Plus agreements (Tham 2010). Second, developing countries like Malaysia may lack the negotiating capabilities and capacities to negotiate an agreement that can accommodate to its development needs when negotiating with developed countries like the USA or EU that have already a fixed template of what they want in terms of market access. For example, the Trans-Pacific Partnership Agreement (TPPA), a Free Trade Agreement that is currently being negotiated by Australia, Brunei, Chile, Malaysia, New Zealand, Peru, Singapore, United States and Vietnam covers traditional FTA elements as well as new elements, including e-commerce; business mobility; government procurement; labour; trade remedies; and legal and institutional matters. The much expanded scope of this bilateral agreement, including an agreement on government procurement, does not augur well in terms of accommodating both the economic and race paradigms in Malaysia's trade policy.

At the same time, the economic imperatives appear to be more binding after the AFC in 1998 due to the drop in economic growth and private investment, including FDI and current stated aspirations of the country which is to shift out of the middle to a high income economy, by 2020 (NEAC 2010). The New Economic Model (NEM), Economic Transformation Plan (ETP) and Tenth Malaysia Plan that were launched in 2010 all emphasize the use of a private sector driven growth strategy, with private investment including FDI, as the catalytic agent for transforming the economy while the government is positioned to be just a facilitator of this process (NEAC 2010; Pemandu 2010; Malaysia 2010). Part of the trade strategy used to enable Malaysia to compete globally is the pursuit of FTAs that are seen as important means to open market access for Malaysia's exports. It is also hoped that these FTAs will help to revive foreign investor interest in Malaysia.

CASE STUDY ON PROTON AND PERODUA

The first national car project (NCP) was approved as part of the heavy industries programme in the country. A partnership between the HICOM and the Mitsubishi Motor Corporation (MMC) and the Mitsubishi Corporation (MC) was formed in 1983. The choice of Mitsubishi was because they were the only willing partners from Japan. Besides, former Prime Minister Mahathir, who initiated this project, did not consider the Europeans or the Americans as suitable partners as they were already losing their market share in Malaysia and elsewhere (Mahathir 2011, p. 513).

PROTON was launched in 1985 with the roll out of the Proton Saga as the pioneering model. The car was protected by high tariffs amounting to 140–300 per cent for passenger cars as well as import quotas and approved permits (APs) for completely built up units (CBUs). Import and excise duties were also imposed on completely knocked down (CKD) units which are assembled locally. These tariff and non-tariff measures immediately caused a price difference of 20–30 per cent between the national car and non-national cars (Mahidin and Kanageswary 2004). For example, in 1987, the price of a 1.3cc Proton Saga was RM21,000 while the prices of similar cars in the same range cost between RM28,000–29,000. This price difference allowed the Saga to capture 65 per cent of the market share in 1987 and PROTON's market share grew to about 73 per cent in 1988.

However, its market share has since dropped to around 25 per cent from 2006–10 (Fong 2011) due to competition from the second national car project (PERODUA) that was started in 1993 and an increase in imported cars as a result of the proliferation in Approved Permits (APs) given. Nevertheless, PROTON is still protected[4] and continues to receive preferential treatment in terms of public procurement as it is the official government car for civil servants who are entitled to a car by virtue of their post.

The national car status of PROTON inevitably meant that its development and achievements has attracted considerable academic as well as media attention from both inside and outside Malaysia. Starting with the motivation, Mahathir (2011, p. 511) in his memoir explained that he was motivated to build a Malaysian car in order to maximize the local content of the country and for Malaysians to learn about engineering. He did not believe that Malaysia could become a developed country by being merely consumers of industrial products from other nations.

The academic literature as well as some media reports has also highlighted the motivation for increasing Bumiputera participation in the automotive industry (see for example, Alavi and Hasan 2001; Rosli and Kari 2008; Wad and Govindaraju 2011; *News Straits Times*, 16 July 1991). In the Review of the National Automotive Policy (NAP) conducted by MITI in 2009, enhancing Bumiputera participation in the domestic automotive industry is also clearly stated as one out of the eight objectives for the NAP review (MITI 2009). Mahathir in his assessment of the achievements of PROTON concluded that "Proton helped us to realize the objectives of stimulating Malaysian engineering industries and the NEP objectives of getting Bumiputera into business as well" (2011, p. 520).

This conclusion is certainly supported by academic analysis on the development of the local content in the automotive industry based on the number of automotive component manufacturers in the country, which is reported to be 690 in 2010 (MIDA 2010). PROTON is reported to have 220 vendors, of which 77 are Muslim vendors in 2007 (Syed Zainal undated).[5] The reported annual business volume for Muslim vendors amounted to RM1.3 billion or 45 per cent of the total component purchase value. Besides this, PROTON has 8,290 employees, 95 per cent of whom are Muslims and an annual employee cost of RM300 million for the Muslim employees and 232 total sales dealers, of which 148 or 64 per cent are Muslims with an annual business volume of RM1.7 billion for Muslim dealers only. Clearly, PROTON has contributed towards increasing Bumiputera employment and income in the country. It has also enhanced skill development through technology transfer and learning from the foreign technology partner, Mitsubishi to PROTON's primarily Bumiputera employees (Tham 2004; Kadir and Cheah 2010).

Apart from tariff and non-tariff measures, direct government intervention was used to develop local content through local material content programme (LMCP) and the vendor development programme (VDP). A mandatory deletion programme (MDP) was also introduced in 1980, whereby a list of thirty items were identified to be deleted from import when the local parts manufacturer is able to supply the original equipment market requirement for the assembly of automobiles in the country (Alavi and Hasan 2001).

The literature hotly debates on the viability of PROTON, the vendor development programme, and the competitiveness of the Bumiputera entrepreneurs that have been cultivated from prolonged years of protection in the automobile sector. This debate has intensified with the arrival of AFTA and Malaysia's commitments in AFTA as well as the increasing importance of bilateral free trade agreements in the country.

The viability of PROTON without protection is often queried as Malaysia's automotive exports amounts to 0.6 per cent of total merchandise exports in 2007 and the country is still a net importer of automotives, despite twenty-six years of protection. PROTON in 2009 exported 23,407 units as opposed to a domestic sales volume of 148,785 units, or 14 per cent of the total sales volume for that year. It is also reported that PROTON (and also PERODUA) are being exported to other countries at prices even lower than the home market, implying the possible usage of export subsidies (Fong 2011). The revealed comparative advantage (RCA), a commonly used indicator for export competitiveness, for transport equipment, was a mere 0.05 in 2001 and although this indicator has grown to 0.13 in 2009, this is still far from the necessary indicator of above one that is commonly used to show export competitiveness. So equally clearly, Malaysia has not established export competitiveness in the automotive sector, after prolonged and continued protection due mainly to the fact that export conditions were not imposed on the protected sector and there was no sunset clause for the phasing out of protection.

Similarly, Malaysia is still a net importer of auto components and parts. In particular, the viability of the local vendor system, including Bumiputera vendors, have been questioned in the literature, in view of findings that show the superior economic and financial performance of foreign suppliers over local suppliers, including Bumiputera suppliers (Alavi 2001; Rosli and Kari 2008). This is despite the extensive support given to Bumiputera vendors in the Proton Bumiputera Vendor Scheme whereby these vendors are granted financial facilities as well as technical assistance.

The use of APs in the automotive sector is also unlikely to create viable Bumiputera entrepreneurs since an AP is a license issued to a vendor to sell foreign cars with no local content. Fong (2011) reported the total number of APs issued in 2004 was 51,559 and this decreased to 27,838 in 2007 but increased again to 40,886 in 2008 before reducing to 20,000 in 2009. Mahathir (2011) blames the AP for the decreased share of PROTON while media attention tends to focus on the lack of transparency in the selection of AP holders who hold monopolistic gains, and the tendency for APs to be abused. In fact one of the key aims of the National Automotive Policy (NAP) that was first introduced in 2006 was to abolish the AP system by 2010. But in its review in 2009, the deadline for the abolishment of the AP system was shifted to 2015 and 2020 respectively for the open and franchised AP (Izwan Idris, *Starbizweek*, 31 October 2009). Therefore, while the initial idea to supply protection came from the government, prolonged protection has created vested interests and demanders for continued protection.

Navigating between the economic and race paradigms has become more complex because the emergence of demanders of protection has come at a point in time when trade policy commitments made by the government requires the withdrawal of protection. Thus in the case of the TRIMs, although Malaysia was granted two extensions for the removal of its local content programme that was used to develop the automotive component industry, it had to phase out its local content requirements on 1 January 2005 (Tham 2008).

In the case of AFTA, Malaysia has managed to delay the liberalization of the automotive sector by initially placing this sector in the temporary exclusion list. Consequently, although the original ASEAN-6 had agreed to lower tariffs to a maximum of 5 per cent by 2003, the automotive sector was excluded and it was only in 2005 when Malaysia reduced its tariffs for CBU cars from other ASEAN countries to 20 per cent and from non-ASEAN countries to 50 per cent. An increase in excise duties was then used to offset the reduction in tariff revenue, with the national cars reportedly exempted from a certain percentage of these excise duties. This was subsequently brought down further to 5 per cent and 0 per cent respectively, for CBU and CKD from other ASEAN countries but the excise duties and sales taxes are again used as compensation for the loss in tariff revenues (see Table 7.1). The opening up of the ASEAN market means that car-makers in ASEAN, including Malaysia, can source cost-competitive components from ASEAN countries and benefit from potential economies of scale (MIDA 2010).

Given the sizeable presence of Japanese automotive makers in Southeast Asia, it is not surprising that the automotive sector is the main sector of interest for Japan in its bilateral free trade negotiations with Malaysia (Higashi 2008). In 2005, Malaysia concluded its first bilateral agreement, namely the Japan-Malaysia Economic Partnership Agreement (MJEPA). In this agreement, liberalization of automobiles is scheduled as shown in Table 7.2.

Since PROTON produces cars generally of a smaller engine capacity, the elimination of tariffs for imported cars (CBUs) from Japan for this range of cars has been pushed to 2015, while tariffs for cars with bigger engine capacities are scheduled for earlier reduction.

The on-going negotiations under the Trans Pacific Partnership (TPP) agreement and the Malaysia-European Union (EU) Free Trade Agreement

Table 7.1
Import and Excise Duties for Imports from ASEAN and Non-ASEAN Countries
(2010)

	Imports from ASEAN Countries		Imports from non-ASEAN Countries	
	Import Duties	**Excise Duties**	**Import Duties**	**Excise Duties**
CKD vehicles	0 per cent	60–125 per cent	0–10 per cent	60–125 per cent
CBU vehicles	5 per cent	60–125 per cent	30 per cent	60–125 per cent
CKD motorcycles	0 per cent	20–50 per cent	0–10 per cent	20–50 per cent
CBU motorcycles	5 per cent	20–50 per cent	30 per cent	20–50 per cent

Source: MIDA (2010).

Table 7.2
Tariff Reductions in Auto; Auto Components and Parts in Malaysia, under the MJEPA

Auto and Auto Parts and Components	Tariff Reductions
CKD	Immediately eliminated
Auto components and parts, other than the CKD	0–5 per cent in 2008 and eliminated by 2010
Passenger cars exceeding 2,000 cc and up to 3,000 cc, multipurpose vehicles (MPVs) exceeding 3,000 cc, trucks exceeding 20 tonnes, and buses	Gradually eliminated by 2010
Passenger cars exceeding 3,000 cc	0–5 per cent in 2008 and eliminated by 2010
All other CBUs other than the above	Gradually eliminated by 2015

Source: Tham (2008).

is also bound to affect the tariffs in the automotive sector, given the precedence in the MJEPA as well as the interests of the American and EU automobile producers in the Malaysian market. It should be noted that ASEAN and the MJEPA agreements have left government procurement untouched. This is unlikely to be the case for the potential TPP and free trade agreement with the EU. Indeed the scope of the latter agreement is just as potentially extensive as the scope in the TPP.

The academic literature and public discourse in general expresses doubts on the viability of PROTON, especially when compared with the more competitive Thai automobile sector. Thailand has been dubbed as "Detroit of the East" (see for example, Mahidin and Kanageswary 2004; Rosli 2006; Nag et al. 2007). The future of PROTON appears to be pessimistic: first there is global excess manufacturing capacity of reportedly 20 million units in conventional cars (Fong 2011).

Second, Malaysia does not have a large domestic market, unlike China and India, and these two countries are also eyeing the automobile market beyond their respective shores. It has been reported that generally car companies need to sell at least one million cars a year to remain profitable (Cheong 2011). In contrast, the Malaysian domestic car market size is estimated at around 550,000 vehicles per year. Thailand with a population base of 67 million and a car registration number of 800,000 vehicles per year is closer to the size that is needed for sustaining a viable domestic manufacturing base. Kuchiki (2007) argues that the domestic demand conditions in Malaysia does not satisfy the minimum size level that is needed for realizing a minimum average cost of production that is so essential for cost competitiveness in the globalized automobile industry.

Third, the auto sector requires huge expenditures on R&D and capital with high entry barriers and demanding economies of scale, scope and speed, rendering national automobile projects that produce for small domestic markets futile endeavors (Fong 2011; Wad 2011). Thailand is one of the six countries in the world housing Toyota's global R&D operations and one of the eight countries in the world hosting Bridgestone's auto tyre test track and proving ground for tyre development (<http://www.toyota-global.com/company/profile/facilities/r_d_center.html>; Cheong 2011).

Fourth, conventional cars that continue to rely on fossil fuels are not sustainable, especially in the case of Malaysia, where fuel subsidies and poor public transportation have supported the high demand for automobiles. Unless PROTON is able to innovate and shift to green vehicles, as well as partner a global partner with a global reach, its future is uncertain, especially with deeper liberalization that impinges on other forms of protection besides just tariff (Tham 2004; Wad and Govindaraju 2011; Wad 2011; Fong 2011). In this regard, PROTON has been seeking a global technology partner unsuccessfully for the last few years. The renewed technology collaboration with Mitsubishi in 2006 and 2008 does not involve equity transfer but it remains to be seen if this will lead to substantial technology transfer and green innovation since in Japan, the current leaders of hybrid cars are Toyota and Honda. PROTON has also announced recently an intention to mass produce hybrid cars in two years (that is by 2013) (*The Star*, 15 September 2011).

The government has been searching for a partner for PROTON after the Asian Financial Crisis in 1998. However, negotiations to sell Khazanah's (a government-linked company that is holding the government's share in PROTON) fell apart in 2007 due to the government's insistence to keep PROTON as a domestically-owned company. Subsequently, there was also a discussion of a merger between PROTON and PERODUA in order to obtain scale and technology from PERODUA's foreign technology partner, namely Toyota. It has been reported that PERODUA is less enthusiastic of a merger (Barrock 2011). Finally, in January 2012, Khazanah sold its entire stake in PROTON to DRB-Hicom, a privately owned Bumiputera company that is a leading car distributor and importer as well as assembler of various car brands. It should, however, be noted that despite its extensive network of partners with global car companies, DRB-Hicom is essentially a car assembler and it remains to be seen whether divesting PROTON to a private Bumiputera company can propel PROTON to be a global car manufacturer, that is based on its own designs.

While much has been written on PROTON, there is considerably less literature on PERODUA. Part of the reason could be the public perception that the car is no longer a national car since its equity restructuring in 2001 as its manufacturing arm, Perodua Auto Corporation Sdn. Bhd., has 41 per cent of its equity owned by Daihatsu Motor Co. Ltd. and 10 per cent owned by Mitsui & Co. Ltd. (Aminar Rashid 2010). Hence, its manufacturing is effectively controlled by Daihatsu which is a subsidiary of Toyota, with a strong niche focus on the compact car segment in Malaysia. This has two important implications. First, in terms of R&D, PERODUA can leverage on the technology of its parent company, Toyota. This lowers the production costs of PERODUA as there is less investment in R&D. The eight models churned out in the last seventeen years were not built from scratch from the drawing board but they were mainly adapted from Daihatsu or Toyota models. The focus of the plant in Malaysia is reportedly on pressing, painting and assembling (Kuchiki 2007). Local touches are used to improve the styling of the cars to meet local demands.

Second, its production system is planned from the perspective of Toyota's supply chain management in Asia (Kuchiki 2007). Hence the decision on whether the Malaysian plant should import parts and components from other plants in ASEAN are based on costs of transportation and the size of the domestic market. This enables the company to overcome some of the problems associated with economies of scale and which has and continue to plague the production of PROTON. It also helps to explain why PERODUA is much more profitable than PROTON. The net profit of PERODUA for the year 2008 is reportedly RM294.9 million, compared to PROTON's RM184 million for the same year (Francis 2011). Moreover, net tangible asset for PERODUA in the same year stood at RM5.4 billion as opposed to RM1.8 billion for PROTON. The former also achieved a return on equity of 16 per cent for the same year as opposed to 3 per cent for PROTON.

The greater profitability of PERODUA does not imply that it is export competitive. Although there is no data on the export of its cars, the overall car export data for Malaysia shows that this cannot be significant. Protection, without export constraints, has led to a more profitable and popular car-maker in PERODUA due to the greater equity control given to Toyota. This has enabled it to capture the domestic demand for compact cars but it has not created an export competitive automobile sector for Malaysia. Domestic demand continues to be high due to poor public transportation and facilities.

However, like PROTON, PERODUA has also contributed to the employment of Bumiputera in the automotive sector. Total number employed as at October 2010 is 10,630 (Aminar Rashid 2010) and although employment by ethnic groups is not given, it is likely that the majority of these are Bumiputera. Similarly, 59 of the vendors (or 42 per cent of total vendors) serving PERODUA are Bumiputera. Hence the second national car project has also contributed towards the fulfillment of the redistributive requirements in the NEP.

CONCLUSION

Before the establishment of WTO, trade policy in Malaysia could and did accommodate to both the economic and race paradigms in the NEP as export promotion catered to the need for growth while selective protection is used for heavy industries. The use of this dual track policy and flexibility in the implementation of trade restrictions such as foreign equity constraints enabled Malaysia to fulfill both the economic and redistributive objectives of the government. The supply of protection for the development of industrial linkages as well as Bumiputera entrepreneurs and their involvement in automobiles can be attributed to former Prime Minister, Mahathir. Global trade rules did not affect the trade policy choices of Malaysia as developing member countries were exempted from the obligations of the multilateral agreement on trade or GATT.

However, the progressive and successful reduction of tariff barriers in the world has led to a greater focus on non-tariff barriers for multilateral trade liberalization, especially during the Uruguay Round negotiations that immediately preceded the establishment of the WTO. This development brought to the fore domestic regulations and practices that may not be protectionist in intentions but that can still affect imports, such as preferential rules. Nevertheless, the type of agreements concluded under the Uruguay Round provided ample space for Malaysia to pursue both export promotion and import protection. This is due to the modalities used that allowed developing countries to choose their commitments and at the same time to limit the extent and depth of their liberalization. Malaysia could also choose not to be a member of the Plurilateral Agreement on Government Procurement. At the same time, Malaysia also garnered her negotiation capabilities to work with other developing countries to block further work on the inclusion of government procurement in the new set of rules that is being negotiated in the Doha Round that was started in 2001. But, the stalling of the Doha Round worked to the detriment of developing countries as trade liberalization can only be pursued at the regional and bilateral levels. Bilateral trade negotiations and agreements are more demanding as they seek to be WTO-Plus.

The case study on PROTON and PERODUA shows that protection in the country has successfully contributed to the redistribution requirements of the NEP by creating Bumiputera entrepreneurship, employment, skills, and technology development through the national car projects. The welfare cost of such protection is typically borne by the whole society due to inefficiencies in terms of resource allocation. But continued protection without export disciplines and sunset clauses as well as relatively slow progress in technology development has led to a lack of export competitiveness in the automotive sector. It has also created demanders for protection within the sector that makes protection typically difficult to dismantle.

Although Malaysia has acquired some competencies in automotive development, the global development in the hugely competitive automobile sector has increasingly made national car projects untenable due to the requirements of scale, scope and speed. Baldwin (2011) shows that the globalization of production after the second unbundling has led to the rapid development of global supply chains. Successful industrialization no longer means building the complete domestic supply chain at home. Instead, harnessing the global supply chain for industrialization is increasingly the way forward for industrialization. Countries have two choices, either join an existing global supply chain or to strive to become a headquarter economy. Unfortunately, the latter has not materialized for the national cars after prolonged years of protection.

Global trade rules are also increasingly impinging on non-tariff protection measures used to protect PROTON such as public procurement practices. The changing requirements of global trade rules and increasing resistance to liberalize from the demanders of protection inevitably mean that hard choices have to be made by the government. The new external realities are exacerbated by increasing competitive pressures from China, India as well as fellow member countries of ASEAN. At home, the stalling of growth and investment after a decade long high growth rates before the AFC is escalating the economic imperatives to seek for higher growth as necessitated by calls to shift to a high-income economy by 2020. Tariff barriers in the automotive sector are being reduced and this already signals the weakening ability to protect while the strengthening of rules against non-tariff barriers is also eating into the policy space to accommodate both the economic and race paradigms of the country. It may no longer be possible for trade policy in Malaysia to accommodate both the economic and race paradigms in the not too distant future.

Notes

1. On 30 June 2009, the Government announced the liberalization of the Foreign Investment Committee (FIC) guidelines, including the repeal of FIC Guidelines on the acquisition of interests, mergers, and takeovers (WTO 2010). However, the dismantling of the FIC is not equivalent to the removal of Bumiputera requirements for approval of FDI as the licensing system in the country requires approval from the respective ministries before a license can be obtained. It has merely reduced a dual process of approval, namely from the FIC and the appropriate ministry to a single approval by the appropriate ministry.
2. It should be noted that the literature review in this chapter covers only the discourses that are articulated in English. It is possible that the public discourse in Bahasa Malaysia or the Malay language, especially in the Malay media, may be more supportive of heavy industries and its use for the development of Bumiputera entrepreneurs.
3. This means countries list only the sectors that they are committed to liberalize.
4. WTO (2010) reports some protective measures that were adopted in the wake of the global financial crisis (GFC) that also promote the development of national cars. For instance, under Malaysia's temporary auto-scrapping scheme, the government rebates RM5,000 for consumers replacing a car aged more than ten years with a national brand vehicle (PROTON and PERODUA) in 2009.
5. There is no published data on employment of PROTON by ethnic groups. However, data on Muslim vendors and employees can be viewed as a fairly close approximation of the ethnic distribution of vendors and sales dealers since all Malays in the country are Muslims and it is unlikely that vendors and sales dealers are foreign Muslims. Data on Muslim employment may overstate the data on Malay employment as it may include foreign workers who are also Muslims.

References

Alavi, R. *Industrialization in Malaysia*. London: Routledge, 1996.

Alavi, R. and S. Hasan. "The Impact of TRIMS on Malaysian Automotive SME Vendors". *Kajian Malaysia*, vol. XIX, no. 2 (2001): 38–57.

Aminar Rashid Salleh. "Supporting Effective and Smart Partnership: Government and Private Sector Working Together Towards A Competitive Corporation", 2010. Available at <www.intanbk.intan.my/i-portal/dl/ppa2010/aminarrashid.pdf> (accessed 20 October 2011).

Ariff, M. and S. Nambiar. "International Trade and Trade Policy". In *Malaysia: Policies and Issues in Economic Development*. Kuala Lumpur: Institute of Strategic and International Studies (ISIS) Malaysia, 2011.

ASEAN Secretariat. "Highlight on Malaysia's Homepage: Trade Policies", undated. Available at <http://www.aseansec.org/12387.htm> (accessed 7 June 2011).

Baldwin, Richard. "Trade and Industrialization after Globalization's 2nd unbundling: How Building and Joining a Supply Chain are Different and Why It Matters", 2011. Available at <http://nber.org/punlic_html/confer/2011/MECf11/Baladwin.pdf> (accessed 21 October 2011).

Chee, P.L. "Heavy Industrialization: A Second Round of Import Substitution". In *Japan and Malaysian Development in the Shadow of the Rising Sun*, edited by Jomo K.S. London: Routledge, 1994.

Gawande, Kishore, Pravin Krishna, and M.J. Robbins. "Foreign Lobbies and U.S. Trade Policy". NBER Working Paper Series. Working Paper 10205, 2004.

Gomez, T. and K.S. Jomo. *Malaysia's Political Economy: Politics, Patronage and Profits*. 2nd ed. Cambridge: Cambridge University Press, 1999.

Higashi, Shigeki. "The Policy Making Process in FTA Negotiations: A Case Study of Japanese Bilateral EPAs". Institute of Developing Economies (IDE) Discussion Paper No. 138 (2008). Available at <http://hdl.handle.net/2344/727> (accessed 8 March 2011).

Jesudason, J.V. *Ethnicity and the Economy: The State, Chinese Business and Multinationals in Malaysia*. Singapore: Oxford University Press, 1989.

Jomo, K.S. *Industrialising Malaysia: Performance, Problems, Prospects*. London: Routledge, 1993.

Kadir, A. Jasin and C.S. Cheah. *A Saga: Proton's 25-year Story*. Sungai Buloh: Superior Press Sdn. Bhd., 2010.

Kuchiki, Akifumi. "A Flowchart Approach to Malaysia's Automobile Industry Cluster Policy". Institute of Developing Economies (IDE) Discussion Paper no. 120. Tokyo: IDE, 2007.

Ladewig, J.W. "Domestic Influences on International Trade Policy: Factor Mobility in the United States, 1963–1992". *International Organization* 60 (2006): 69–103.

Lim, D. "Economic Development: A Historical Survey". In *Malaysia: Policies and Issues in Economic Development*. Kuala Lumpur: Institute of Strategic and International Studies (ISIS) Malaysia, 2011.

Machado, K. "Proton and Malaysia's Motor Industry". In *Japan and Malaysian Development*, edited by K.S. Jomo. London: Routledge, 1994.

Mahani Zainal Abidin. "The NEP: Private Sector and Economic Growth". In *Malaysia: Policies and Issues in Economic Development*. Kuala Lumpur: Institute of Strategic and International Studies (ISIS) Malaysia, 2011.

Mahathir, Mohamad. *A Doctor in the House: The Memoirs of Tun Dr. Mahathir Mohamad*. Kuala Lumpur: MPH, 2011.

Malaysia. *The Second Malaysia Plan: 1971–75*. Kuala Lumpur: National Printing Department, 1971.

———. *The Fourth Malaysia Plan: 1981–1985*. Kuala Lumpur: National Printing Department, 1981.

———. *Tenth Malaysia Plan 2011–2015*. Putrajaya: The Economic Planning Unit, 2010.

McCrudden, C. and S.G. Gross. "WTO Government Procurement Rules and the Local Dynamics of Procurement Policies: A Malaysian Case Study". *The European Journal of International Law*, vol. 17 no. 1 (2006): 151–85.

MIDA. "Malaysia's Automotive Industry", 2010. Available at <http://www.mida.gov.my/en_v2/uploads/Publications_pdf/BO_MalaysiaAutomotive/Automotive_FA.pdf> (accessed 7 July 2011).

Ministry of International Trade and Industry (MITI). "Review of National Automotive Policy", 2009. Available at <http://www.miti.gov.my> (accessed 14 May 2011).

———. "Client's Charter", 2010. Available at <http://www.miti.gov.my>.

Mohd Uzir Mahidin and R. Kanageswary. "The Development of the Automobile Industry and the Road Ahead: Department of Statistics", 2004. Available at <http://www.statistics.gov.my/portal/images/.../V204_AUTOMOBILE.pdf?> (accessed 8 June 2011).

Nag, Biswajit, Saikat Banerjee, Rittwik Chatterjee. "Changing Features of the Automobile Industry in Asia: Comparison of Production, Trade and Market Structure in Selected Countries". Asia-Pacific Research and Training Network on Trade (ARTNet) Working Paper Series, no. 37 (July 2007).

National Economic Advisory Council (NEAC). *The New Economic Model for Malaysia*. Putrajaya. Available at <www.neac.gov.my> (accessed 22 August 2010).

Pemandu. *Economic Transformation Programme: A Roadmap for Malaysia*. Putrajaya: Pemandu, 2010.

Rajapatirana, S. *The Trade Policies of Developing Countries: Recent Reforms and New Challenges*. Washington, D.C: The American Enterprise Institute (AEI) Press, 2000.

Rasiah, R. "Free Trade Zones and Industrial Development in Malaysia". In *Industrialising Malaysia: Policy, Performance, Prospects*, edited by K.S. Jomo. London: Routledge, 1993.

———. "Industrialization and Export-led Growth". In *Malaysia: Policies and Issues in Economic Development*. Kuala Lumpur: Institute of Strategic and International Studies (ISIS) Malaysia, 2011.

Rosli, Mohd. "The Automobile Industry and Performance of Malaysian Auto Production". *Journal of Economic Cooperation* 27, no. 1 (2006): 89–114.

Rosli, Mohd. and F. Kari. "Malaysia's National Automotive Policy and the Performance of Proton's Foreign and Local Vendors". *Asia Pacific Business Review*, vol. 14, no. 1 (January 2008): 103–18.

Syed Zainal Abidin Syed Mohamed Tahir (Managing Director of PROTON). Memperkasa Ekonomi Ummah Melalui Pemantapan Jaringan Tempatan dan Penerokaan Berkesan Dalam Pasaran Global: Persiapan Mendepani Cabaran Baru Ekonomi Dunia, undated.

Tham Siew Yean. "Foreign Direct Investment Policies and Related Institution-Building in Malaysia". In *Foreign Direct Investment in Selected Asian Countries: Policies in Related Institution Building and Regional Cooperation*. United Nations Economic and Social Commission for Asia and the Pacific, Development Papers No. 19. ST/ESCAP/1809, 1998.

———. "Malaysian Policies for the Automobile Sector: Focus on Technology Transfer". In *Production Networks in Asia and Europe: Skill Formation and Technology Transfer in the Automobile Industry*, edited by Rogier Busser and Yuri Sadoi. London: RoutledgeCurzon, 2004.

———. "Trade Liberalization and National Autonomy: Malaysia's Experience at the Multilateral and Bilateral Levels". In *Globalization and National Autonomy: The Experience of Malaysia*, edited by J.M. Nelson, J. Meerman and A.E. Rahman. Singapore: Institute of Malaysian and International Studies (IKMAS) and Institute of Southeast Asian Studies, 2008.

———. "Evolution of Trade Policy Formulation in Malaysia". In *Complexity of FTAs: A Key Issue in Malaysian Trade Policy*, edited by Wan Khatina et al. Kuala Lumpur: Khazanah, 2010.

Toyota website on its R&D centres in the world. Available at <http://www.toyota-global.com/company/profile/facilities/r_d_center.html> (accessed 7 July 2011).

Wad, Peter. "The Automobile Industry of Southeast Asia: Malaysia and Thailand". *Journal of the Asia Pacific Economy*, vol. 14, no. 2 (May 2011): 172–93.

Wad, P. and C.V.G.R. Govindaraju. "Automotive Industry in Malaysia: An Assessment of Its Development". *Int. J. Automotive Technology and Management*, vol. 11, no. 2 (2011): 152–71.

Woo, Wing Thye. "The Changing Ingredients in Industrial Policy for Economic Growth". Paper presented at the Asia-Pacific Research and Training Network

(ARTNet) Symposium "Towards a Return of Industrial Policy?" United Nations Economic and Social Commission for Asia and the Pacific, Bangkok, 25–26 July 2011.

World Trade Organization (WTO). "Trade Policy Review: Malaysia". Geneva: WTO. WT/TPR/S/156. Available at <www.wto.org/english/tratop_e/tpr_e/s156-2_e.doc> (accessed 7 July 2011).

———. "Trade Policy Review: Malaysia". Geneva: WTO, 2010. WT/TPR/S/225. Available at <http://www.wto.org/english/tratop_e/tpr_e/tp325_e.htm> (accessed 7 July 2011).

Newspapers

Barrock, J. "Advisory Council to Study Proton-Perodua Merger". *The Edge Financial Daily*, 18 April 2011.

Cheong, Hans. "National Automotive Policy (NAP) Report Card". *News Straits Times*, 29 June 2011.

Fong Chan Onn. "Burden or Catalyst? Focus, Sunday Star", 1 May 2011, F38–39.

Francis, Isabelle. "Government will not force Proton-Perodua merger, but does it have to be?". *The Edge Financial Daily*, 26 January 2011.

Izwan Idris. "Coming to Grips with APs". *Starbizweek*, 31 October 2009.

The Star. *Proton Delivers First Batch of Electric Cars to Government*, edited by Zuhrin Azam Ahmad, 15 September 2011.

8

NATIONAL SECURITY CONCEPTIONS AND FOREIGN POLICY BEHAVIOUR
Transcending the Dominant Race Paradigm?

K.S. Nathan

INTRODUCTION

The scope, goals, approaches and strategies of Malaysian national security reflect the struggle to build a nation out of a state inherited from British colonialism — an effort which is increasingly premised on broader notions of comprehensive security incorporating the political, military, economic, socio-cultural, psychological, and environmental dimensions of national survival and advancement. Malaysian conceptions of national security are therefore informed by factors based on history, geography, political culture, pluralism, Malay nationalism and ethno-religious identity, the character of political and economic development, problems and goals of national unity and integration, as well as perceptions regarding the nature of internal, regional, and international conflicts.

Ethnicity or race has played an important role in national and international politics. In America, the Jewish lobby is known to exercise disproportionate influence in terms of the numerical size of the Jewish community. In India, for instance, "caste" can be substituted for race to produce a similar effect, i.e. affirmative action policies are constitutionally endorsed for protecting and promoting the welfare of "schedule castes". In the Malaysian context a Malay-dominant political elite has emerged with attendant consequences for foreign as well as domestic politics — with the management of foreign policy largely in the hands of the politically dominant Malay/Muslims. The impact of domestic, regional and international developments such as the drive towards modernization, industrialization, regionalization and globalization has impelled the national leadership to redefine and reinvent the nation by infusing a new sense of purpose and direction that would strengthen national security as well as regional peace and prosperity. In pursuing this thrust, the UMNO-dominant political leadership has attempted to maintain and even consolidate the dominant race paradigm anchored in Malay hegemony.[1]

This conceptualization of security in Malaysia contains both domestic and external dimensions. Conceptions of domestic security clearly continue to emphasize internal peace, law, and order so that the daily business of governing and fulfilling the needs and demands of a multiracial society is not disrupted by chaos leading to violence. Internal tranquility is a *sine qua non* for development and progress, and in Malaysia it carries the idea of a Malay race whose political dominance remains paramount while its economic strength depicts an upward trajectory. Hence legal instruments, even if they are draconian, are essential if not inevitable in legitimating the government's authority and its capacity to manage a plural society like Malaysia. Conceptions of external security, however, are based on an assessment of the nation's defence capability as well as the dynamic operations of the regional and global balance of power. National security, therefore, connotes the idea of strategic survival both internally and externally.

National security conceptions can also be gleaned from the instruments used to promote them. Foreign policy itself can be viewed as the vital instrument that provides the nexus between internal and external conceptions of security. Foreign policy then becomes the vehicle for expressing the national interest. This chapter examines the scope, referent units, goals, threats, and approaches governing Malaysian security conceptions and their linkages to foreign policy behaviour. It argues that while the dominant race paradigm may be salient to the understanding of Malaysia's domestic politics, and sense of internal security, the conduct of foreign policy — even if it is led by a Malay-dominant leadership — is governed more by a shrewd, rational, and pragmatic calculation of how best the national interest can be advanced in the context of regional and international politics. It should therefore be noted at the outset that Malaysian foreign policy is not couched in terms of addressing the "Malay World", the "Chinese World", or the "Indian World" merely because of the presence of significant components of ethnic Chinese and Indians in the Malaysian population. The ruling elite, while although Malay-dominant and also being cognizant of the internal character of Malaysian society, pursues a foreign policy that is grounded in the characteristics of the national political economy as well as trends in the global political economy. Such an approach is invariably guided by the ideology of pragmatism in pursuit of "the national interest".

DOMESTIC FOUNDATIONS

All societies are influenced by their own past record in coping with internal and external challenges, formulating social, political, and economic structures and policies designed for self-survival as well as for national aggrandizement, and initiating new directions that have domestic and global impact well beyond original expectations. For Malaysia, the strongest ideological compulsion driving its anti-communist domestic and foreign policies was the bitter experience with the communist insurgency from 1948 until 1960. Defeating internal communism and containing if not defeating international communism became a cardinal principle of strategy for Malaysian decision-makers entrusted with the security of the nation. The success of the Maoist revolution in China in 1949 heightened fears of a Beijing-led Asian communism engulfing the entire Southeast Asian region. This apprehension was strengthened by the ethnic character of the Malaysian communists, the overwhelming majority of whom were Chinese. The presence of a sizable ethnic Chinese population in Malaysia fuelled official concern about their potential role as fifth columnists in the service of the Communist Party of Malaya (CPM) and the Communist Party of China (CPC).

The essential nature of the Malayan communist political agenda — with its primary objective since its formation in 1930 "to carry on the struggle for national liberation, formulate a military program for the overthrow of imperialism and feudal aristocracy and to establish the Soviet Republic of Malaya by the coordinated efforts of the proletariat and peasantry" (Hanrahan 1971, p. 43) — was anathema to the Malays, who generally viewed Chinese involvement in the anti-colonial and communist activities as "assisting one form of Chinese domination to replace another" (Fisk and Osman-Rani 1982, p. 9). It is quite apparent, then, that ethnicity has combined with ideology to produce a particular security orientation since the early days of independence. Malaysia's post-independence security conceptions incorporated this historical, ideological, and ethnic security orientation into policies and strategies for molding the nation.

The rejection by the United Malays National Organization (UMNO) of the Malayan Union proposals put forward by the British also bore testimony to rising Malay political consciousness, as did pressures for a Malay-led Malaya (later Malaysia) following independence in 1957. These events also portended increasing Malay insecurity — which had its origins in political developments in the years preceding and succeeding the World War II. Moreover, British colonial rule had encouraged the growth of "a Malay bureaucratic class which, after independence, continued to dominate the key organs of the state — the bureaucracy, judiciary, military and police — and provided the leadership of the United Malays National Organization or UMNO" (Crouch 1993, p. 136). Thus the referent units of Malaysian security were to be principally Malay in character — determined almost exclusively by the Malays to whom power was transferred constitutionally by the British colonial masters on 31 August 1957.

MALAYSIAN SECURITY/MALAY SECURITY

Constitutions are essentially political-legal documents outlining the powers, functions, and limitations of the social groups and institutions that compose the body politic at a given time. A constitution reflects the interests of prevailing power groups in society regardless of the manner in which they have been constituted. Politically dominant groups write into national constitutions their own interests, privileges, ideologies, aspirations, and goals — all of which establish a framework for a viable and orderly interaction among various groups in society. Although constitutions as social documents evolve with time as reflected by amendments, certain provisions are regarded as sacrosanct despite radical changes taking place in society. Amendments affecting entrenched provisions threaten the security of those groups who have benefited from special provisions granting them political, economic, and social privileges *vis-à-vis* other communities and presumptive territorial rights to the land.

In short, a nation's constitution can serve as an important source of national security — even if this notion is selectively applied to legitimize the interests of a particular ethnic group. Article 153 of the Malaysian

Federal Constitution — providing for special position and rights for Malays and other natives with respect to public service jobs, education, scholarships and training, and business licenses — remains an entrenched provision even after nearly fifty-five years of Malaysian independence, in spite of the fact that the political dominance of the Malays remains assured while their economic position *vis-à-vis* the non-Malays has significantly improved.[2] Moreover, the concept of "Bumiputera" (literally, sons of the soil) that gained currency after Malaysia's 1969 racial riots, as well as the onset of the New Economic Policy, represents a further political attempt to preserve this entrenched provision — even if the economic position of the Malays happens to overtake that of the non-Malays. Article 153 and "Bumiputera" must be viewed as two sides of the same coin in entrenching Malay dominance and strengthening Malay feelings of security in relation to the other communities in Malaysia.

The citizenship provisions of the Federal Constitution shed additional light on Malay perceptions of national security. Stringent provisions under Articles 14 to 31 ensure tight controls over citizenship acquisition by non-Malays and foreigners, including foreign wives of Malaysian citizens (Article 15). Indeed, "there is no similar provision for the granting of citizenship to husbands who were married to women who were citizens of the Federation" (Sinnadurai 1978, p. 76). Such provisions are designed to preserve the Malay character of the Malaysian Federation — and hence the constitutional security of the politically dominant Malays.

As other chapters in this volume make clear, Malaysian politics is still by and large communal politics: the ruling Barisan Nasional (BN) coalition is itself a political and electoral arrangement along ethnic lines. Thus the whole notion of individual, group, and organizational security is closely tied to the communal character of the Malaysian political system. Attempts to form multiracial conceptions of political security through multiracial parties have either foundered because of the ethnic factor or have been stifled by official intervention. This compulsion for ethnic security has also found expression in the suppression of the left in the post-war period — thereby virtually eliminating any prospect of non-ethnic ideological discourse. Since the late 1960s, and especially after the 13 May 1969 racial riots, "ethnicity has increasingly dominated Malaysian political culture" (Jomo 1989, p. 36). The Gerakan Rakyat Malaysia (Malaysian People's Movement), originally conceived as a multiracial party, has degenerated into essentially a party promoting Chinese interests. In Sabah, the multiracial Parti Bersatu Sabah (PBS; Sabah United

Party) has faced strong challenges from the federal government in Kuala Lumpur, especially under Mahathir's premiership, until it was finally ousted from power in 1995. Sabah is now ruled by a UMNO-dominated state government resembling the ethnically oriented political model in Peninsular Malaysia.

Given the dominant role of the Malays in Malaysian political life, Malay security is invariably equated with Malaysian security. Malay feelings of insecurity are invariably translated into policies and strategies of coercion and accommodation designed to promote Malay ethnic interests. The New Economic Policy from 1970 to 1990 is perhaps the classic example of how the Malays attempted to overcome their insecurity in the aftermath of the 1969 general elections, which appeared to threaten their political dominance. Strategies of excessive state interventionism in the 1970s in support of Malay interests were gradually replaced by economic policies in the 1980s and 1990s that reduced the state's role in the economy but were animated by the same objective of strengthening Bumiputera control of the Malaysian economy. Such strategies of Malay ethnic survival and security included Prime Minister Mahathir's programme of "Malaysia Incorporated," deregulation, the suspension of NEP implementation (Jomo 1989, p. 42), and the establishing of the Heavy Industries Corporation of Malaysia (HICOM) for the production of Malaysian-made cars. The government's privatization policy in the mid-1980s was clearly designed to "accelerate growth, improve efficiency and productivity, trim the public sector, reduce the government's financial and administrative role, and redistribute wealth to the Bumiputeras" (Jomo 1995, p. 48).

Although the New Economic Policy (NEP) has been replaced by the National Development Policy (NDP), the basic contours of Bumiputera supremacy in Malaysia's political economy remain intact. The new UMNO elite created largely by the New Economic Policy is loath to make any concessions that are seen to be eroding the privileged position of the Malays. Economic nationalism in Malaysia strengthened the link between Malay ethnicity and Malay economic security (in contrast to a focus on *Malaysian* economic security) by official preference for transnational capital rather than domestic Chinese capital, strongly influenced as it was by concerns about Chinese wealth accumulation in the nation (Jomo 1993, p. 11). If Malaysian security equals Malay supremacy, then any perceived erosions of that supremacy must necessarily endanger Malay (and therefore national) security — regardless of how this notion affects the security of the non-Malays.

One thing is clear: today the basic domestic structure of Malaysian security is built around Malay ethnic identity. As one Malaysian political activist notes: "The classification of Malaysians into Bumiputeras and non-Bumiputeras has long been an issue of contention in our political arena. Perhaps no other issue divides our people as much as this one" (Fan 1995, p. 175). Indeed, the ideology, policy, and practice of "Bumiputeraism" has effectively intervened between Malay nationalism based on monoethnicity and the emergence of a truly Malaysian nationalism based on multi-ethnicity — even after fifty-five years of independence. It is therefore hardly surprising that virtually no serious reference is made to the existence of a Malaysian nationalism. After five decades of independence, the Malaysian state-nation is still in the process of building the Malaysian nation-state — and also a more pluralistic as well as inclusive conception of national security.

MALAY STATE, ISLAM, AND LANGUAGE

The concept of Malaya (the name of the country until 1963) as comprising essentially the Malay state is embodied in the Malay-language reference to the country as "*Tanah Melayu*", or Malay land. This basic Malayness was also preserved in the new name of "Malaysia", when Malaya was expanded to include Singapore (until 1965) and the North Borneo territories of Sabah and Sarawak. The security and sovereignty of the Malay state are preserved by constitutional provisions pertaining to the role of the nine Malay sultans who also serve as heads of the Muslim religion in their states. The sultans therefore function as legitimizers of Malay sovereignty over Malaysia, a position that cannot be challenged under the constitution. In the years preceding Malayan independence, Malay rulers warned against the erosion of traditional Malay loyalties by stressing communalism — especially by pointing out the incompatibility of Islam (embraced by the Malays) and communism (largely a Chinese phenomenon) (Hua 1983, p. 98). Besides the institution of the Malay rulers, the Malay language or Bahasa Melayu (also known as Bahasa Malaysia) furnishes an additional tool of legitimacy for Malay dominance of Malaysia. The use of the national language as the main medium of instruction at all levels of education — primary, secondary, and tertiary — as well as the medium of official communication with government is yet another integral element of preserving Malay ethnic security and, by extension, Malay dominance in a multiethnic society in which other racial groups are individually as well as collectively weaker in the political domain.

Islam's pre-eminent status — as the nation's official religion — is a further source of Malay/Muslim security, and it cannot be challenged under any circumstances. The Muslim-dominated leadership, however, practises a moderate form of Islam to accommodate the multi-religious sentiments of Malaysian society and, more important, to ensure that Islam does not become a tool reinforcing Malay backwardness but instead serves as a vehicle of progress so that the socio-economic status of Muslims is at least on par with non-Muslims. Modernist interpretations of Islam also reinforce ethnic security in the sense that they allow a focus on nationalism, not religion, as the dominant ideology. In employing Islam to strengthen Malay nationalism, however, UMNO faces a challenge arising from the transnational force of Islamic universalism.

To be sure, modernists reject theocracy as being incompatible with development and modernity (Mehmet 1990, p. 99). Deviance in terms of sectarianism or contradictory interpretations of the Koran is strongly discouraged if not penalized to preserve the ultimate goal of Muslim unity in the Malaysian context. Official concerns that disunity among the Muslims would expose them to political exploitation by outsiders as well as weaken them as a group tend to find expression in strong pronouncements and threats of severe sanctions including the use of the Internal Security Act for non-compliance. The activities of the Al-Arqam movement, headed by Ashaari Mohamed, were viewed as a threat to national security because this sect threatened the core of Muslim orthodoxy as practised in Malaysia. The banning of Al-Arqam in early 1990s, the extraction of confessions from its leadership, the suppression of religious literature and publications by Muslim individuals and organizations that are deemed to subvert Malay/Muslim unity and security — all provide strong evidence of the link between race and religion as referent units of national security in a domestic context.

THE EXTERNAL DIMENSION

Turning from national to external conceptions of security, in the case of regional relations Malaysia's approach is based on a structural response to the character of its own domestic national structure and that of the regional power structure of which it is an integral part. State-directed nationalism and state-directed growth, coupled with a growing need for pooling resources in the drive for modernization, have produced the related phenomenon of Southeast Asian regionalism, which has evolved in the form of the Association of Southeast Asian Nations (ASEAN), inaugurated in 1967. ASEAN regionalism is also reflected in increased bilateralism as a necessary by-product of the nation-building process in Southeast Asia. In Malaysia and Singapore this process is particularly instructive in terms of the role of ethnicity in mutual perceptions, especially the need to sensitize the foreign policy process to the realities of ethnicity: Chinese-dominant Singapore interacts with Malay-dominant Malaysia without questioning the basis of ethnic supremacy governing both societies. Ethnicity is in general an unstated factor in national security perceptions characterizing interstate relations within the framework of ASEAN regionalism. It is a key factor in the way the nation-building process in advanced developing societies such as Malaysia and Singapore links national survival to regional stability and prosperity.

One area in which the race paradigm is significant relates to Malaysia's commitment to the notion of comprehensive security — a notion that places emphasis on striking a balance between strengthening military capability and strengthening the socio-economic and political basis of national security. The adoption of a holistic approach to national defence and regional security — especially with the demise of bipolarity in international relations — has invariably meant a reduction in defence expenditure relative to other sectors of the national economy. The long-term allocation of an average of only 2–3 per cent of total GNP for defence (Najib 1995, p. 38) is strongly indicative of Malaysia's approach to national security: military power is but one dimension of the total equation, while other components such as political, social, and economic security are assigned greater significance in terms of contributing to peace, stability, harmony, and prosperity.

There are parallels between domestic and regional conceptions. For instance, consider the New Economic Policy (1970), which reflected the Malaysian leadership's desire to correct ethnic imbalances and assert indigenous Malay control over politics and economics. The then Prime Minister Tun Razak intended to fill the domestic economic power vacuum with Malay elements, and he extended this concept to region building when he sought to fill the regional power vacuum with greater indigenous regional content. We see here the underscoring of a link between Malay security, national security, and regional security — and, arguably, the relevance to some degree of the dominant racial paradigm to international politics. This trend found expression in the Malaysian call for the creation of a neutralized Southeast Asia following the massive American military withdrawal from Vietnam. Tun Razak's strategic response was to initiate the process of zonal neutrality in the wake of the collapse of American power — and, conversely, the victory of communist power in Southeast Asia. The Kuala Lumpur initiative — giving regional expression to the post-Vietnam balance of power — came in the form of the Zone of Peace, Freedom, and Neutrality (ZOPFAN) Declaration of 1971. Known also as the Kuala Lumpur Declaration, ZOPFAN was endorsed in principle by the ASEAN foreign ministers at their annual meeting in Kuala Lumpur on 27 November 1971. ZOPFAN, so it might be argued, represented an indigenous expression of national and regional empowerment in the sphere of foreign policy.

ECONOMIC REGIONALISM, EAEC AND EAS

The creation of regional economic associations, as well as greater economic integration, is merely a reflection of the congruence of national interests. Malaysia's proposal to set up an East Asian Economic Grouping (EAEG), first announced by Mahathir in December 1990, was a response to the unsatisfactory progress of the now concluded Uruguay Round of multilateral trade negotiations (Nathan 1995, p. 231). Moreover, Malaysia harboured genuine fears over "the emergence of an economic cold war, a vastly more complicated global struggle for economic influence where the powerful seek to dominate, even exploit, the weak".[3] The concept of the EAEG (later renamed East Asian Economic Community, EAEC) — which was to comprise states geographically part and parcel of Asia (including ASEAN, Hong Kong, Taiwan, China, South Korea, and Japan) — aimed to build up negotiating strength *vis-à-vis* other economic groupings. In an important sense, the EAEC can be regarded as the externalization of Malaysia's domestic security conception. Mahathir saw a natural geographical, cultural, ethnic, and historical affinity with other East Asian partners — the emergence, that is, of an East Asian consciousness — thus lending viability to EAEC-style economic regionalism. Here one might posit a convergent perception of regional empowerment having racial overtones between Tun Razak's post-Vietnam conception of regional security and Mahathir's post-Cold War formulation of East Asian regional empowerment.

Furthermore, Mahathir's strategy of downplaying the Chinese threat to Southeast Asia earned the anticipated dividend: China's "explicit and unwavering support" for the EAEC.[4] The conspicuous removal of China as a threat in Mahathir's foreign policy was also designed to strengthen local Sino-Malay business cooperation to capitalize on the "economic opening of China", and thereby boost Malaysia's economic performance. Prime Minister Najib's visit to China in May 2009 to commemorate the 35th anniversary of the establishment of diplomatic relations between Malaysia and the PRC is indicative too of a pragmatic strategy in which a Malay-led Malaysia seeks to harness the entrepreneurial skills of ethnic Malaysian Chinese to the rise of China — a project which guarantees the advancement of mutual national interests. A similar trend is noticeable with the rising India. Here Najib's visit to Tamil Nadu in January 2010 was aimed at underscoring the significance and contribution of the domestic presence of ethnic Tamils, who comprise 85 per cent of the Malaysian Indian community of over 2 million.[5] Evidently, PM Najib was also communicating the message that a Malay-led Malaysia need not be a barrier either to inter-ethnic cooperation within the country, or to cooperation between Malaysia and the two major Asian civilizations which have a historic and contemporary influence on Southeast Asia that cannot be ignored.

ISLAM

Given the dominance of the Muslim/Malay grouping in Malaysia's racial structure, Malaysia's involvement in international Islamic developments is not surprising. As a result of the Muslim world being subjected to Western colonial domination, South-South cooperation and Islamic solidarity are complementary strategies for promoting national security and advancement. In this regard, the establishment of the "Development Eight" in Istanbul, Turkey, represents yet another Malaysian strategy to publicise the compatibility of Islam with modernization and development, thereby promoting Malaysian conceptions of national security and economic progress.[6] Inasmuch as Third World countries have developed common interests *vis-à-vis* the West as part of the decolonization process, the Muslim world developed strong feelings of Islamic solidarity *vis-à-vis* their ex-colonial masters. For the Muslim world, "the idea of Islamic solidarity gave them a framework for increased cooperation among themselves in social, political, and economic fields" (Noor Ahmad Baba 1993, p. 42).

Malaysia has taken the initiative in building Muslim solidarity since the early 1950s, culminating in the Rabat Summit Conference (22–25 September 1969), which formalized the establishment of the Organization of the Islamic Conference (OIC). Although the achievements of the OIC as a forum for international Muslim solidarity might be negligible in terms of restructuring the world order in favour of Muslim interests, its existence as a symbol of Muslim identity and security and its potential role as a political and economic force cannot be ignored.

For a Malay/Muslim-dominant multiethnic and multi-religious Malaysia, the search for identity and security in the Muslim world represents the external dimension of the internal quest for ethno-religious identity in a plural setting. Following Mahathir's accession to the premiership, he attempted to broaden Malaysia's Islamic credentials by creating the Islamic Bank and the International Islamic University in 1983, accelerating the government's mosque-building programme, and strengthening ties with other Islamic countries — efforts designed to strengthen Malay ethno-religious identity while "reinforcing UMNO's Islamic legitimacy among the Malays without kindling a degree of unease in the other ethnic communities" (Camroux 1994, p. 20).

Regionally, Malaysia has expressed concern over the fate of Muslims in southern Thailand and southern Philippines. In both cases, a Malay/Muslim identity component is obviously driving Malaysia's perspective and approach to the two conflicts. In the case of the Muslim minority in southern Thailand, while expressing concern over the plight of Muslims, the Malaysian government has nevertheless been careful in not openly supporting the insurgency, or be seen to be aiding the insurgents. On the one hand, any expressions of support must be viewed in the context of domestic politics in terms of not losing the initiative to the opposition Pan Malaysian Islamic party (PAS), and externally in terms of the government strengthening its credentials with the Muslim World as an "Islamic State".[7] On the other, as a Member State of ASEAN supporting principle of non-interference in the internal affairs of other members, it is not in Malaysia's interest to support the Muslim insurgency in southern Thailand. Similarly, Malaysia views the conflict in southern Philippines as a threat to its national security arising from the flow of illegal immigrants and refugees from that region.[8] Malaysia's mediatory role in resolving the conflict between the Moro Islamic Liberation Front (MILF) and the Philippine Government on 6 October 2012 was acceptable to the Muslim rebels because of Malaysia's Muslim credentials, and equally acceptable to Manila in the spirit of both being members of ASEAN.

Internationally, Malaysia closed ranks with the OIC by taking a strong stand on Bosnia, which is viewed as an issue to strengthen Islamic solidarity. At a special meeting on Bosnia-Herzegovina of the OIC Contact Group and countries contributing troops to the United Nations Protection Force (UNPROFOR) in Kuala Lumpur on 14 September 1995, the then Foreign Minister Abdullah Badawi stressed that "so long as we allow ourselves to be manipulated by the West, and for as long as we remain indecisive, we will not be able to help our brethren, even when they are under threat of extermination".[9] In a very different sphere, the international Koran reading competitions held annually in Malaysia are another manifestation of this desire for identity and security.

In recent times PM Najib has become conscious of the weaknesses of his predecessor's "Islam Hadhari" (Civilizational Islam) policy. He has also shown an awareness of the 9/11 impact in terms of rising Islamophobia in the western world. In this context he has sought to project internationally Malaysia's internal capability in managing multi-culturalism, stability and development via the "1 Malaysia" project. In particular, he is keen that Malaysian Islam be projected as moderate, tolerant, progressive and highly adaptive to the changing trends and demands of globalization. At all costs, Najib wishes to refute the international negative image of Muslims as a backward people prone to terrorism and violence to achieve their goals. Malaysia as a Malay/Muslim majority country, he believes, can provide a beacon of hope for those wishing to advance materially and spiritually in this world — marked as it is by tremendous economic, political, cultural, ideological and social pluralism. Externally, his "1 Malaysia" project[10] gives him a platform to market Malaysian foreign policy via the proposal to create "A Global Movement of the Moderates". Najib declared in his address before the United Nations General Assembly on 28 September 2010 that:

> The real issue is not between Muslims and non-Muslims but between the moderates and extremists of all religions, be it Islam, Christianity or Judaism. Across all religions we have inadvertently allowed the ugly voices of the periphery to drown out the many voices of reason and common sense. I therefore urge us to embark on building a "Global Movement of the Moderates" from all faiths who are committed to work together to combat and marginalize extremists who have held the world hostage with their bigotry and bias.

> It is time for moderates of all countries, of all religions to take back the centre, to reclaim the agenda for peace and pragmatism, and to marginalize the extremists .... This "Global Movement of the Moderates" will save us from sinking into the abyss of despair and depravation. This is an opportunity for us to provide the much needed leadership to bring hope and restore dignity for all. With greater will and collective determination, we will build a more peaceful, secure and equitable world.[11]

CONCLUSION: THE DOMINANT PARADIGM IN MALAYSIAN FOREIGN POLICY: CHALLENGES AND PROSPECTS

Malaysia's security conceptions — as expressed in its domestic and foreign policies — can be stated as follows: national sovereignty with emphasis on political integrity and the territorial unity of the Malaysian Federation; economic development and social justice in the context of a multiracial society; preservation of constitutional monarchy, Islam, and the special rights of the Malays; a firm commitment to ASEAN and promotion of other forms of economic regionalism that advance national interests; promotion of regional stability and security via ZOPFAN; and a commitment to promote South-South cooperation aimed at enhancing the economic welfare of the less developed world and supporting human rights and social justice worldwide.

Such conceptions of national security invariably call for adroit diplomacy to bridge the gap between national aspirations and international realities — in other words, the gap between desirability and possibility. In this context, the Malaysian leadership has evidenced a commendable degree of pragmatism in managing relations at all three levels: bilateral, regional, and global. Strategic management of domestic and foreign security policies has informed the present success enjoyed by Malaysians in terms of political stability, economic growth, social peace, and national prosperity. Malaysia's ability to manage structural constraints — such as multi-racialism, economic, political, religious and cultural diversity — and convert them into positive forces for development and prosperity has, in the main, contributed to an expanded regional capacity to sustain and promote micro-level and macro-level regionalism. PM Najib has proudly remarked that "Malaysia's experience in integrating cultures, languages and religions over the past half century had proven that the unity forged had resulted in stability, security and peace."[12]

The current scenario would undoubtedly be different without a strategic vision and the ability to manage difficulties while promoting possibilities. Indeed, in the regional sphere, such a strategic vision was already in place as early as 1967 when ASEAN was formed. Succeeding years merely witnessed the consolidation of that vision in the form of national and regional resilience — an Indonesian concept that has become ASEAN-ized owing to its relevance, practicality, and potential. Thus ASEAN has enabled Malaysia and its ASEAN partners to manage bilateral relations on the basis of tolerance and mutual respect. Such an approach to national security at both the Malaysian national level and the regional level has in turn strengthened the foundations of regional cooperation and prosperity through ASEAN. It lends credence, as well, to the success of nascent regional economic and security agendas for the post-Cold War era such as those embedded in the EAEG/EAEC, the ASEAN PLUS 3 (which can be viewed essentially as a triumph for the EAEC ideal), the ASEAN Regional Forum (ARF) and now East Asia Summit (EAS) — all ASEAN-led regional institutions.

The critical link between regionalism and nation building lies in the fact that the former cannot succeed without the latter. Internal stability in each of the regional partners determines their individual as well as collective capacity to cooperate and advance at the regional level. In this regard, Mahathir's remarks are noteworthy: there is a strong correlation, he has said, between rapid economic growth and strong stable governments in East Asia, for together they provide the stability and consistency so essential to long-term investment and economic progress.[13] The ASEAN experience has confirmed this fundamental political condition of healthy regionalism.

Nation building is an ongoing process for many developing countries that were colonies of the European powers. The management of interethnic relations has been one of the most challenging tasks for Malaysia and other multiracial states. Finding the right formula requires political maturity, economic wisdom, and even occasional use of repression to promote the government's legitimacy and the regime's security. Indeed, the "national security" imperative can serve as a convenient device for regime legitimation and continuation of ethnic-based discrimination as a "temporary evil" in order to achieve the presumably greater good of national unity, and the professed vision of a united Malaysian nation. Meanwhile, the concept and practice of national security might well perpetuate Malaysia's status as a state-nation, strengthened as it is by a record of good governance, political stability, and economic prosperity, without having to confront the real challenges posed by a genuinely constructed nation-state.

In Southeast Asia, with the possible exception of Thailand, which was never colonized, the state came before the nation. The task of the independent state, therefore, was to create a nation — that is, to commence the nation-building process while at the same time maintaining racial harmony, social security, political stability, and economic development, all vital elements of national security. The Malaysian record of dealing with the multifold challenges of post-independence nationalism and regionalism is a record of strong state intervention in the management of the political and economic dimensions of national security.

As stated at the opening of this chapter, Malaysian foreign policy is driven above all by the concern to promote national interest. As we seek the somewhat nebulous link to the ethnic dimension — examining such areas as China relations, policy toward the Islamic world, and the link between domestic security strategies and regional objectives — it makes sense as well to consider the sometimes acrimonious relationship between Malaysia and Singapore. Following Singapore's exit from Malaysia in 1965, the bitterness of separation was evidenced by the many bilateral issues that remained unresolved over nearly five decades. These issues — namely: (a) supply of water to the republic, (b) sovereignty over Malayan Railway land in Singapore, (c) customs, immigration and checkpoint (CIQ) disagreements, (d) pension funds of Malaysian workers withheld by Singapore, (e) territorial claims over Pulau Batu Putih (Pedra Branca), (f) the use of Malaysian airspace by RSAF aircraft, and (g) a new bridge to replace the Johor-Singapore Causeway built in 1923 — have all bedeviled the relationship, but the difficulties are also compounded by the injection of racial overtones between Malay-majority Malaysia and Chinese-majority Singapore.

Since the departure of Mahathir in 2003, it should be pointed out, his successors Abdullah Badawi and Najib Tun Razak have categorically debugged the emotional/racial content, thus paving the way for pragmatic approaches to resolving bilateral issues. Conflicting claims over Pulau Batu Putih were finally resolved by a decision of the International Court of Justice on 28 May 2008, awarding the rocky island to Singapore. Second, the seventy-nine-year Tanjong Pagar Railway Station was closed on 30 June 2011, thereby fully resolving the CIQ issue. In the context of globalization, stiffening competition and expanding development opportunities in Malaysia, Singapore was awarded handsome infrastructure and service contracts in the Iskandar Malaysia region (situated in Johor).

Malaysia-Singapore economic, trade and investment relations have considerably improved since the Badawi era.[14] Evidently, the Najib government is much more focused on discarding historical baggage and promoting good neighbourly relations based on history, geographical proximity, cultural and familial ties, and a strong sense of interdependence. These considerations, it is hoped, can trump the penchant for evoking racial sentiments whenever convenient on the Johor side of the Causeway, with the media on both sides fuelling the fire to the detriment of both parties. Both sides are also equally aware that bilateral Malaysia-Singapore trade alone accounts for 50 per cent of intra-ASEAN trade.[15] It would appear, therefore, that the ethnic dimension of Malaysia-Singapore relations — although having the potential to exacerbate tensions — is being effectively suppressed.

With respect to domestic security in Malaysia, state-directed development and intervention in the economy will remain a continuing feature of the political economy of this and other states in the developing world. Malaysia's development programmes since the Seventh Malaysia Plan (1996–2000) have envisaged a much larger role for the private sector in growth — though the role of the state in infrastructural and human resource development is still viewed as instrumental in providing economic security.[16] In Malaysia, the expansion of the state "in terms of both the spatial and policy range of its activities" is closely paralled by the role of ethnicity and the rise of UMNO's political-economic power (Brown 1989, p. 8). Thus any attempt to shift this power from state to society through Western conceptions of democracy — whether at the domestic level or through blocs such as APEC — will be resisted by the government (Nesadurai 1996, p. 52), particularly on grounds of national security.

In sum, then, Malaysia's conception of security is a corporate aggregate of its own historical experience, its multi-ethnicity, its ethno-national vision, and its desire to seek recognition for its changed status from "object" to "subject" in international relations. To see how this foundation is undergirded by Malaysia's dominant racial paradigm, it is important to examine the policies of the Malaysian prime ministers, who have been the principal architects of the nation's survival strategies. In particular, the conception of Malaysian security held by Mahathir Mohamad — who injected a personal vision into national security formulation, and was singularly instrumental in gaining Malaysia its present high profile — emphasizes the notion that leaders of multiethnic societies must continuously reinvent the nation to strengthen national security and promote regional stability. His successor, Abdullah Badawi attempted, with limited success, to instrumentalize "Islam Hadhari" for profiling Malaysia as a modern, democratic and progressive Muslim-majority Nation. The "Najib Doctrine", if it may be called that, is anchored in the promotion of the ideology of moderation in domestic and international policy in all the key dimensions of human existence: politics, ethnicity, culture, religion, economics, development, peace, security and stability.

Taking this approach, Najib could rightly claim to be strengthening the tradition of Malay political and economic empowerment in a changing domestic, regional and international context.[17] Ensuring regime legitimacy, political stability, multi-ethnic harmony and economic progress in a changing and uncertain global environment is the major challenge confronting his administration. Consequently, the success of Najib's ambitious two-pronged agenda — "1 Malaysia" (for internal consumption), and "A Global Movement of the Moderates" (for external consumption) — depends very much on whether he can practise what he preaches. He is confronted by rising ethnic and religious cleavage as well as economic polarization in Malaysian society — all of which pose additional, perhaps serious challenges to maintaining and transforming the dominant paradigm to justify its continuing relevance in both domestic politics and foreign policy. A major economic downturn could pose a major test as well as threat to his New Economic Model, thereby eroding the very basis of moderation which has to this point been the primary vehicle for Malay empowerment and Malaysia's success as a modern nation-state. In this way, ethnic issues would present a strong ethnic challenge to Malaysia's domestic security — and, indeed, a potent imperative to drive Malaysian policy in the international sphere.

Notes

1. This chapter draws substantially from an earlier work that has been published. For details see, K.S. Nathan, "Malaysia: Reinventing the Nation", in *Asian Security Practice: Material and Ideational Influences*, edited by Muthiah Alagappa (Stanford, California: Stanford University Press, 1998), pp. 513–48. However, newer arguments and analysis have been introduced to fit into the broader theme of the book's project on dominant and competing paradigms.
2. *Federal Constitution, Malaysia* (Kuala Lumpur: MDC, 1993), pp. 148–51.
3. "Malaysian Foreign Policy in the 1990s". Address by Foreign Affairs Minister Datuk Omar to the Malaysian International Affairs Forum (MIAF) on 3 May 1990. *Foreign Affairs Malaysia* 23, no. 2 (1990): 7.

4. *New Straits Times*, 14 July 1993, p. 14. See also Deputy Prime Minister Anwar Ibrahim's statement during his August 1994 visit to China; *New Straits Times*, 27 August 1994, p. 1.
5. Veera Pandiyan, "Najib Proud to Visit Tamil Heartland", *The Star Online*, 24 January 2011, available at <http://thestar.com.my/news/story.asp?file=/2010/1/24/nation/5535925&sec=nation> (accessed 15 May 2011).
6. Established on 15 June 1997 at the end of a four-day summit in Istanbul, the D-8 nations comprise Bangladesh, Egypt, Indonesia, Iran, Malaysia, Nigeria, Pakistan, and Turkey, with the declared aim of strengthening development cooperation among members. See *New Straits Times*, 13 June 1997, p. 2.
7. For an insightful account, see S.P. Harish, "How Malaysia Sees Thailand's Southern Strife", *Asia Times Online*, 8 February 2006, available at <http://www.atimes.com/atimes/Southeast_Asia/HB08Ae01.html> (accessed 15 January 2013).
8. *The Star Online*, "Southern Philippines Framework Peace Pact will Benefit Malaysia, says Ahmad Zahid [Malaysia's Defence Minister]", available at <http://thestar.com.my/news/story.asp?sec=nation&file=/2012/10/9/nation/12143178>, 9 October 2012 (accessed 15 January 2013).
9. *Foreign Affairs Malaysia* 28, no. 3 (September 1995): 27.
10. "1Malaysia" is an on-going programme designed by Malaysian Prime Minister Najib Tun Razak on 16 September 2010, calling for the cabinet, government agencies, and civil servants to more strongly emphasize ethnic harmony, national unity, and efficient governance.
11. Cited in James Fallows, "A Global Movement of Moderates: Speech of a Muslim Prime Minister", *The Atlantic*, 28 September 2010 <http://www.theatlantic.com/international/archive/2010/09/a-global-movement-of-moderates-speech-of-a-muslim-prime-minister/63689/> (accessed 5 June 2011).
12. "PM: Better Multilateral Cooperation Needed", Keynote Address at the 10th International Institute of Strategic Studies Asia Security Summit, Singapore. *New Straits Times*, 4 June 2011, p. 2.
13. *New Straits Times*, 6 December 1993, pp. 1–2.
14. For details, see "Roundtable on Singapore-Malaysia Relations: Mending Fences and Making Good Neighbours", *Trends in Southeast Asia Series* 16 (Singapore: Institute of Southeast Asian Studies (ISEAS), 2005).
15. For a complete analytical account of the dynamics of bilateral relationship, see K.S. Nathan, "Malaysia-Singapore Relations: A Bilateral Relationship Defying ASEAN-Style Multilateralist Approaches to Conflict Resolution", in *International Relations in Southeast Asia: Between Bilateralism and Multilateralism*, edited by N. Ganesan and Ramses Amer (Singapore: Institute of Southeast Asian Studies, 2010), pp. 254–86.

16. *Seventh Malaysia Plan 1996–2000* (Kuala Lumpur: Malaysian National Press, 1996); see Foreword by Prime Minister of Malaysia, pp. vi, 19.
17. Khadijah Md. Khalid, "Malaysia's Foreign Policy under Najib: A Comparison with Mahathir", *Asian Survey*, vol. 51, no. 3 (May/June 2011): 429–52.

References

Ahmad, Abdullah. *Issues in Malaysian Politics*. Singapore: Singapore Institute of International Affairs, 1988.

Alagappa, Muthiah. The National Security of Developing States: Lessons from Thailand. Dover, Massachusetts: Auburn House, 1987.

Ayoob, Mohammed. "The Quest for Autonomy: Ideologies in the Indian Ocean Region". In *The Indian Ocean Region: Perspectives on a Strategic Arena*, edited by W.L. Dowdy and Russel B. Trood. Durham, North Carolina: Duke University Press, 1985.

———. "The Third World in the System of States: Acute Schizophrenia or Growing Pains?". *International Studies Quarterly*, vol. 33, no. 1 (1989): 67–79.

Brown, David. "Crisis and Ethnicity: Legitimation in Plural Societies". *Third World Quarterly*, vol. 7, no. 4 (1985): 988–1008.

———. "Ethnic Revival: Perspectives on State and Society". *Third World Quarterly*, vol. 11, no. 4 (1989): 1–17.

Camroux, David. "Looking East and Inwards: Internal Factors in Malaysia's Foreign Relations During the Mahathir Era, 1981–1994". *Australia-Asia Paper* 72. Queensland: Griffith University, 1994.

Crouch, Harold. "Malaysia: Neither Authoritarian nor Democratic". In *Southeast Asia in the 1990s: Authoritarianism, Democracy and Capitalism*, edited by Kevin Hewison, Richard Robison, and Gary Rodan. St. Leonards, New South Wales: Allen and Unwin, 1993.

———. "Government and Society in Malaysia". Ithaca, New York: Cornell University Press, 1996.

Fan Yew Teng. "Class Race, and Ethnicity". In *Political Culture: The Challenge of Modernization*, edited by Murugesu Pathmanathan and Robert Haas. Petaling Jaya: Centre for Policy Sciences, 1995.

Fisk, E.K. and H. Osman-Rani, eds. *The Political Economy of Malaysia*. Kuala Lumpur: Oxford University Press, 1982.

Gomez, Edmund Terence. "Political Business: Corporate Involvement of Malaysian Political Parties". Townsville, Australia: James Cook University, 1994.

———. "Electoral Funding of General, State, and Party Elections in Malaysia". *Journal of Contemporary Asia*, vol. 26, no. 1 (1996): 81–99.

Haftendorn, Helga. "The Security Puzzle: Theory-Building and Discipline-Building", *International Studies Quarterly*, vol. 35, no. 1 (1991): 3–17.

Hanrahan, Gene Z. *The Communist Struggle in Malaya*. Kuala Lumpur: University of Malaya Press, 1971.

Hua Wu Yin. "Class and Communalism in Malaysia: Politics in a Dependent Capitalist State". London: Zed Books, 1983.

Jomo K.S. "Malaysia's New Economic Policy and National Unity". *Third World Quarterly*, vol. 11, no. 4 (1989): 36–53.

———. "Industrializing Malaysia: Policy, Performance, Prospects". London: Routledge, 1993.

———. "Privatizing Malaysia: Rents, Rhetoric, Realities. Boulder". Colorado: Westview Press, 1995.

Kennedy, Paul. "The Rise and Fall of the Great Powers: Economic Change and Military Conflict from 1500 to 2000". London: Fontana, 1988.

Khoo Boo Teik. "Paradoxes of Mahathirism: An Intellectual Biography of Mahathir Mohamad". Kuala Lumpur: Oxford University Press, 1995.

Mahathir Mohamad. *The Malay Dilemma*. Kuala Lumpur: Federal Publications, 1970.

Means, Gordon. *Malaysian Politics: The Second Generation*. Singapore: Oxford University Press, 1991.

Mehmet, Ozay. "Islamic Identity and Development: Studies of the Islamic Periphery". Kuala Lumpur: Forum, 1990.

Morrison, Charles E. and Astri Suhrke. "Strategies of Survival: The Foreign Policy". *Dilemmas of Smaller Asian States*. New York: St. Martin's Press, 1978.

Muzaffar, Chandra. *Islamic Resurgence in Malaysia*. Petaling Jaya, Malaysia: Penerbit Fajar Bakti, 1987.

Nathan, K.S. "Nationalism and Foreign Policy: A Case Study of Indonesia Under Sukarno". *NUSANTARA* (Journal of the Arts and Social Sciences of Southeast Asia), vol. 10 (1983): 28–47.

———. "The Role of Malaysia and Singapore in Nation-Building and Southeast Asian Regionalism". Unpublished seminar paper delivered at the Fourth Malaysia-Singapore Forum, Petaling Jaya, Malaysia, 8–11 December 1994.

———. "Malaysia: The Challenge of Money Politics and Religious Activism". In *Southeast Asian Affairs 2006*, edited by Daljit Singh and Lorraine C. Salazar. Singapore: Institute of Southeast Asian Affairs, 2006.

Nesadurai, Helen E. "APEC: A Tool for U.S. Regional Domination?", *Pacific Review*, vol. 9, no. 1 (1996): 31–57.

Noor Ahmad Baba. "Organization of the Islamic Conference: Conceptual Framework and Institutional Structure". *International Studies*, vol. 30, no. 1 (1993): 35–51.

Razak, Mohamad Najib Tun. "Asia-Pacific's Strategic Outlook: The Shifting of Paradigms". Petaling Jaya, Malaysia: Pelanduk Publications, 1995.

Rejai, Mostafa, and Cynthia H. Enloe. "Nation-States and State-Nations". *International Studies Quarterly*, vol. 13, no. 2 (1969): 140–58.

Sandler, Shmuel. "Ethnonationalism and the Foreign Policy of Nation-States". *Nationalism and Ethnic Politics*, vol. 1, no. 2 (1995): 250–69.

Singh, Hari. "UMNO Leaders and Malay Rulers: The Erosion of a Special Relationship". *Pacific Affairs*, vol. 68, no. 2 (1995): 187–205.

Sinnadurai, Visu. "The Citizenship Laws of Malaysia". In *The Constitution of Malaysia: Its Development, 1957–1977*, edited by Tun Mohamed Suffian, H.P. Lee, and F.A. Trindade. Kuala Lumpur: Oxford University Press, 1978.

Thambipillai, Pushpa. "The ASEAN Growth Triangle: The Convergence of National and Sub-National Interests". *Contemporary Southeast Asia*, vol. 13, no. 3 (1991): 269–314.

Zainah Anwar. "Islamic Revivalism in Malaysia: Dakwah Among the Students". Petaling Jaya, Malaysia: Pelanduk Publications, 1987. Institute of Strategic and International Studies (ISIS) Malaysia, 1994, pp. 13–14. *Security Policy in the 1990s*. New South Wales: Allen and Unwin, 1996.

INDEX

www.ingramcontent.com/pod-product-compliance
Lightning Source LLC
Chambersburg PA
CBHW070240290326
41929CB00046B/2211
* 9 7 8 9 8 1 4 5 1 7 9 1 1 *